Richard Holt Hutton

Essays, theological and literary

Vol. 1

Richard Holt Hutton

Essays, theological and literary
Vol. 1

ISBN/EAN: 9783337809874

Printed in Europe, USA, Canada, Australia, Japan

Cover: Foto ©Lupo / pixelio.de

More available books at **www.hansebooks.com**

ESSAYS

THEOLOGICAL AND LITERARY

By RICHARD HOLT HUTTON, M.A. (Lond.)

TWO VOLUMES

Vol. I.—THEOLOGICAL ESSAYS

STRAHAN & CO., PUBLISHERS
56, LUDGATE HILL, LONDON
1871

LONDON:
PRINTED BY WILLIAM CLOWES AND SONS, STAMFORD STREET,
AND CHARING CROSS.

PREFACE.

THESE Essays need no preface beyond the explanation that most of them appeared some years ago in the 'National Review,' while a few have been published since in other periodicals. All have been carefully revised, and some re-cast and partly re-written. With regard to the first volume, on theological subjects, it may be well to add that the essay last in order was almost the first written, and that though it expresses a view which I still earnestly hold, I do not think it does full justice to the theology of Mr. Maurice, to whom indeed, but for a certain feeling that dedications have become a somewhat unreal mode of acknowledging mental obligations, I should have wished to dedicate these Essays. To him more than to any other living man, I certainly owe my belief that theology is a true science, that a knowledge of God in a true scientific sense, however imperfect in degree, is open to us. But for what I venture to think the great living principle of Mr. Maurice's writings, the first volume of these Essays, and a considerable portion of the second, could scarcely have been written. That principle I take to be that all beliefs *about* God are but inadequate intellectual attempts to justify a belief *in* Him which is never a merely intellectual affirmation, but rather a living act of the spirit by no means confined to those who consciously confess His presence. Grant this, and it follows that all attempts to limit our living relations with God by beliefs about Him,—whether those beliefs are negative, and deny His power to reveal Himself at all to beings so narrow,—or positive, and affect to express His essence exhaustively in a number of abstract propositions,—are mistakes of the same origin and root. Only where a belief about God helps us to explain a more real belief in Him, and only so far as it does so, has it any true value. Scepticism and dogmatism are but different forms of the attempt to accommodate infinite living claims upon us to our human weakness. The former, which declares God "unknown and unknowable," makes our weakness a sort of fastness in which we fortify ourselves against Him; the latter, which insists on set formulæ as alone representative of real spiritual life, dilutes the divine nature with human limitations to make an image more commensurate with ourselves. It seems to me that it has been the one purpose of all the divine revelation or education of which we have any record, to waken us up out of this perpetually recurring tendency to fall back into ourselves. If the essays of the first volume have any worth in them, they owe it to the coherent application of this principle in a good many different directions; and my grasp of it I date entirely from my study of Mr. Maurice's writings.

R. H. H.

14th January, 1871.

CONTENTS OF VOL. I.

(THEOLOGICAL ESSAYS.)

I.
PAGE
THE MORAL SIGNIFICANCE OF ATHEISM 3

II.
THE ATHEISTIC EXPLANATION OF RELIGION 30

III.
SCIENCE AND THEISM 45

IV.
POPULAR PANTHEISM 68

V.
WHAT IS REVELATION 95

VI.
THE HISTORICAL PROBLEMS OF THE FOURTH GOSPEL .. 144

VII.
THE INCARNATION AND PRINCIPLES OF EVIDENCE 227

VIII.
M. RENAN'S 'CHRIST' 285

IX.
M. RENAN'S 'ST. PAUL' 310

X.
THE HARD CHURCH 336

XI.
ROMANISM, PROTESTANTISM, AND ANGLICANISM 375

THEOLOGICAL ESSAYS.

I.

THE MORAL SIGNIFICANCE OF ATHEISM.

IF ever the dark shadow of Atheism were suddenly to envelop the earth, would the crash of falling churches, the disbanding of ecclesiastical classes, and the vanishing of all conscious individual intercourse with God, be necessarily accompanied by the yielding of all moral ties and the dissolution of every sacred social organisation? Before it is possible to answer such a question, it is necessary to call to mind a very obvious but a strangely-forgotten truth, that human trust does not create God, and that human distrust would not annihilate Him. There is a thoroughly atheistic way of shuddering over Atheism, which is apt to express itself as if the spread of human disbelief would not only overcloud but *empty* Heaven. Although the darkness which we have supposed would hide God from us, it would not hide us from God; nor should we ever be beyond the reach of His moral influence. When people assume that an Atheist *must* "live without God in the world," they assume what is fatal to their own Theism. I believe that by far the greater part of all human trust does not arise, as is commonly supposed, from our seeking God, but from God's seeking us; and this, too, without any clear admission or confession on our part of His influence upon us;—that a great deal of it is trust in goodness rather than in any personal God, and might possibly be held along with intellectual disbelief of His personal existence; in short, that if you could blot out on the one hand all acts of self-confessed trust in God,—if you could blot out all private and public worship, properly so called, spurious or genuine, all churches, all creeds, all pharisaism, and all pure conscious devotion; and if, on the other hand, you might leave all this, and blot out of the earth all unconscious and unconfessed acts of surrender to the divine influence in the heart,—all that *might* possibly be connected with purely intellectual Atheism,—you would blot out more of true "religion," more of that which "binds together" human society, more of God's true agency on the earth, in the latter case than in the former. Of course I do not mean that the truest unconscious trust in God's influence is not generally to be found in the same minds which, *at other times*, also consciously confess Him; but only this, that if in every life, whether of faith or doubt, you numbered up the acts of trust which are not rendered to God personally, but to the instincts and impulses which so often represent Him in the heart, and which might continue to represent Him even when the cloud of conscious doubt of His existence had intervened, you would probably have numbered far more acts which really originate in divine influence than could possibly be found animated by a conscious personal belief.

And if this be so, as I think most men will admit as much from self-knowledge as from knowledge of the world, it is a fatal blunder to attempt to prove to the Atheist, that, in consequence of his doubt, he has been and is living totally without God; that his eyes need opening, not in order that they may recognise One who has been ever with him, but that they may help him to find a distant and alienated power. There is no teaching more mischievous in its effects than that which makes human belief in God the *first* regenerating power in human society, and God Himself the second; which makes God's blessing a consequence of man's confession, and which therefore limits that blessing to the narrow bounds of the confession. In fact, this delusion tends to depress rather than to exaggerate ordinary men's estimate of the value of faith. Hearing it constantly implied that God influences men's hearts only so far as they confess His influence; that He will do nothing for them, morally and spiritually, unless they render the "glory" where it is due; and yet, seeing that in point of fact this *sine qua non* of divine influence is anything but a true mark of actual goodness, being often only the crowning element in evil,—a school of thought has sprung up which depreciates the value of faith altogether, which delights in discovering that the greatest good is, after all, to be found hidden under a mask of scepticism and self-mockery, in short, a school which replaces the religious ascription of all goodness to God's grace, by light ridicule of a human nature that does not pretend to be so assisted, but rather does the best it can for itself in an unostentatious way. This disposition to compare keen self-mockery with formal belief, and to give the preference to the former, is perceptible enough in the whole tone of our literature. Thackeray's writings are throughout tinged with the feeling that thorough self-mockery is one of the highest moral virtues of which men in general are capable. And until even honest self-exposure, and every other sort of goodness, so far as it is goodness, be attributed to God's Spirit working in man, far though it be removed from the theological virtue of faith, faith itself will never recover from the discredit into which its undue isolation has brought it. As soon as God is confessed to be far greater than our faith, we shall begin to make the effort to render our faith more worthy of God: but while men own so many things to be noble which are never claimed as divine because they are unaccompanied by this conscious faith, so long they will care little what that faith does or does not include. Men have found the faith-classification of human actions so narrow and unjust, they have seen so much goodness without faith, and so much faith without goodness, that they begin to preach justification by sincerity as a more human, if it is not a more divine formula than justification by faith.

In showing, then, that Atheism is false to human nature, that trust in God is the natural atmosphere of our moral life, it must not be taken for granted, as is so often done, that belief in God as God, and belief in goodness, are one and the same thing. We must grant the Atheist his unexplained impulses to good, the *implicit* God of his conscience, and show how he mutilates and dwarfs human nature by denying it. all explained impulses to good, the explicit God of faith. Though guarding against the error that distinct acknowledgment of God must accompany all virtual obedience to His word, it is of course manifest that, so far as human action is self-conscious as well as voluntary, blindness to God's existence must entail a large and constant loss upon the blind. Although other and deeper springs of divine influence be not closed, although these may be yet (except in the cases in which intellectual Atheism is the dulness produced by moral Atheism) far more effectual means of inward guidance still accessible to God's providence than those which any deadness of insight can obstruct,—yet all the tone of the reflective life must be greatly injured by the exclusion of this great object from the field of the inward vision. Not to see what exists must of course modify constantly the whole range of action and thought which has a real (though in this case unperceived) reference to that existence. As our ancestors, who did not know that air had weight, reaped unconsciously most of the benefits of the all-permeating atmospheric pressure, but of course lost that which depended on the actual recognition and conscious use of its weight, so those who do not know that God is, while they experience, almost as much as any, the blessing of His existence and His character, cannot have the blessing which arises only from taking account of the fact of that existence and character; and therefore it is, I believe, that, in proportion as mental culture increases the horizon of man's experience, and reduces more and more of his life beneath the eye of his thought, is the moral loss serious and deep which arises from this mental blindness. Those who have but little inward life, whose busy routine of occupation, or natural one-sidedness of character, leaves room only for a narrow moral horizon, suffer indeed, and bitterly, from blindness to the only great and tranquillising reality of life, but not at all in the same proportion as those whose whole nature is awake and sensitive to human emotions, without including the belief in God. Of all merely intellectual Atheisms, hard material Atheisms betray *least* strikingly and painfully the absence of the power of faith. There are so many natural obstructions in such minds to the permeation of religious conviction throughout the whole nature, that its absence is not striking; there would be so many clouds as to hide the sun even if it were up. But thoroughly cultivated and refined Atheisms are always intensely startling and painful, like the blotting of the sun out of a clear sky. The actual loss is greater;

proportionally far more of God's influence would naturally come through conscious channels with the cultivated than with the uncultivated man; proportionally less strength and warmth can be received unconsciously from "behind the veil."

Now, first of all, look steadily at the startling fact which meets one on the threshold of this question—the fact, namely, that it is so much as possible for a sincere truth-loving mind to doubt of God's existence—that the greatest of all realities appears so frequently, in the history of nations as well as in individual life, rather in the shape of a whispered haunting suggestion than of a fully illumined truth. Can any answer be found to the argument, "You tell us that this faith is the one pure spring of all the conscious purity and strength to which human nature has access. Why, then, is it at best a faith, and not a conspicuous fact? Why can it ever, even for a time, be inaccessible to eager search? And why, when attained, does it still linger in the background of your mind, as it were, being usually, even to yourselves, more audible than heard?" The common and dreary answer is, of course,—on account of the mists of human corruption. But it seems strange that the very remedy which is to heal the blindness should be applicable only when the blindness is already healed. I believe, too, that this difficulty is not explicable by the suggestion of a distinguished theologian, that trust is imposed on us as a kind of probationary venture of the will—a courageous risk of ourselves by a dim twilight, in order to test whether we would not rather serve even a probable God than a certain self-love. I do not deny that we ought to do so, if it were possible for Him thus to experimentalise upon us; but it seems to me that it is a most unworthy representation of the divine character to represent Him as tempting us by self-concealment.

Probably the account which most true men would give to themselves of the mystery is this: that while faith fosters, sight must arrest, the growth of our moral nature,—nay, that there may even be peculiar stages of individual and social life when the absence of faith alleviates instead of aggravating the danger of moral evil. I suppose that a constant *vision* of God would be an injury to almost all men,—that there are periods when even utter scepticism is the sign of God's mercy, and the necessary condition of moral restoration. A real independent moral growth would be impossible to natures that had not been shaded, as it were, by a special veil from the overwhelming brightness of a divine character ever present with us. Either everything human must have been changed, so as to make us impervious to personal influences, or there must be a special film to screen from our sensitive passive nature, at least during the growth of our character, the intense impressions proceeding from spiritual beings greatly superior to ourselves. Every one knows that, even amongst men, a powerful massive character, though it be nearly perfect, often positively injures those within the circle of its influence. They lose the spring of their mind beneath the overwhelming weight of its constant pressure. They are crushed into an unconscious mechanical consonance with all its ways. Nay, even affection, not pressure, may do the same thing. Moral preference, moral freedom, moral character, may be superseded altogether by the single unanalysed predominance of another's wish. This it was, probably, which rendered the removal of Christ the first condition of the moral growth of the apostles. "It is expedient for you that I go away." In the case supposed we should lose the power of growing up to be "fellow-workers" with God, through mere unmoral captivity to His infinite influence. Faith means the discernment of His character without subjugation of the small finite personality to the infinite life. To exchange faith for sight on earth would be to exchange Theism for Pantheism—moral education for moral absorption.

Again, I think it true, for a converse reason, that there are stages in human culture when even utter scepticism may be a divine remedy for moral evil. When civilisation has become corrupt, and men are living below their faith, I think it may often be in mercy that God strikes the nations with blindness,—that the only remedy lies in thus taking away an influence they resist, and leaving them to learn the stern lesson of helpless self-dependence. The shock of a lost faith often restores sooner than the reproach of a neglected faith. Nay, often before any real faith can be attained at all, scepticism may be, I believe, a discipline of mind and heart, given not in retribution but in love. The painful groping of an uncertain footing amidst immortal wants and affections is often the only means by which, as far as I can see, we could have our eyes opened at once to their meaning and to our own responsibility.

It is in *growing* characters, maturing in the culture of all the finer elements, as well as in mere intellect, that scepticism seems most evil in its influences—characters needing the genial influence of trust, and yet held fast in some of the many intellectual traps of human speculation. In other cases it cannot be regarded as unmixed evil. But, as I have said, in refined and cultured minds there is, I believe, no influence that can secure constant progress apart from personal trust; and long-continued doubt, whether arising from personal unfaithfulness or from other causes, must in the end ossify the higher parts of mind and distort the whole.

What, then, is the atheistic type of character? In other words, what is the type of character which a fully realised disbelief in the existence and influence over us of any spiritual nature higher than our own (however faithfully our own may be accepted and trusted) *tends* to produce? Vividly to realize the import of Atheism to human character, even though it be not moral Atheism (or disbelief in ultimate moral distinctions), is the first step towards its disproof.

It is clear that Atheism necessarily tends to reduce relatively the influence of the higher intellectual and moral faculties (even where the real existence of these is not disputed), as compared with that of the senses, social impulses, and those energies which tell most directly upon the world. And this it does both involuntarily and unconsciously, by eradicating from the imagination that haunting image of the divine character which most stimulates these faculties into action, and also voluntarily and consciously, because the Atheist must in consistency believe that the Theists' worship gives them an unfair prominence. Holding that the human mind is in direct contact with no other mind, but is the latest and highest consummation of forces pushing upwards from a lower stage of existence, the Atheist cannot regard his own highest mental states—conscience, affection, and so forth—as having any independent illumination of their own,—as skylights opened to let in upon human nature an infinite dawn from above,—but rather as a polished arch or dome completing and reflecting the whole edifice beneath. To him the highest point of human culture is the absolutely highest point in the mental universe; mere non-existence roofs us in beyond; and of course, therefore, the highest faculties we possess must derive their sole validity and their sole meaning from the lower nature to which they add the finishing touch. No doubt he will admit that new power and insight is gained, the higher our self-culture is pushed; but the new power is not power from beyond human nature, the new insight is not insight into a region above it; it is only the stronger grasp of a more practised hand, the keener vision of a more comprehensive survey. Hence, by dismissing the faith in God, Atheism necessarily props up the higher faculties of man completely and solely on the lower organisation, and denies them any independent spring. Moreover, the Atheist is led to justify and fortify himself in this natural result of his modes of thought by assuming, as Feuerbach does, that the object of man's worship, if there be any, ought to be a perfect *man*, and that the Theist's God is not even strictly a magnified shadow of humanity, but only of a special and arbitrarily selected portion of humanity. This kind of worship, therefore, gives, he maintains, a factitious and disproportionate influence to certain so-called "higher parts" of human nature. An injurious and morbid reduplication is given, he thinks, to the faculties called moral and spiritual by this rapt attention to a fanciful religious echo of them, while the physical organisation and common-sense understanding are left to assert themselves. And so the Atheist, denying any special or original sources of life for the highest part of man's nature, sets it to take lessons from the lower, and look down instead of looking up. Hence, I believe, Atheism is far more uncomfortably and consciously alive to the material conditions under which it works, and the physiological laws it so anxiously consults, than would be the case if man had no moral nature at all. There is the same kind of soreness in the alliance between the moral and physical nature, under this levelling theory, that there usually is between essentially different ranks, where the higher is induced by some theoretic conviction to disavow its special birthright.

Again, atheistic theory in one still more important respect diminishes the influence that must be given to the moral nature of man. It necessarily regards good and evil as ideas attained and attainable only by human capacity, —as depending on natural genius and insight only,—as wholly limited by natural disposition. Hence not seeing in them any movement of an independent character towards us, but only an exercise of human capacity,— cases of moral difficulty are apt to be given up or slurred over as insoluble, which the Theist feels *must* be and are capable of solution if he can only trustfully follow, step by step, and without impatience, the gradual indications of God's purposes. There is all the difference in the world between the view of right and wrong which treats it as a mathematical problem which a man can solve or not according to his capacity, and the view of it as something which depends on the faithfulness of a personal relation—something certain to become clearer and clearer, not through our capacity, but through the free illuminating power of another's influence, if we use the dim light we have in beginning to go where it leads. Right and wrong are usually considered as extremely simple to see—difficult only to do. This is very false, however, especially when weakness and sin have already complicated human relations. And at this point the atheistic and theistic views of conduct necessarily become essentially different in the relative importance they assign to moral instincts. Neither Atheist nor Theist can see anything but thick darkness perhaps, and both are utterly incompetent to find their own way to the light. But the Atheist has only his own powers to trust, and, finding them shackled and paralysed by a thousand chains, can but despair, and find no help in the flickering conscience, which only seems to mock the gloom. The Theist, if he can still believe in the infinite love of God, can trust implicitly that every step into the darkness will be into a darkness less complete, and show the way to the step beyond. Hence he can never believe but that right is *attainable*, if he will follow on; that the little insight he has must be implicitly obeyed, and not thrown away because it seems utterly inadequate to his need. If you don't believe that "good" is living and free—that it is a person—you cannot believe that it will find *you* out; and you may be truly as incompetent to find *it* out as to leave the earth for the sun.

And just in the same way as the absence of trust tends to nourish a despondency in deep moral difficulty, and a neglect of the inadequate faculty we have, in the case of the individual,—so it is also fatal to the healthy progress of nations. The Atheist says, "Even you admit that God helps only those who help themselves. Well, we help ourselves, and therefore God, if He exists, helps us; if He does not, we have all the help we can. *Science* is the true providence of man. We lay no faith on 'personal god;' we use our own faculties." Very well; but let men only realise your negative creed, and you will find they have not the heart, or perhaps the temerity, on great occasions, to help themselves any longer. *Trust* is the postulate of the capacity to help ourselves in any great or noble work. It becomes impossible to do our part bravely without this perfect reliance on the co-operation of God. What is to justify trust in a mere sudden gleam of light,—a streak just flashing over a universe at midnight,—except the conviction that it comes from One who will send more and more, as the occasion demands, if that be followed? Luther's intense saying, "We tell our Lord God plainly, that if He will have His church, He must look after it Himself. We cannot sustain it; and if we could, we should become the proudest asses under heaven," is the inspiration of all great action. No man will dare to follow a gleam of conviction which tends to overturn a world, unless he is sure that he is but the interpreter of a Power who gave him that conviction, and can guard it after His interpreter is gone. Luther took no responsibility in the case, except the responsibility of his own individual life. How could he have done what he did with a sense of the uncertain fate of Europe when the Roman Church should be gone, resting on his individual conscience? A small anxiety oppresses a man, if it be only his own uncertain judgment that he trusts. St. Paul was insupportably anxious about the measures he took to defend himself from Corinthian ill-will. Luther was depressed into a state of chronic melancholy by the difficulties of marriage-questions referred to his ecclesiastical jurisdiction. Yet St. Paul snapped the chain which bound Christianity to the formal Judaism with the serenest equanimity; and Luther was never so calm and loftily certain as in the act which rent Christendom and cut history in two. If there is no one else who has looked into the future for you, and distinctly told you how to act, then you are bound to look into the future yourself, and take the awful possibilities you initiate upon your own shoulders. Who could do this, on great or even small occasions, without a paralysing dread? Atheism should tend to make prudent men and nations anxious, timid, hesitating, disinclined to place ample confidence even in such moral insight as they have.

And further, Atheism shakes the authority of the moral faculties of man, by doing away with all adequate means of *expressing* the infinite distinction between right and wrong. Neither admitting that right action opens human eyes to a vision of Infinite Holiness, nor that it survives for ever in the immortal life it assists to build up,—Atheism has no language by which it can express the infinite nature of moral distinctions. Right and wrong, like all other qualities of human life, can, then, only be expressed in finite terms,—can only be symbolised by objects which are immediately swept away by the drift of time,—which are mere invisible points in the infinite universe of space. The Atheist has no infinite calculus applicable to human actions. He may say, indeed, that considerations of right and wrong differ from all others in their imperativeness, but he cannot believe that any infinite result in any way attends moral choice more than any other act of finite life. Why should the aged be anxious about the regulation of their hearts, for example? It may be absolutely right; but how can we single out a right action as distinct from all others of trivial and temporary nature? In this case, it affects no external life; it will almost immediately cease to affect any internal life. As is one act, so is another. All alike are temporary—all alike limited. Immortality—the communion with God—these are the only living expressions which the struggling nature of man, intensely conscious of the infinite character of duty and sin, can give to that infinitude. It is not, as is falsely said, that right and wrong take their distinctions from measures of duration, or from the arbitrary will of God; but that faith in infinite personal life, and in our communion with, or separation from Infinite Good, is the only articulate utterance which our conscience can find for its sense of the absolutely boundless significance it sees in every moral choice. A rejection of these realities must react on the conscience itself, and force it to resign its "absolute and infinite" distinctions.

Again, a fully realised Atheism will undermine the worth of personal human affections; not merely indirectly, by losing sight of immortality, but still more by cutting off the chief spring of their spiritual life. If that fine wide-spreading network—hidden from all human eyes—the winding, crossing, blending, diverging threads of human affection which hold together human society, be indeed conceived as issuing everywhere out of everlasting night,—as spun, snapped asunder, and again repaired by the mere automatic operation of Nature's unconscious and impersonal energy,—the personal affections lose quite the richest and most permanent of the *conscious* influences at least which minister to their life and growth. If we cease to believe in the infinite spiritual presence mediating between mind and mind, and try to expel that conception from our thoughts, we must become more and more completely dependent for the growth of the higher human ties on the conditions of physical intercourse. The awkward and constrained intercourse of human beings, so rarely interchanging the real secrets of the heart, and often most frigid when covering the intensest life, is not adequate to sustain the growth of deep affections. It supplies the occasions, not the sources of that growth. If there be no Eternal Depository of our resolves and fears, and hopes and trusts, there is little new moral strength consciously poured into these higher human relations at all. He who supposes that his nature can never be directly addressed from the spiritual side at all—that it remains rooted in unconscious energies—may indeed indulge impassive emotion, when it arises spontaneously within him,—nay, may entertain and welcome it; but he cannot regard affection as claiming constant *service* from him, even where it has no external duty,—as a *trust* which he is bound to reverence; he cannot feel it matter of self-reproach if he grow cold; it is to him no withdrawal of a voluntary gift; it cannot be regarded as a personal and moral matter at all; it is the ceasing of that which he did not cause; it is the subsiding of a wave; he has no passionate dream that God is taking away that which was not treasured,—and that, even now, higher self-sacrifice, truer devotion, would bring back the receding tide. It is gone back out of the heart whence it came; and that is but a fiction which would make it appear a result of moral conduct on our part,—an expression of the character of a vigilant God.

The atheistic theory thus tends to reduce the life of human affection to dependence on the *visible* relations between man and man. It leaves some sense of responsibility towards the living and present object of affection, but it cancels all idea of moral responsibility to the Inspirer of affection. It would tend to make us measure the self-sacrifice due from us by the self-sacrifice deserved by others, instead of measuring it by the eternal purposes and the immeasurable love of God. It destroys in this way the fulcrum on which human affection is sustained; for while we can feel the claim of another upon us, yet to hear it selfishly advanced is utterly destructive of its power;—only the great Mediator between the severed minds of men can revive the fading sense of duty, and melt the mind into bitter memory, without further estranging the rebellious heart; and if no such Mediator be recognised, all conscious seeking of His influence or submission to His prompting is of course impossible. All the promises, the prayers, the self-reproaches, the resolves which assume both a providential origin, and a divine influence, for our spirits, are rendered impossible, and Atheism thus clips the life of human affection down to the mortal type which atheistic theory assigns to it. Of course Theists are in this respect often practical Atheists, and Atheists may unconsciously treat as a moral trust and result of providential government that which their theory should represent as an involuntary, inevitable event. But just so far as the conscious life influences us at all, just so far theoretic Atheism dries up the sources of personal affection, by sweeping away that searching moral relation to the Inspirer of affection in which, even far more than in its relation to human objects, its safety and strength consists. The best and purest part of conscious self-sacrifice and devotion is not that which passes directly between men, but that which goes round by God, and is sifted and purified in the very act of submission to His eye. If you sweep this away, there is no little danger of falling back into the jealous, exigeant, selfish type of affection which at best weighs out with scrupulous care the exact debt. Moreover, there is nothing more narrowing to the character than even true human love devoid of a deep faith. Its very nobleness, being without trust, tyrannises over the mind, and would take the place of Providence in anxious guarding against fate. The Atheist can scarcely admit any claim higher than a strong personal affection, since he believes that no *better* being is claiming his service, and that no immortality can ever repair the final evil of separation. Yet the narrow anxiety that would thus supplant a hopeful trust, and limit the aims and activity of man in order to cheat separation a little longer of its pain, is apt to foil its own end, and cool the affection which thus unnaturally limits the range of life. Once realise Atheism, and it will soon appear that affection must burn itself away, without that separate life of responsibility to its Inspirer which it does not acknowledge; and further, if that could be otherwise, that it would soon eat into the healthy energy of man, if it had no Infinite Love to trust, while it had a certain impending fate to fear.

But turning now from this tendency in Atheism to impair the authority of the moral faculties and the worth of the personal affections, consider how far it affects the worth of that one great idea for the sake of which it considers all these sacrifices as nothing. If God be dislodged from our thoughts, will *Truth* cover a wider area, and gain a deeper significance? Will it spread itself over that world of thought from which the image of God is banished, absorb into itself the sacred attributes with which Theists invest Him, and supply anything analagous to the softening influence of personal reverence? Clear the mind of God, and truth is reduced almost to mere knowledge—true "information." The aggregate of the actual and temporary relations between the short-lived intelligent beings, the animals, the plants, the stones, the forces, which are thrown together in more or less permanent connection in this big round and rather empty sphere of space, would then constitute Truth. The highest truth would be the account of observed and quite momentary influences of human minds upon each other, such as the relation of the vestiges of Shakespeare's mind to the quickly vanishing generations of his successors,—in short, the momentary relations of minds ceasing to have relations to anything in a few brief years. The most permanent truth would be the lowest,—facts about cohesion, gravity, and mineral life. Nay, suppose that—what is quite possible—physical science discovers some gradual destructive agency, which would, in the course of years, remove man wholly from that universe in which for a few centuries he has managed to live in curious wondering contemplation of the irrational silence around him. This agency, when discovered, would itself be a part of this "sacred" truth which Atheism worships in the place of God. It would be to man the most important inference from actual fact hitherto attained. The knowledge that a time was coming when the law of gravitation (or perhaps not even that) should be left in undisputed possession of the limitless blue spaces, and when there would not even be any one anywhere to know that the "eternal truth" of nothingness had survived its evangelists—this knowledge, I say, if it were attainable, should be "sacred" to the minds of the discoverers, if, at least, it is to bare fact, as such, that sacredness belongs—if it depends only on the *certainty* of the fact announced, and not in any way on the *quality* of that fact—*i. e.* on the kind and number of the influences it puts forth over our nature.

With the Theist, "The Truth," as distinguished from

mere reality, signifies the whole web of durable personal influences which he believes to bind together God with man, and man with man through God. It is therefore "sacred" to him as affecting the highest life of man, and as affecting it eternally. But blot out this eternal centre of creation, and what is left for truth to include except a *rationale* of relations of which the least human are then believed to be the most permanent, and the highest of all are not only almost momentary for individual men, but perhaps quite transient for the race itself? If we believe in no immutable Reality, truth itself must change with history, and at best is nothing more than a rough computation of the law of change. To tell how human lives influence each other for the present, and are likely to influence each other while things go on in the main as they do now,—and how they stand related to the rocks, and the ocean, and to light, and to the worlds of plants and animals,—this is the highest import of "truth" to the Atheist's mind. The man who could resolutely keep down his conception of "truth" to this standard would scarcely feel it very sacred, or worthy of much costly sacrifice. It is the ever-retreating horizon of an eternal life, and faith in the inexhaustibly fresh possibilities of every opening relation between character and character, and awe at the new insight into our dependence on God, which unconsciously or consciously give their fascination and sacredness to the search after "truth." The tendency of Atheism is to lower these feelings into mere curiosity craving "information."

It seems, then, that Atheism, in proportion as it is fully realised, cannot but tend to weaken and even shatter the authority of conscience; to sow despondency both as to personal and human progress; to cast the personal affections in a much narrower and more selfish type; and to dispel all the highest fascination and grandeur of the conception of Truth. The Atheist may fairly reply, of course, that this only shows that the existence of a personal God may be *desirable*, not that it is real, that men would benefit by believing in Him if they could only see ground to believe in Him. As Mr. Holyoake insists, human wants and wishes must not be allowed to create a delusion merely for their own satisfaction. Presentiments must not be regarded as proofs of external existence. On the contrary, the Atheist may maintain, as Feuerbach does, that it is precisely in these human wants and presentiments that we find the explanation of the mirage of Theism,—a view of the case which I must reserve for discussion in another essay. But, in point of fact, I believe we are so constituted that no sincere Atheist is really able to think that any illusion is better for human nature than Truth. This is exactly the point at which Atheists show themselves to be above their opinions. Where is the Atheist who does not encourage himself to disclose his unpopular opinions expressly on the ground that the extinction of the old illusions will give the highest play to the energies of human nature? Yet in assuming this, the Atheist assumes that truth must be morally best for the mind, and conversely that whatever is morally best for the mind is true,—an assumption of a "pre-established harmony" between human nature and the universe, which evidently covers the old "superstition," as the Atheist would call it, of Providence, under another name, and bears remarkable testimony to the truth that God besets even the intellect of the Atheist "from behind," though He be hidden from him "from before."

So much of Atheists. But of these there are, in the higher walks of literature, at present very few. And though modern science is generally believed to strike more or less at the faith in a personal God, it is not true to say of even the most negative of the men of science that they are Atheists. They themselves vehemently dispute the term, and usually prefer to describe their state of mind as a sort of know-nothingism or Agnosticism, or belief in an unknown and unknowable God. This is Professor Huxley's phrase. This also is Professor Tyndall's, if I may judge by his recent assertion that the ideal man of science has "as little fellowship with the Atheist who says there is no God as with the Theist who professes to know the mind of God," and by his professed sympathy with Goethe's view of matter as "the living garment of God." Mr. Herbert Spencer, the most eminent of the metaphysicians of this school, even maintains, I believe, that the attitude which it is reasonable for the mind to assume towards the inscrutable Cause of the Universe, may some day be seen to be as much higher than the personal dependence of a Theist of Christian type on his God, as the mental attitude of the Theist is generally supposed to be than that of the Polytheist. This clinging to the name of God when coupled with such adjectives as "unknown and unknowable," this deep-rooted belief that there is and must be something higher in the feeling towards the inscrutable Cause of the Universe, than in that of the ordinary Theist who supposes that he has a clear glimpse of God's character, seem to me to betray the belief that the ultimate Cause is not quite so "unknown," "unknowable," and "inscrutable" as the language of these distinguished men suggest. Why should a name be claimed for the Unknown and Unknowable so full of personal conceptions, as "God" if personal conceptions are altogether misleading? Why should the feeling of awe directed towards the inscrutable Cause of the Universe be *higher* than the personal dependence of the ordinary Theist, unless there be some positive and discernible quality in the object of awe to exercise this influence? It seems clear that, for a *completely* unknown Cause, no one would ever care to claim the name of God; and that towards an utter inscrutability, the attitude of mind could hardly be either high or low, but must be one of pure marvel. The Agnostics, the adorers of Inscrutability, clearly limit their own very strong language as to the unknowability of the primal Cause by the very claim they make that it provides them with an equivalent for religion, and one which must in the end prove higher than that which they suppose it destined to replace. This seems to me a very remarkable testimony to the ineradicable belief that the highest truth leads to goodness and the highest goodness to truth,—a belief for which I never could see any speculative justification, unless righteousness in some more or less *human* sense be attributed to the primal Cause.

However, one may, I suppose, say as much as this of the know-nothing school of religion,—that the further it diverges from the ordinary Theism, the more nearly the preceding sketch would apply to it, and that so far as that sketch would misrepresent it, it would be because the know-nothings really feel towards God as if they knew *something* of Him, and something which inspires an approach to trust and love. The attitude of mind towards a mere Enigma can only differ from that towards a pure vacuum, in so far as one really guesses at the solution of the enigma and relies on the truth of one's own guess. What is true of a deliberate Atheist is true of a religious know-nothing—just so far, and only so far, as he sedulously repudiates the trust and love with which the true Theist regards God.

II.

THE ATHEISTIC EXPLANATION OF RELIGION.[1]

THE "essence of Christianity" is pronounced by Feuerbach, the ablest of the atheistic thinkers of Europe, to be the trust of man in himself or in the dignity of his own nature. God is but the magnified image of man reflected back upon space by the mirror of human self-consciousness. As pilgrims to the Brocken often observe, during an autumn sunrise, shadows of their own figures enormously dilated confronting them from a great distance, bowing as they bow, kneeling as they kneel, mocking them in all their gestures, and finally disappearing as the sun rises higher in the sky, so the German Atheist maintains that in the early dawn of

---

[1] 'The Essence of Christianity,' by Ludwig Feuerbach, translated from the second German edition, by Marian Evans. Chapman, 1854.

human intelligence, man has been deluded by such a Brocken-shadow of himself, which has been childishly worshipped as an independent being and named God, but which must vanish soon. Feuerbach attempts to prove this assertion in precisely the same fashion in which travellers to the Brocken have satisfied themselves that the great spectre of the mountain is but their own shadow. Look, Feuerbach virtually says, at the accounts which those men give of God who have from age to age recorded their religious experience. Where man has been savage, earthly, and fierce, and his joys those of animal excitement, this spectre also has been seen to brandish spears, or to be draining wine-cups. Where man was sensuous, cultivated, joyous, reflective, artistic, — the spectre, too, was graceful, intellectual, smiling, calm, contemplative. Where man was imperious, ambitious, inflexible, administrative, the spectre was cold and haughty, and made stern gestures of command. Where man was scrupulous, self-accusing, longing, loving, conscientious, — the Brocken-spectre he beheld was also a spiritual, just, loving, and gentle apparition. And so argues this writer, if we can detect no gesture in this figure which the spectator has not himself previously made,—if all our human peculiarities are mimicked by the mysterious phantom before us,—is it not evident that instead of man's being dependent on this moral spectre, the spectre is dependent on man? If the initiative can always be detected in the heart of the worshipper, only vivacity of imagination is needed to see the action or the emotion reiterated by that vague image of himself which the fancy of man is taught to paint upon the clouds.

Thus Ludwig Feuerbach goes through all the attributes ascribed to God, and detects their human origin. Reason, Moral law, Love—the three principal Divine attributes—are clearly recognised as divine in God, because felt to be divine in man. Human suffering for others' sake is deified by historical Christianity in Christ. In Roman Catholicism, even the peculiar beauty of feminine excellence has attained a certain kind of deification in the worship of the Virgin. Yet while suffering is recognised as divine in the deification of Christ, immunity from suffering, or abstract impassibility is equally recognized as divine in the Father. And hence arises, says Feuerbach, the moral and intellectual contradiction in the doctrine of the Trinity. Man, sensible that his capacity for emotion and for suffering arises from limitation in his nature, ascribes no such limitation to God. Yet equally conscious that his endurance of suffering for others is a noble endurance, he does ascribe this endurance to God, and is obliged to get out of the contradiction, as best he may, by a separation of the two Divine persons, wherein also lies this additional gratification to the religious nature, that God, instead of being conceived as eternally lonely, is conceived as having had an eternal object of love in the Son. Then, again, in the doctrine of creation, man seeks to reconcile the contradiction between the conception of Nature and his own human idea of God as its cause, by representing the powers of nature as proceeding out of the pure will of a being constituted like himself. God is to be conceived as a "person," *i.e.*, says our author, as man, although man stripped of certain finite limitations; but there is nothing in the mind of man at all analogous to the genesis of physical life in nature; in order, therefore, to humanise the cause of the universe, man represents creation to himself by the analogy of human "making or fashioning" a totally different conception, and affirms that by some instantaneous act of mere volition, God made the world out of nothing. Feuerbach therefore truly represents all *miracle* (such as Christ's multiplication of the loaves) and *creation*, in this sense as identical, inasmuch as in both cases the natural and ordinary constituents of the result were not present, and their place was supplied by the mental exertion of a supernatural will.

When our author approaches the spiritual evidences of religion, he still feels no kind of embarrassment. The peace of prayer he ascribes to the delusive self-confidence of human feeling, which, when most excited, is so conscious of its own sacredness, that it believes no obstacles to be worthy eventually to obstruct its wishes, and feels itself certain to triumph in the end over the merely physical limitations against which for the present it may be struggling in vain. "Prayer," says Feuerbach, "is the certainty that the power of the heart is greater than the power of nature,—that the heart's need is absolute necessity, the Fate of the world. . . . In prayer

man forgets that there exists a limit to his wishes, and is happy in this forgetfulness." "What else is the Being that fulfils these wishes but human affection, the human soul giving ear to itself, approving itself, unhesitatingly affirming itself?" Thus everywhere Feuerbach goes through the modes of thought of a religious mind, only asking himself in point of fact, — "If Religion *be* an illusion, what would be the best explanation of this?" and then, after finding the best answers he can for each case, he considers them as constituting a proof that Religion *is* an illusion. The reasoning of the whole book is indeed one long expansion of the following passage:—
"Man's nature demands as an object goodness, personified as God; but is it not hereby declared that goodness is an essential tendency of man? If my heart is wicked, my understanding perverted, how can I perceive and feel the holy to be holy, the good to be good? Could I perceive the beauty of a fine picture if my mind were æsthetically an absolute piece of perversion? Though I may not be a painter, though I may not have the power of producing what is beautiful myself, I must yet have æsthetic feeling, æsthetic comprehension, since I perceive the beauty that is presented to me externally. Either goodness does not exist at all for man, or if it does exist, therein is revealed to the individual man the holiness and goodness of human nature. That which is absolutely opposed to my nature, to which I am united by no bond of sympathy, is not even conceivable or perceptible by me. The Holy is in opposition to me only as regards

the modifications of my personality, but as regards my fundamental nature it is in unity with me. The Holy is a reproach to my sinfulness; in it I recognise myself as a sinner; but in so doing, while I blame myself, I acknowledge what I am not, but ought to be, and what, for that very reason, I, according to my destination, can be; for an 'ought,' which has no corresponding capability, does not affect me, is a ludicrous chimera without any true relation to my mental constitution. But when I acknowledge goodness as my destination, as my law, I acknowledge it, whether consciously or unconsciously, as my own nature. Another nature than my own, one different in quality, cannot touch me. I can perceive sin as sin, only when I perceive it to be a contradiction of myself with myself—that is of my personality with my fundamental nature. As a contradiction of the absolute, considered as another being, the feeling of sin is inexplicable, unmeaning."

The argument here developed is the kernel of Feuerbach's system, and reappears so constantly in sceptical writings that it deserves the most careful consideration. Its burden is that as the righteousness of God could not be discerned at all without a moral faculty in man, and cannot be apprehended except in proportion to the development of that moral faculty, it is philosophically gratuitous and superfluous to attribute any reality to this divine Object which only comes into our theory along with our conscience, and stands for the index of its discriminating power. But if this be final, it will apply just as well to cases where it would yield a false conclusion. Were Newton's mind presented to a series of learners in each successive stage of mathematical culture, each would only discern and admire as much of his power as his own gifts and study had enabled him to appreciate—all the rest would only affect the student with a vague unmeasured sense of power, as going beyond the margin of his own comprehension. What does not disprove, then, the real existence of a human mind, cannot disprove the real existence of a divine mind. Because Newton would be conceived by the child only as one who had unlimited powers of counting, by the boy as one who could even deal easily with fractions, and had all Euclid in his head, by the youth as one whose conceptions of space were close and vivid to an extraordinary degree, and whose powers of imagination and combination were never confused by the variety and complexity of abstract processes,— it of course would not follow that no real Newtonian intellect existed at all, but only some imaginary ideal conception, *named* the intellect of Newton, differing according to the mind of the observer.

How, then, are we to discriminate between a real and an imaginary object which varies with the individual mind and only has the same *name* in each case? Feuerbach thinks that the only criterion of a real existence is physical sensation. If there is a real object, then there must be something which affects my sensorium, he says. He would not pretend to doubt Newton's existence merely from the various estimates formed of him, but he would admit it only because a human *body* so named once produced certain effects on the sensoria of men existing in a certain century and certain place—effects which were "not dependent on their own mental spontaneity or activity, but by which they were involuntarily affected." He does not doubt the existence of mind and will, and affection, but he entirely disbelieves in their existence *separate* from the body.

"Personality, individuality, consciousness, without Nature is nothing; or, which is the same thing, an empty unsubstantial abstraction. But Nature, as has been shown and is obvious, is nothing without corporeality. The body alone is that negativing, limiting, concentrating, circumscribing force, without which no personality is conceivable. Take away from thy personality its body, and thou takest away that which holds it together. The body is the basis, the subject of personality. Only by the body is a real personality distinguished from the imaginary one of a spectre. What sort of abstract, vague, empty, personalities should we be if we had not the property of impenetrability—if in the same place, in the same form in which we are, others might stand at the same time? Only by the exclusion of others from the space it occupies, does personality prove itself to be real."

Hence, unless something affects my *senses* without my concurrence or consent, Feuerbach refuses to believe that it does not originate in me. In any *other* case, he virtually says, "You suppose this influence not to originate in your own mind; but that is an error. You admit that it did not affect you through your senses, and anything that affects your mind only, must have originated in your own mind."

Thus Feuerbach says expressly:—"Real sensational existence is that which is not dependent on my own mental spontaneity or activity, but by which I am involuntarily affected, which is, when I can not, when I do not think of it or feel it. The existence of God must therefore be in space—in general, a qualitative, sensational existence. But God is not seen, not heard, not perceived by the senses. He does not exist for me if I do not exist for Him. If I do not believe in a God, there is no God for me. If I am not devoutly disposed, if I do not raise myself above the life of the senses, He has no place in my consciousness. Thus He exists only so far as He is felt, thought, believed in,—the addition 'for me' is unnecessary. His existence, therefore, is a real one, yet, at the same time, not a real one,—a spiritual existence, says the theologian. But spiritual existence is only an existence in thought, in feeling, in belief; so that His existence is a medium between sensational existence and conceptional existence, a medium full of contradiction." It is hard to call this series of reiterated assumptions reasoning; it is mere tenacious assertion that sensation is the only conceivable evidence of independent existence. It is not even clear what Feuerbach means. I have no sensation of the attraction exercised upon me by the matter of the earth and sun. Reasoning alone persuades me that there is such an attractive force. Am I then to disbelieve in the independent existence of that attractive force? Feuerbach will, indeed, hardly be supported even by the members of his own school in maintaining that there can be no evidence of independent existence except what is derived through the senses. Men of science would laugh at him for an assumption which would at once dispose of most of their discoveries—gravity, an undulating ether, the velocity of light, and a host of others.

Passing by, however, this obvious blunder, of which it would be absurd to take advantage, it must of course be admitted that we do mean by evidence of an "independent existence," evidence of an existence "by which I am involuntarily affected, which is when I can not, when I do not think of it or feel it." If God be not that, the Atheists are right. If He cannot be shown to our own minds to be that, the religious sceptics, "agnostics," or "know-nothings" are right. But, curiously enough, Feuerbach never really grapples with this question, never discusses any other criterion of independent existence than this false criterion of the evidence of sensation. We have seen that the religious phenomena on which he harps so much are capable of two explanations,—the gradual unfolding of human faculty to apprehend a really existent God, and the mere "projection" of its own conceptions into the external universe. But the latter explanation is bound to show also *why* man is so deceived by the phantom of himself as to believe universally in his own dependence on that phantom, instead of sooner discovering, with Feuerbach, the dependence of that phantom upon him. Surely an explanation ought to be found for this extraordinary illusion. So far as it goes, it is at least a consideration against Feuerbach's explanation that man has so universally accepted the opposite view. It is at all events, for so universal an error, one of an exceptional kind. We do not usually "project" our Ariels or Calibans, our visions of imaginary worlds, into a fanciful reality. I think I can show that, on the contrary, we have a real criterion, of which Feuerbach takes no notice, that God's existence is independent of ourselves.

Feuerbach avoids altogether the consideration of that experience of moral obligation which chiefly compels man to believe in a universal mental power distinct from himself and unfettered by limits of space and time; that is, he never touches the deepest of all roots of our faith in the supernatural, the moral root. The consciousness of moral obligation, and that of moral freedom which accompanies it, are due to no abstracting process such as Feuerbach uses to explain our conceptions of God. They are the essential characteristics of a very positive experience, which, from its universality, and at the same time its absolute independence of space and time-relations, forces on us the sense of a Power which besets our moral life, while absolutely penetrating all the physical conditions of our existence. "Thou hast beset me behind and before, and laid Thine hand upon me,"—"Oh! whither shall I go from Thy Spirit, and whither shall I flee from Thy presence? If I go up into Heaven Thou art there; if I go down to Hell Thou art there also;"—are no vague utterances of the imagination, striving to set free its ideas from the limits of finite existence. This is but the natural language of the mind that truly describes the pressure and the absence of pressure—it is either and it is both—of *duty* upon it. Accustomed as man is to feel his personal feebleness, his entire subordination to the physical forces of the universe—unable as he is to affect in the smallest degree either the laws of his body or the fundamental constitution of his mind—it is not without a necessary sense of supernatural awe that, in the case of moral duty, he finds this almost constant pressure remarkably withdrawn at the very crisis in which the import of his action is brought home to him with the most vivid conviction. Of what nature can a Power be that moves us hither and thither through the ordinary courses of our lives, but withdraws its hand at those critical points where we have the clearest sense of authority, in order to let us act for ourselves? The absolute control that sways so much of our life is waived just where we are impressed with the most profound conviction that there is but one path in which we can move with a free heart. To what end, then, are we allowed this exceptional liberty to reject that path, unless a special interest attach to our use of it? And, if so, are we not then surely *watched*? Is it not clear that the Power which has therein ceased to *move* us, has retired only to observe, to see how we pass through this discipline of self-education? The sense that a supernatural eye is upon us in duty is so strong, because the relaxation of constraint comes simultaneously with a deep sense of obligation; as the child is instinctively aware when the sustaining hand is taken away, that the parent's eye is all the more intent on his unassisted movement. The sense of *judgment*, of a constant vigilance exercised over the secret exercise of free will, can never be obliterated from the human breast. The mind is pursued into its freest movements by this belief that the Power within could only voluntarily have receded from its task of moulding us in order to keep watch over us as we mould ourselves. And this instinctive conviction of the supernatural Life surrounding us in the exercise of our moral responsibility, is taken up and strengthened by that mysterious guidance through the labyrinth of outward circumstances which almost all observant consciences feel to be full of purpose in its adaptation to their individual moral wants. That sense of an internal spiritual vigilance over us which is first and most deeply impressed on the mind in every experience of moral obligation is echoed by the experience of outward influences, as we see those moral situations prepared for us which are most needed to discipline our special gifts, or supply our special deficiencies, or bring home to us our special sins. The experience of moral responsibility first inspires, and the personal appeals of Providence deepen, the trust in the moral Power that embraces us.

According to the conception of Feuerbach, the blind agencies of the universe only first develope into consciousness in man—a belief which renders the whole experience of moral obligation utterly inexplicable. Like a mountain summit, the human mind then stretches upwards into vacancy, while it covers a mass that is rooted in the earth. The moral nature must, then, be wholly determined by the physical agencies on which it is reared. And to suppose that they could give a power of self-determination of which they are not themselves possessed, or issue in a sense of obligation, when they are a mere bundle of helpless forces, is to suppose Nature at once free and servile, vigilant and asleep.

Take another test whether or not the moral constitution of man contains in itself any distinct evidence of independence or dependence, of being in itself the summit of creation, or of showing its highest perfection in that receptive and listening attitude which implies that there is a source beyond and above it from which it may receive and hear what is most essential for its guidance. A great discoverer, or a great genius in purely human arts, is a man who, after he has learned all he can, shows a deep self-reliance and an imperious audacity in making new combinations and striking out new enterprises. In such arts a man who jealously restrained his own impulses of self-confidence would be at once felt to be second-rate,—to be a copyist. How is it that by the universal assent of mankind this is otherwise in relation to moral excellence, that the ideal character—the character which we even regard as morally the most original, that is, as embodying the most of true creative genius—is of the opposite type? How is it that humility, or the habit of waiting to be ruled by some power that is acknowledged to be often mortifying to self—not enterprise or the ambition of boldly striking out the path most in harmony with previous theory and experience—is regarded as affording the highest type of moral excellence? If a real revealing character draws men on, in proportion as they have faithfulness and trust, this is natural enough. But if spiritual progress is all self-caused, and our religion is only the high-tide mark of our self-attained practice, it would seem that a certain boldness and self-dependence and natural arbitrariness would be the best means of access to new and better standards of moral conception. Yet it is the very basis of a religious character, and of the essence of that prophetic power which has most influenced the fate of men, it is even the essence of such characters as that of Socrates, no less than that of Christ, to be utterly dependent on guidance from within. It is no accident that the highest and finest minds are essentially of the leaning type, and marked chiefly by humility. This truly indicates that those learn most of moral truth who are most willing to be passive in the hands of God. Were God only the glorified image of man, those who had the greatest amount of intrinsic self-reliance and inborn impetuous impulse would be as much leaders in the spiritual and moral as they are in the secular world.

III.

SCIENCE AND THEISM.[1]

THERE is a vague, general dread that Science, if fairly faced, is atheistic in its tendency. Men are haunted with the phantom of a power that they dare not challenge, which is rumoured to have superseded and exposed natural theology, and to be gradually withdrawing every fold of mystery from the universe, without disclosing any trace of God. I am anxious to show that, though Science cannot be expected to reveal God, it is nevertheless far more favourable to Theism than to Atheism, indeed that it presents to the thought a spectacle of incredible incoherence without the theistic nexus. On every side alike—in the absence of this ground-faith—analysis unravels the component threads of reality,

---

[1] 'Principles of Psychology.' By Herbert Spencer. Longmans, 1855.
'On the Origin of Species by means of Natural Selection, or the Preservation of Favoured Races in the Struggle for Life.' London. Murray, 1860.

but dissipates, by some strange sleight of hand, the living force that wove them, and leaves us at last with a so-called "equivalent" for concrete fact, which, like dry colours scraped off a picture, has indeed been fetched out of actual existence, but which no power could ever constitute into it again.

The object of all science is said truly to be the attainment of unity. But unity is an ambiguous word; and there are two ideas concerning scientific unity in vogue, one of which is synonymous with generality or high abstraction, the other with the idea of a real tie or bond. The one notion of unity is derived from each single science, and is related to concrete fact exactly as universal truths are related to particular cases. Here the unity is really the unit of which the individual elements are fractions; there is no uniting, because there is no possibility of real separation even in thought. The special cases illustrate the abstract whole; they cannot be bound up together, because they are only different aspects of the same thought. The other notion of unity is derived not from single sciences, but from the conjunction of many, and denotes the vinculum, or sheath, under which branches of thought or existence, really different in kind, are taken up into a single complex root or stem. In the former case the unity and the variety are both purely formal, and the tie or bond is purely intellectual,—standing for a power in our intelligence to explain different examples by the same rule; in the latter case the unity is a *power*—holding together positively divergent provinces, distinct forms of existence. Now Science, properly regarded, aims, I believe, at reaching both these kinds of unity,—each in its right place. In each single science it aims at generalising the particular cases into the abstract formula which includes them all— at getting back to the fundamental conception of the science from studying to comprehend all its phenomena in one law. But true universal Science does not attempt to ignore real differences of kind between the special phenomena of its various branches; and therefore it aims not at falsely identifying radical distinctions, but at finding out how they may be really united without being confounded.

The real unity, then, at which true Science aims is unity of conception. Where it can identify apparent varieties as mere modifications of one and the same conception, it does so, and creates *a* science. Where, on the other hand, it can make the universe conceivable to us only by admitting, to the full, specific and ultimate differences of kind in its phenomena, it admits those differences, and studies to find a higher unity, not by further generalising, but by looking for a uniting *power*. The only test we have of the truth of scientific hypothesis is the degree of aid it gives us in representing to ourselves at will the facts of the universe without distinct individual study of each. Hence nothing is less scientific than any hypothesis which tries to run one set of facts into another without justification, in order to evade the admission of a distinct root. Instead of increasing our means of representing the universe, such a procedure confuses and disturbs them. Why was Copernican astronomy preferred to the old Ptolemaic astronomy? First, because it rendered the mental representation of the facts studied simpler than before; next and most, because it suggested new and true representations of relations not hitherto represented to the mind at all. It was one step towards a justification, to find that we could conceive as simple relations what had hitherto been conceived as most complex relations; but when that mode of conceiving the planets' motions suggested modes of including quite other relations (such as the motion of bodies on the earth's surface) in the same thought,—that is, not only simplified what had before been reduced to definite conceptions, but reduced other facts within the scope of the same definite conceptions,—the thing was regarded as certainly established. Of course it could not be *proved*. No one can see what force keeps the earth in her orbit, or the moon in hers, or what draws the stone to the ground. It is still quite conceivable that no such forces exist at all, but quite different and far more complicated forces, producing the same effects. But the belief in the new astronomy is grounded on the assumption that whatever hypothesis gives our reason the best means of representing actual fact, gives us that means just because it is the reflected image of actual fact. For instance, why do scientific men daily attach more and more credit to the wave-theory of light, and less and less (I believe) to the atom-theory of matter? Simply because the former not only enables them to represent all that is hitherto known, but daily increases their power of representing to themselves hitherto unknown relations of light and colour. It is a working hypothesis, opening up ever new explanations of relations hitherto more or less outlying and unattached. The latter (the atom-theory) has, on the other hand, never represented anything but the combining proportions of chemical substances, and is a mere arbitrary form of that. It is a dead addition to the law of combining proportions, suggesting nothing beyond it.

All science, then, aims at enabling us to represent fact more and more completely to our own minds.. It takes accurate representative power as its best test of reality. Hence any attempt to merge the *distinctive* characteristic of a higher science in a lower—of chemical changes in mechanical—of physiological in chemical—above all, of mental changes in physiological—is a neglect of the radical assumption of all science, because it is an attempt to deduce representations—or rather misrepresentations—of one kind of phenomenon from a conception of another kind which does not contain it, and must have it implicitly and illicitly smuggled in before it can be extracted out thereof. Hence, instead of increasing our means of representing the universe to ourselves without the detailed examination of particulars, such a procedure leads to misconstructions of fact on the basis of an imported theory, and generally ends in forcibly perverting the least-known science to the type of the better known.

These remarks apply almost necessarily to any view of science that excludes the conception of a primary mind in the universe; unless, indeed, it be bold enough —which it never is—to assert that at every stage in the evolution of the universe new phenomena throng into existence, self-created, which had no previous equivalent, no spring or source of being at all,—which admit, in short, of no analysis into any antecedent phenomena. If this be admitted, then Science is a body of thought, which, starting from concrete reality, utterly loses a thread at every step back into the past, till it unravels into the "Absolute Nothing." Mental phenomena fall off first into the "Absolute Nothing," as they rose last out of it; then vital phenomena drop away, then organic, then chemical, then mechanical, lastly geometrical; and Science has rendered her account by gradually wiping out her score. This system, which deifies the creative power of Zero, is the boldest but also absurdest form of Atheism. In it Science boasts to be identical with Nescience. No one ever seriously held it, though of course it has been maintained.

But, Nihilism apart, science can only be atheistic through the confusion of the two kinds of unity I have mentioned — *i.e.* through that extreme analysis which admits no radical differences of kind in the phenomena of the universe at all, and proposes therefore to deduce all the complex combinations from the more simple, and these again, ultimately, from some highly abstract and simple formula or unit of existence—the nutshell of the universe—by pure analysis of that unit into its constituent elements. This danger might be escaped, if such speculators chose to maintain that Reason is absolutely incapable of uniting the particular sciences into a single whole, and can neither analyse one into the other nor find any living tie or knot by which to combine them, but must be content to bring their common analogies to light, and keep their distinctive phenomena apart. But this is exactly what Atheism almost always will not do. Indeed, could Atheism take this course, it could scarcely long survive as Atheism. To admit the reality and irreducible nature of mental phenomena—to admit that they cannot anyhow be analysed into physical—is either to put a period to all inquiry as to cause, or to open a broad way into Theism; and the less men believe in an Infinite Being, the more thirsty usually is their curiosity about the supposed genesis of our mental nature.

The result is, that the problem of all atheistic philosophers has been, not to find the *real* ultimate link between the different classes of natural force and life, but to soften away as much as possible the one into the other, so as to make the transition imperceptible, and so introduce a thoroughly new creative force *as if* it were but an expansion of that beneath it. It is a mere self-deception of philosophy, to accept the graduality of the stages by which life ascends from the gravitating force of inorganic matter to the highest pinnacle of human reason as any sort of evidence that the universe was all implicitly involved in its earliest stage. There can be no reason in assuming, contrary to all evidence, that all forces and all organisms, and all life and all reason, lie shut up implicitly (*i. e.* without any manifestation or possible symptom of existence) in that which seems possessed of no force and no organism, and no life and no reason. If this assumption be not made, then, as we know only of one great power totally escaping sensible analysis and yet able to effect sensible changes—the power of mind,—the natural assumption is, that the actual and sensible additions to existence come out of that power. What is gained by showing the *graduality* of the transition from one creative process to another? Because only a small addition has been made to the living resources of the world—is it any the more possible to identify it with that which it is not? Because the boundary between vegetable and animal life is but little distinct, can we any the more ignore the fact that some fresh power has been given to the world when a locomotive capacity gradually creeps into it? Because the creeping is so gradual, is it any the more possible to identify it with no-creeping? Because the automatic action in the infant very slowly opens into consciousness, is consciousness at all the more capable of identification with automatic action? Because instinct and habit are the unconscious instruments of adapting means to ends, and intelligence the conscious and voluntary adapter of means to ends, shall we talk of the *germinal intelligence* in the processes of the bee? As correctly, or more correctly (for the act *may* become semi-conscious and semi-voluntary), might we talk of the intelligent cough by which a man adapts the action of his lungs to the removal of an obstruction in the windpipe.

This attempt to analyse away the positive additions of creative power, by merely noting how gradually they steal into the universe, appears to show most strikingly how the absence of theistic faith tends to expel reality from science, and to make philosophy the universal solvent of fact, instead of the spirit which investigates the order, correspondence, and the ultimate connections of all fact in the concrete and complex unity of the highest life. Thus, by far the most able recent writer of this school, Mr. Herbert Spencer, who, as I said in my first essay, utterly disclaims Atheism, but yet recognises no evidence that the inscrutable Cause of the Universe is what the Theist means by a personal God, looks for his definition of "life" from a survey of all the phenomena, vegetable, physiological, and psychical, of which it is ordinarily predicated. He defines it thus: "Life is the continuous adjustment of internal relations to external relations;" or more at length, but less simply: "Life is the definite combination of heterogeneous changes, both simultaneous and successive, *in correspondence with external coexistences and sequences.*" Now if Mr. Spencer only means by this to indicate, that which *all* forms of what is ordinarily termed life have in common, we should be grateful for this contribution to the analysis of a most complex conception. But he slides in immediately a very favourite axiom of the religious know-nothing school, that all differences between the phenomena of the lower and higher sciences are differences of degree—differences in the *stage* of expansion—not differences of *kind;* and so proceeds to deduce that the highest mental life has nothing more in it than is indicated in this definition. He first overlooks, ignores, rejects, the special characteristics of personal life—which would be legitimate in forming an abstract idea—and then, forgetting that it *is* abstract, and that all the differentia of the highest kind of life has been neglected, he clips down that highest kind of life to the limits of his definition. There is positively nothing in his conception of the higher life to indicate a real difference of kind between man and a vegetable. He must therefore, of course, reject originating power—free-will in man. He does so: and thus defends his position:—

"Respecting this matter, I will only further say, that free-will, did it exist, would be entirely at variance with that beneficent necessity displayed in the progressive evolution of the correspondence between the organism and its environment. That gradual advance in the moulding of inner relations to outer relations, which has been delineated in the foregoing pages—that ever-extending adaptation of the cohesions of psychical states to the connections between the answering phenomena, which we have seen to result from the accumulation of experiences, would be arrested, did there exist any thing which otherwise determined their cohesions. As it is, we see that the correspondence between the internal changes and the external coexistences and sequences must become more and more complete. The continuous adjustment of the vital activities to the activities in the environment, must become more accurate and exhaustive. The life must become higher and the happiness greater—must do so because the inner relations are determined by the outer relations. But were the inner relations to any extent determined by some other agency, the harmony at any moment subsisting, and the advance to a higher harmony, would alike be interrupted to a proportionate extent; there would be an arrest of that grand progression which is now bearing humanity onwards to perfection."

—which only means that Mr. Spencer thinks free-will *à priori* unlikely, because it is not a self-adjusting *apparatus*, but a self-adjusting spirit; because it is not determined absolutely by the external world, but determines itself after free intelligent judgment on both worlds, internal and external. "The psychical states," as Mr. Spencer denominates a *man*, "cannot determine their own cohesions." I do not know a more remarkable instance of the confusion between the *unity* of the sciences and the *identity* of the sciences, than is given by this development of voluntary life out of the idea of vegetable life. In the vegetable, Mr. Spencer says, the self-preservative correspondence between internal and external changes is simple, limited to a narrow region of space, and almost limited to the present moment in time. In the animal, with the gradual growth of a nervous system, the correspondence becomes much more full—extends over a wider region in space (as when the bee is driven far and wide for its honey), and reaches over a longer time (as in the instincts which provide against the future emergencies of seasonal change). In the intellect of man it reaches its acme by the ripening of forecasting instincts into a widely-ranging consciousness. The "afferent" nerves bring reports to the brain,—the common-hall through which, now, almost all sensations pass, and where they establish a mutual understanding, so as to have their reports compared, connected, and enlarged. Here, too, ensues the conflict as to which of the "afferent" nerves shall get the command of the "efferent" nerves which convey motory impulses from the brain. This conflict is what we mean by voluntary choice. The psychical states, which are too weak to win, and are merely candidates for an "efferent" nerve, are our passive memories, emotions, and the like. The victorious candidates are our volitions. And this is the *rationale* of our moral nature!—physiology excluding from mental life all that does not suit the scientific analogies in her own domain! Have I not some reason for saying that this is a confusion of the sciences, not a unity of the sciences? Is it not clear that this positive method puts into the higher science as little more than it gets from the lower science as it can possibly help?—that it strives to varnish over their distinctions, instead of to combine them? How could even the semi-intelligent life of the higher animals be described merely as a cohesion of psychical states, if the notion did not come up from the vegetable world beneath? The unity that was not in the source cannot be in the result. A cohesion of simultaneous and serial changes is all that is seen in the vegetable, and therefore a cohesion of simultaneous and serial changes is all that can be found in the man!

There is, however, as is generally supposed, a much stronger stronghold of the non-theistic view of the

Universe in Mr. Darwin's recent physiological discoveries, than in the view of those who believe in the ultimate identity of all sorts of forms, physical and moral, and who explain away, as a mere change of form, the gradual accession of power which is gained at every step in the ascent from the force of gravity to the force of will. Mr. Darwin has discovered that very many of the more important modifications, and especially the *improvements* in animal and vegetable organization, are ultimately due to what looks at first sight very much like a fortunate *accident*. At least he shows that of an indefinite number of individual variations in the type, that one which tends to give an advantage to the individual in the struggle for life in any particular region of the world, tends also to be perpetuated in that region, while any variation that tends to cause a disadvantage to the individual in any particular region, tends also to be extinguished in that region. The mode in which this happens is very simple. A creature with any variety of organization useful to it, is in a position to avoid danger or to procure food more easily than its fellows which have not that variety ; it is therefore likely to have a less difficult and disturbed existence, and a more numerous family, many of which will inherit the variety: on the other hand, all creatures born with a variation of organization that is unfavourable to their escape from beasts of prey, or to their power of procuring their own food, will tend to die off exceptionally soon, or, if they live to breed, will breed descendants probably inheriting the unfavourable variety, and therefore in special danger of extinction. Hence Mr. Darwin has apparently discovered a principle which accounts for the selection of improved types,—improved, that is, in reference to the evasion of danger or the command of the means of subsistence,—and for the extinction of deteriorated types—deteriorated, that is, in relation to the same conditions—without assuming that there was any more special *design* in the elaboration of the former than of the latter. It is as if Paley's imaginary watch, which immediately disposes the finder to believe that it was made by design, were traced to a manufactory containing a great variety of other instruments, varying through all degrees of usefulness and uselessness; the more useful, however, having been at once valued and preserved and multiplied through the appreciation of the external world, while the vast number of useless ones had been neglected and allowed to go to decay. If this were so, people would at once be apt to infer that the useful articles had been originally no more designed than the useless ones; though, once produced, they had been taken better care of, and multiplied in much greater numbers. If it were discovered that a certain poet had written nineteen or twenty senseless stanzas, and nine hundred or a thousand stanzas of little meaning, for every stanza of pure poetry, though the latter had all been carefully preserved and published by a delighted world, while the former had been at once forgotten, such a poet would probably be supposed to have written his more popular pieces by accident; though, when written, it was not accident which caused them to be valued and sedulously preserved. And, in the same way, Mr. Darwin's discovery that an improvement of organization is only a single one amongst many changes which are not improvements, and many of which may be changes for the worse, suggests to many minds that there was no more design in the improvement which is perpetuated simply because it helps the animal to live, than in the variations for the worse which were soon lost, simply because they made it more difficult for the animal to live. In a word, Mr. Darwin's discovery seems to bring back the idea of *luck* into the modification of the forms of vegetable and animal existence. The varieties which succeed are those which *happen* to be in harmony with the external needs of the creature; those which are extinguished are those which *happen* to be out of harmony with those needs. The old conception of Natural Theology rested on the notion that design anticipated all the wants of the different classes of creatures, and gave them at once and exactly what was most suited to those wants. What is the difference, it will be said, between trying a hundred experiments in organization which fail, to one that succeeds, and playing at a game of chance where the odds are a hundred to one against you?

I will try to answer this. What Mr. Darwin has discovered is, a general system or constitution for the modifying of physical organisms; and, as soon as any general constitution is established in the place of what looked like individual acts of adaptation or design, the jurisdiction of the inquiry as to design is clearly removed from the domain of the individual organism to that of the general constitution under which it is liable to be modified; so that the true matter to be inquired into obviously is, *not* "Is there any more special design in the variation of type which profits an animal than in the variation of type which is disadvantageous to it?" but rather, "Is the system, as a whole, one which implies design or not?" Now, in discussing this, I must note, first, that struggle and competition for food—the preying of one tribe of animals upon another—is not by any means a new fact, but is one of the old puzzles of natural theology; but that which is a new fact of Mr. Darwin's discovery is that this struggle and competition are the direct means of adjusting the organisms of the vegetable and animal world more completely to the conditions in which they live, *i. e.* of *improving* the physical type of the various tribes of vegetables and animals. So far, I think, Mr. Darwin's discovery tends to diminish rather than to increase the old difficulty of animal conflict, and of the preying of one order on another, since the effect of all this is to introduce a greater perfection into organization, and a greater economy into the whole system; the tribes of plants and animals which are capable of economising their means most, gaining a great advantage over those which are incapable of it, and so gradually superseding them.

Dr. Hooker has pointed out a very remarkable illustration of this, in showing that the plants and animals of the old world, which have, of course, had a far more complete sifting by the process of natural selection than those of recently discovered lands, have acquired so great a superiority over the plants and animals of New Zealand and South America, that they almost always beat the latter directly they are imported from home. Thus the English fly soon supersedes entirely the disgusting and enormous blue-bottle of New Zealand. The English rat drives out the Maori rat. The little clover competes successfully even with the *phormium tenax*, the sword-flax, " a plant of the coarsest, hardest, and toughest description, that forms huge matted patches of woody rhizomes, which send up tufts of sword-like leaves six to ten feet high, and inconceivably strong in texture and fibre." This is " the weak things of the world confounding the mighty " over again, though in a purely physical sense :—the explanation, no doubt, being that in the old countries only those kinds of vegetables and animals whose habits of life and growth have become in the highest degree economical, survive ; and that these, when transplanted to regions where natural selection has not yet formed such habits of economy, drive everything before them,—the grasses sucking away nourishment from the great indigenous ferns and flax, the rats and flies exploring and appropriating, with habits of ancestral economy and cunning, the storehouses of the native rats and flies. Hence, surely, it is obvious that the competitive system of nature, which, before Mr. Darwin's discoveries, looked simply purposeless and cruel, is now at last shown to evolve higher and more economical types of organization, types which are more consistent with the wants of man, and less likely to come into collision with him. This is the removal of a difficulty, not the addition of one.

But, then, is not this self-acting arrangement for weeding the universe of its inferior organisms capable of being interpreted as a *substitute* for a sovereign mind, as the explanation of what mimics the action of a sovereign mind, rather than as the indication of a real sovereign mind? Does it not, like the nebular theory of astronomy, seem, if once assumed to be in action, to be as sufficient for the phenomena which come out of it, as the theory of an intellectual and conscious Creator? That must, surely, depend rather on its *relative* place and importance in the universe, than on any examination of its particular operation. You cannot adequately judge whether geological causes might have produced the flint axes and knives or not, till you can compare, on a wide scale, what is actually produced by purely geological causes, with what is actually produced by human purpose. Now, I observe that the Darwinian theory starts from the assumption of organic types competent to reproduce themselves, and needing external food for their perpetuation, as its point of departure, and does not profess to go back for its origin to what I may call the ante-tentative and ante-competitive era of the universe, when the store of forms was as little variable as the store of forces. Moreover, it is obvious that the Darwinian theory is quite incapable of explaining the specifically human phenomenon of the rise of what may be called an anti-Darwinian conscience, which restrains and subordinates the principle of competition, inspiring pity for those degraded types of nature which, on Darwinian principles, simply stand in need of extinction, and expending the best elements of human energy on the rescue of weakness and the redemption of sin.

In other words, the selective power of the competitive principle is limited to the functions of physical life in the universe; cannot explain at all how physical life, capable of reproducing itself, comes into being from that which is not capable of reproducing itself; can explain still less how, out of a system sharpened and improved solely by competition, comes an order of beings who put strict limits on competition, curb it in the higher parts of their own nature, and recognize that he who will not "break the bruised reed" is higher far than he who labours to extinguish a low type of humanity, however unpromising for the purposes of future "selection," instead of to use and elevate it. Taken, then, in its true place in the universe, the Darwinian explanation of the laws of organic progress seems to me to make for the theistic argument instead of against it. The evidence that the world is weeded of its lower organic types by the success of the higher, is no explanation of the growth of life out of that which is not living, and is no explanation of the growth of love out of that which is not loving.

I think Mr. Darwin's discovery rather supports than weakens the impression that all these subordinate systems or constitutions in the universe are raised one above the other by a being who embraces in Himself the full scope of all. Certainly, in showing that the bitter conflicts of animal (as of vegetable) life lead to higher types and greater economy of function, it somewhat dispels the darkness of a sufficiently difficult problem. That which seemed to be mere war is now seen to be war that weeds the world of what is worse adapted to its particular place in it, for the sake of what is better adapted to that place.

And here seems the right point to note that neither the scientific principle of what is called the "correlation of forces" (that is the equivalence of forces which seem to be of very different kinds, like heat and motion, or heat and nervous action, or nervous action and thought), nor the Darwinian law of selection by conflict for existence, seems to throw the smallest glimpse of light on the origin of human free will, and that sense of responsibility of which free will is the absolute condition. As for the Darwinian law, it is simply inconceivable, supposing you deny free will to the lower types of organic beings, out of which, in his conception, the higher species are gradually elaborated by natural selection, that an accidental variation should introduce free will; and, as we have seen, Mr. Spencer asserts that if (by any possibility) it could be so, it would be a change so fatal to the harmony between "the vital activities" and "the activities in the environment," that the individuals burdened with so fatal a quality would soon succumb in the conflict for existence. It is, however, inconceivable that any law of *transmission* should introduce an element of freedom which was entirely absent from the universe before. All that is supposed to vary in the qualities derived from ancestors is the proportion in which they are mingled, and, so to say, the mode of application to the universe outside. But that a necessary being should give birth to a being with any amount, however limited, of moral freedom is infinitely less conceivable than that parents of the insect or fish type should give birth to a perfect mammal. An accidental variation only means a variation of which you cannot determine the direction; but you can determine that the direction of variation will not outrage all the laws of parentage.

But if the Darwinian principle wholly fails to render such a fact as free will in the offspring of absolutely determined natures, even conceivable, so equally does the supposed scientific principle that all the higher forms of force are mere highly-refined and complex equivalents of the lower forms. If all the lower laws of force and life are absolutely fixed and inviolable, then they cannot revoke their own constitution when they issue out of the region of physiology into that of moral life. If it be the essence of all things to follow fixed laws, if there is nothing but unchangeable force moulding the universe by its gradually concentrating strength, then the conscience of man is a delusion, and his sense of responsibility and freedom must be explained away. But if the pressure of necessity is really removed just at the very point where the sense of the awful importance of our choice is most intensely realised,—if the iron chain of events by which our course is guided is unclasped, and we are permitted to go either to the right hand or to the left, just when we are most distinctly conscious that a false step is an irretrievable and infinite evil—then we cannot be the offspring of law, or embodiments of definite force. The logic of Science is consistent, but it does not explain freedom. We know that we are morally free; and we know that a free person cannot be the issue of helplessly unfolded laws. It is impossible for necessity to emancipate itself. Only if the observed necessity has been the "must" of a divine free will, can that "must" be withdrawn, and freedom restored wherever the materials for self-determination have been granted. The identity of all the sciences is assumed only at the expense of the falsification of some, and the total abrogation of one. The main facts of man's moral nature,—all those which assume personal responsibility, duty and sin, merit and demerit, praise and blame, reward and retribution,—all those on which the great interests of mankind centre, all which are the life of reverence and love,—are swept away into meaningless unreality by the absolute identification of moral science with the natural sciences on the summit of which it stands. It is dangerous enough to scientific reality to confuse intelligence with instinct, and to describe memory as "a weak form" of perception; but it is the suicide of a science to manufacture a theory of moral obligation out of the materials of physical necessity—a theory of vision for the blind.

IV.

POPULAR PANTHEISM.[1]

MR. FOX'S conception of the Religious Ideas makes faith not the controlling and regenerating power of human life, but the natural completion and embellishment of an otherwise maimed and fragmentary existence. He presents us with a kind of popular Pantheism, which adds the last beautifying touches, as it were, the intellectual finish to the temporary happiness of earthly existence. He assigns to man his place in the universal order, pieces the human mind into its proper niche in the great scenic display of Creative power, and shows man's adaptation alike for a God and a future. He discovers a religious firmament so sublime and universal that it bends equally over all aspects and developments of human nature, and is the ornament of all. He argues

---

[1] 'On the Religious Ideas.' By William Johnson Fox, M.P. London: Charles Fox, 1849.

for God and immortality, and the final extinction of the negation which we call evil, on principles derived from a disposition to trust universal human hopes and to complete the cycle of human progress. In a word, the sense of harmony—the æsthetic faculty—seems to require a religion for man, and, therefore, such religion as will satisfy this sense of harmony must be true. Such seems to be the general drift of Mr. Fox's Pantheism. Indeed his book gives us so slight and rhetorical a statement of this æsthetic phase of religion, that were it not for the attraction which this kind of artistic religion seems to have, especially for those who make up for the absence of a real faith by the poetic religiosity of their views of the universe, it would hardly perhaps be very useful to point out what appear to be its chief deficiencies. But its eclectic width of sentiment, its generous promise of harmonizing a satisfying faith with all positive religions on the one hand, and with all modern science on the other, its really liberal tone to more positive forms of faith, and its imposing dress of illustration, are so representative of a certain school of easy-going æsthetic religion, as to deserve to be regarded as a distinct type.

Mr. Fox gives as the Religious Ideas which are the constituents of all forms of faith, Revelation, God, Creation and Providence, Redemption, Human Immortality, Duty, Heaven, and proceeds to discuss the grounds on which he considers them not merely subjective, but representative of realities beyond the mind. This discussion is not an important part of his book, and I may pass it by with the remark, that did anything essential depend on this part of his reasoning, he would have built upon very precarious ground. A philosophy which puts the evidence of religious faith on the same ground of certainty with the presumption that the most natural of Shakspeare's characters either do exist, have existed, or will exist (p. 27), and makes mere "*congruity with the laws of nature indicative of reality*" (p. 26), would not win any very general assent. It is, however, quite unnecessary to deal with these general remarks on the criteria of objective existence, because in the succeeding chapters Mr. Fox begins all over again with each of his religious ideas, when he considers them separately. After urging the usual difficulties against the possibility of any positive revelation, that is not sanctioned by the mind of man, Mr. Fox gives his own completely pantheistic idea of revelation—pantheistic, I mean, in the sense that it advisedly confuses the personalities of God and man,—thus :—

"Wherever moral and spiritual truth suggests itself to the mind, grows in that mind, passes from it to other minds, there is revelation."—P. 45.

And again :—

"There is a state of mind to which it comes—not preternaturally—there is no conjuration in the case, there is no violation of law; it comes in harmony with the great laws of matter, mind, spirit. When a man has meditated in solitude or discussed in society—if he has become familiar with antique volumes, or has listened to living teachers—whenever and wherever he has felt himself most at one with the scheme of things in which he exists; when, his mind retiring from petty struggles and petty enjoyments, or seeking relief from its weight of sorrows, allowing the course of his thoughts to run freely, he has perceived, amid the various confusion of things, some moral truth as it were beaming from above,—there has been God's revelation; and let him lay it to his heart and cherish it."—P. 46.

Now, inspiration is in truth denied altogether wherever it is reduced to a consequence of laws that act independently of the strictly personal, *i. e.* individual, relation subsisting between each human soul and the mind of God. What God suggests by means of laws that are, to use a mathematical phrase, no *function* of the individual, as *e. g.* the general laws of formal thought, *that* clearly is not inspiration. The truest and highest view of our relation to God, is to regard Him as a distinct person, having laws in His own nature, partially like those which He has given us for our nature; and then what He communicates to us by the general laws regulating the *constitution* which He gave us, and which we have modified, is in the ordinary course of His providence; what He communicates in consequence of prayers of our own,—imploring Him not to leave us to the providential laws which regulate and develop our present self-educated faculties, but to take up a *personal* relation to us in our present state as self-formed beings,—may be regarded as inspirations. The sense I wish to convey will perhaps be best illustrated by a comment on Mr. Fox's explanation of his own meaning. He says:—

"When the impulse came to Gibbon, in the ruins of the Coliseum, amid mouldering walls and deepening shadows—when it blended with his recollections of grandeur passed away, and of its contrast with that other strange form of grandeur which had taken its place—no voice, indeed, from the clouds or from the earth said audibly to him, 'Go and write the history of the Decline and Fall of the Roman Empire, in sentences as gorgeous as the hues of that sunset by which it is typified ;' but the impulse came, came combinedly from without and from within ; it was the sort of occurrence which, told in Oriental phraseology, would be, 'The word of the Lord came to such a one, and said, Go thou and do this great work.'"—P. 58.

Now this example, chosen no doubt expressly on account of the irreverent spirit well known to pervade the great work alluded to, is admirably calculated to illustrate the difference between natural suggestion and divine inspiration. The impulse that came to Gibbon was obviously the consequence of natural capacity, acted on by the laws of association and memory, and stimulated by ambition and a moral spirit that was due to his own free acts, and I am certainly not at all disposed to deny it a place in the general plan of Providence ; still it was the result of the personal acts of his own mind, excited by the objects and sights around him. It was the effect of general laws acting on the particular, partly self-created, character of Gibbon's mind. On the other hand, that would be inspiration which proceeded, not from a regular development of the mind within, affected by its own volitions and laws, but from the spirit of God freely entering into it, whether as a consequence of inward need or entreaty, or for any other reasons such as might be sufficient to the divine mind. The moral distinction between the two cases would be this : Our faculties once given, are under our own control, and their action, when once placed under the government of our wills, is no longer entirely from above, but is affected by every one of our own moral acts, so that their later suggestions are no longer purely from God as at first they might be, but are the complex results of God's providence and of the nature He gave us, taken together with our own free volitions. Here then a term is introduced due to our own free causation, and not of God at all. Inspirations, on the other hand, must be communications given directly and wholly from God, even though they be coloured, and, so to say, reduced by the limitations of the finite nature which receives them. The difference is somewhat the same as that between the conduct that would be suggested by a friend's past relation to us, when received into our mind and modified there by our own actions and history, and that suggested by the *living* friend once more before us. Even in this case there might be misunderstanding, owing to our incapacity ; but the new impulse, the new shock, is from without, and not from our own self. Gibbon's impulse was thus not a direct communication, but the result of his nature modified by the laws that governed his life, and especially by his own voluntary acts ; had it been a pure inspiration, it might have been somewhat similar yet very different, and would have suggested to him to write a history that should attempt to trace in a very different spirit the influences exerted over the world by the moral and intellectual characteristics of the Roman empire. Mr. Fox, in refusing, both philosophically and practically, to make the distinction, appears to me to miss the very essence of religion, at the outset of his work.

Besides, no theory of Religion could be complete that failed to distinguish between mere poetic inspiration (a pre-eminence of original faculty), and that universal inspiration of the Spirit which, so long as it continues to visit us at all, comes direct from God, without being further discoloured than by the inadequacy of our own minds to comprehend fully what is communicated. Mr. Fox banishes this holy spirit entirely from human life by not admitting any personal discourse of God with the mind. Before leaving these remarks on the nature of inspiration, I may just add, that if what I have laid down be true, then the two kinds of God's intercourse with the mind, by faculty and by direct teaching, would coalesce in any being absolutely perfect, since, when untainted by neglect and sin, every faculty would remain the same channel of divine power that it was at first, and God would be as purely represented in the suggestions of a perfect nature educated in strict obedience to divine law, as in any direct discourse: in fact, the two would be identical.

Revelation, Mr. Fox argues, supposes a revealer, and from the very consciousness of *communication* to the mind, of something entering it which was not there before, we reach the conviction of a power, a life, beyond the sphere of our consciousness, and yet able to connect itself with us through those mysterious sources of being that we cannot penetrate. The entrance of pain from unseen sources, of blessing, of beauty, of right, of approval or disapproval, all this necessarily implies a life, nay, a mind, who has access to the hidden springs of our own : and this Being, once conceived of, is invested with the highest functions and powers that are consistent with the education and the wants of the people or individuals who have lifted their thoughts up to Him. Mr. Fox traces the conception of God in the Jewish scriptures, through the stages of Deliverer (when the release from the cruel bondage of Egypt formed the summit of the people's conceptions of beneficent power), of Legislator (when the reduction of the barbaric elements in the Israelitish society to a divine order seemed the most sacred and difficult of tasks), and of a divine Defender in battle (when the inroads of unjust and swollen powers caused the preservation of national liberty to be the greatest need and toil of the people). He then notices the Christian phase of religion which makes God a Father, and seems to regard it as but a temporary phase of the religious life.

"And then came the phase of supplication; the reliance upon pity in the Divinity; the plaintive, childlike cry that called on God as 'our Father ;' then came those thoughts of mercy, and patience, and kindness, forbearance and all long-suffering, which the woes and miseries of humanity have made but too enduring a form of the theological conception."—P. 72.

And this is giving way, he thinks, in our own day, to

a modification of faith which regards God chiefly in his aspect of—

..... "universality, of a pervading power; not only of an impartial providence over all human beings, of all countries and religions, but of an essence, a spirit, a soul of the universe, incorporate with all and in all, which manifests itself in every flower that blossoms, in every star that shines, in every cloud that flits across the sky, as well as in that everlasting arch which bends over all, and proclaims the Infinity co-existing with all these seeming and transitory modifications."—P. 74.

That this so-called higher conception of God's nature is strictly pantheistic, we learn from the next chapter, where, in commenting on the idea of *plurality*, which Mr. Fox thinks has never been excluded from religion, he accounts for the want of sympathy shown towards Christian Unitarianism, by its endeavour to conceive of God as an infinite person, distinct from Nature and humanity. He says:—

"It was a step in the doctrine, though it might at first seem in a backward direction, the ascription of Godhead to Christ. 'God in Christ,' was something towards God in humanity, as God in humanity was a progress towards God in universal nature. There alone we find the infinity which satisfies the thought; and departing from those blended notions that our own habit of conceiving of persons infuses into the mind, there we see one whose countenance towards us is in all that is grand and lovely—who is one with the majestic frame of the heavens and the earth—one with the mighty movements of material nature—one with intellectual and moral development in humanity—who lives, breathes, thinks, feels, acts, in and by all that is—all that is being one with Him, and He all and in all. Such at least is the last effort which the human mind seems to have made in the endeavour more fully to develop this notion of infinity, which so early and so strongly associates itself with the thought of God."—P. 87.

Now in this account of the manner in which the true notion of the great Revealer dawns upon the human mind, Mr. Fox seems to me, like all believers in a pantheistic creed, to destroy what he has set up, and get to so high a conception in the end as to invalidate all the premises with which he started. It is strange how the æsthetic faculty, craving the excitement of absolute infinitude for its contemplation, breaks loose from the restraints that the moral and intellectual nature would put upon it, and leads to a system as destitute of spiritual support as it is full of latent contradictions. The original grounds of faith in a divine cause and inspirer *fail*, the moment the personal faculties which discover Him are surrendered in favour of the newly-found Spirit. Mr. Fox's own arguments are, that fear, gratitude, admiration, and love, arising on occasion of the events of outward or inward life which have no other cause, all *imply an object*, a terrible power, a beneficent giver, a Being beautiful and sublime, an object for affection;—but the newest and highest modification of our conception of this Being, according to Mr. Fox, is that of a universal Essence, an all-pervading life that is as much represented in the fear, the gratitude, the admiration, and the love, as in the object of these emotions. True, it was this power which (in its infinite aspect) startled the fear; but then (in its finite capacity) it directly felt it. And so the supposed discovery turns into a mere childish game at hide and seek, where the finder and the found are identical, and yet each must be evidence for the real existence of the other.

Now, all the real spiritual evidence for the existence of a divine object of our worship is upset at once, the moment we cease to distinguish between the worshipper and the worshipped. It is assuredly as certain that God is an object of recognition for our minds, as matter for our senses, and that too by an exactly similar act of faith, equally irresistible (when the appropriate faculties are awake) and equally incapable of demonstration. But what would be said were any philosopher to reason thus: "I certainly perceive an external world as a reality beyond me, and to that perception I accord my faith; but a truer modification of this conception of the external induces me to say, as a more complete description of the fact, that this external existence beyond me was itself the precipient agency which acted in me at the time"? I am totally unable to perceive any difference between nonsense such as this, and the religious theory which relies on human faculties for reporting the presence of a divine power, by them perceived, and asserted in the very act of perception to be different from ourselves,—producing what we could not produce, giving us what we could not take, feeling differently from us, acting differently, thinking differently, —and which nevertheless presently turns round and says, "This Being is not in fact distinct from us, and we have found out, after all, that while we were searching for a fit object to adore and love, we were only in want of a more perfect knowledge of ourselves to show us, that it mattered not whether we loved the beneficence or the gratitude the most, since both are ultimately identical." The mystery of religion can never be solved by a process which identifies the creature and the Creator, and it were better to place no faith in our spiritual discernment at all, than to credit the witness and yet deny his existence, which is the condition of his credibility.

To my mind the assertion of the Pantheist, "I believe in God," is a contradiction; for when you look for the subject, it has vanished into the predicate, and you have the facts of fear, gratitude, &c., attesting the existence of their object, yet denying the existence of their source,— unless any one is willing to admit that source and object are identical, so that all reciprocal functions in mind are circular, and end where they begin; the fear of the creature flowing out into the power of the Creator, and the power of the Creator renewing the fountains of the creature's fear.

But I have said more than enough on this subject: no one is or can be a consistent Pantheist in thought, and little would the system affect mankind did it end in the mere logical absurdity in which it begins. Unfortunately it is not so; it has always moral consequences, and the attempt to sink the personal distinction between man and God by resolving the former into the latter, is always followed by the loss of those personal relations of affection and conscience between them which are the very life of religion. When the universe is resolved into one mighty Being, and history into His self-developed life, and all human minds are but finite sprouts from the same infinite root, it is impossible that the same importance can be attached to the particular relations of any single being to that great fountain of life with which he is believed to be already necessarily at one, as must belong to the hopes and fears of beings who know themselves to be free to wander from their Creator, and to be bound to Him, if at all, only by ties which they themselves may break. This form of faith necessarily dissolves the personal and voluntary ties between the creature and Creator, in substituting a kind of physical tie which nothing (it is believed) can dissolve. God is *already* at one with, nay in essence identical with, His creatures; He is so by the ties of Being itself; He himself lives in them, their acts are His, their lives are His,—where then is the room for the spiritual ties which can only exist where there is a voluntary connection that might be broken, for the gratitude that requites a free and full obedience, for the love that works willingly that it may win love again, for the prayer that asks what it might not otherwise receive? All the highest portions of human life would be impossible, were the spiritual and voluntary relations between person and person superseded by one vast community of life, which insuring *unity* in the whole, beyond the power of dissolution, would destroy all moral *unison*, and change the everlasting Father of Christ, into the all-pervading Essence of Spinoza. No wonder that Mr. Fox considers the

Christian conception of God a form of the theological conception that has endured too long: for if the infinitude of God is to be conceived of as absolute, and His universality consist in His bearing the same relation to all His creatures, like the physical laws which Mr. Fox takes up as affording us an analogy for His moral nature, then indeed the Christian conception of His rule attributes to Him superstitious partialities and dislikes.

In treating of divine attributes Mr. Fox is, of course, obliged to give up the "holiness" of God, in the common, and, as I conceive it, the true sense of the word. He conceives that to represent Him as of "purer eyes than to behold iniquity," and as "angry with the wicked every day," is an arbitrary and degrading superstition :—

"Wiser he, to our perception, who perceives the relation and sub-ordination of evil to good—who apprehends that the Deity meant virtue to be a progressive thing in human nature, to be attained by trial and struggle; and the comparative and relative perfection of his being only to be reached by strife within and without, from which the spirit mounts stronger and yet stronger after every conflict, until it basks in the brightness of the unclouded rays of the perfectly Holy."—P. 84.

This is so obvious a consequence of the premises Mr. Fox had already assumed, that I need not comment upon it further than to suggest that the theory which makes the subordination of evil to good (so much insisted on by the necessarian scheme), the means of making virtue either intelligible or desirable to man, professes to explain much more than it can: all that, at the most, it could account for would be the introduction of temptation into the world, not of sin. If needed as a background to set off the beauty and glory of virtue, the *possibility* of sin would do as well as its reality; and if sin be not really a moral consequence of liberty, but only a providential contrivance for enhancing the brilliance of virtue, the same effect could be produced by retaining all the moral phenomena of conflict and effort, only with the provision that they should all end in victory. Nor let it be said that this would be a deception which would be unworthy of the Divine Being, and which would fail in its end, because finding that the danger was always surmounted, it would at last be disregarded. The moral struggle is *always* a deception, if it be true that we only deceive ourselves in the belief that two possibilities are really open to us; and it would be as easy to Providence to implant in us the belief that it was only our own effort which prevented us from falling, as it is now to convince us that we have fallen by no necessity, but only by a moral wilfulness of our own. One would think that it might have been as easy to contrast virtue with the *danger* as with the reality of vice; let the traveller's road pass along the brink of an awful chasm, at which his head turns giddy, and he will need no fall to convince him how very wise it is to keep his footing if he can: if the only object is to make a didactic impression on his mind, and show him the blessing of his position, this might surely be as well effected by the terrors of anticipation; and it seems a useless cruelty to add the misery of actual degradation.

The arrangement of Mr. Fox's book is almost as defective as its reasoning. In speaking of God, and drawing out the divine attributes, he argues from the human principles within to the divine character which they reveal. From our fear, he deduces our faith in a Power, from our gratitude, in a Beneficence, around us. It is clear, therefore, that he should have considered the moral faculty in man, before speaking of the holiness of God, to which it corresponds. But this would not, in truth, have suited his purpose; had he done so, he would have forced upon himself the very questions which his previous assumption as to the all-pervading agency of God had led him to predetermine. And so he puts this part of the discussion only at the very close, in time to aid him in determining the destiny of man, but too late to cast any light back upon the character of God. I must just notice how essentially the truer arrangement might have affected the conclusions arrived at, had it been faithfully followed out. The feelings that we have *towards* another being do not teach us to enter into that being's character; gratitude does not explain to us the feeling of beneficence,—nor admiration, the essence of beauty,—nor fear, the hidden nature of power: they tell us *that* some Object of these feelings is, not *what* he is; what we feel for him, not what he feels for us. We must be in his position, dispensing good, creating beauty, wielding power, before we begin to understand the hidden life of him who was the object of these feelings of gratitude, admiration, and fear. Hence we begin to *know* God, not in worship, but in action; not when we are filled with affections *reciprocal* to His, but when we feel the *same* turned upon other beings beneath and around us; and then it is that the moral faculty begins to act, telling us His wishes as to the regulation of our conduct, and so speaking to us implicitly of the law which guides His own. We know that He has been good to us, and when we begin to labour for others we enter into the knowledge of His goodness; we know of His power over us, and when we first wield that power over others we begin to understand divine responsibility; we know His displeasure, and when we begin to blame and punish, we learn something of the emotions that accompany His discipline; but we have no knowledge of His *holiness* till we have formed some conception of the whole character which this detailed experience of right and wrong tends to form in us, and of the relative power of the various springs of action resulting in us after we have either obeyed or resisted these individual moral directions.

By limiting his view to the sentiments we feel *towards* God (which are partly the root of our faith in His being, but explain nothing of His nature), and omitting those that we do or might feel *with* Him, Mr. Fox has missed the very point in the psychology of Religion which might have diverted him from his religious theory. I mean the fact that there are some sentiments which we feel with God, but some that we feel without Him, and in opposition to His, in the actions of our life. Here it is that the separation between the divine being and our own ought necessarily to come in : here it is that we should at once recognise that He is *not* the infinite person that gathers up all being in Himself; here He appears not as a force but as a voice, not compelling but appealing, wishing what we dislike, disapproving what we wish : here is the eternal protest against Pantheism, God not *in* man, but against him, telling us of a life separated from ours as far as the East is from the West ; identifying our *duty* with His *desire*, when our own desire is different from our duty, and so providing us with a case where we may learn that our being is not only distinct from His, but widely divergent. This case of the moral faculty, where we feel that God exerts no force over us, but has sentiments directly contrary to our own, giving us His wish but saying nothing of His will, laying aside His power, and speaking only of right *before* our decision, yet distinctly telling of His pleasure or displeasure afterwards,— this surely would decide for ever that His being and ours are not really one. By considering only our affections *towards* God, which afford no possible means of comparing our natures with His, and deferring the consideration of the moral faculty which exhibits His spirit in close contact with and contrast to our own, till this very meagre survey of the divine attributes was concluded, so that the most complete and obvious means of distinguishing between the human and divine personalities was neglected, Mr. Fox has avoided difficulties that his form of religion can never solve or explain away. He has formed his conceptions of Deity on the analogies of physical science and the newest thought of the age, and only where that fails him, and he can get no account of the future destiny of individual man, does he ask the human conscience to tell him something of the future of humanity, though he omitted to question it as a witness to the nature of God.

It will easily be understood what kind of a moral sense Mr. Fox's system will alone admit: it is a mere taste or tendency in man towards the more beautiful course of conduct, which of course must take its place amongst the other tendencies of his nature. God being in all man's nature and actions, He is in this too, and, it would seem, more essentially, more permanently, in this than in the others; but still the fatal vice of all-pervading power comes in, so that even this becomes only one mode of the manifestation of that power, and cannot therefore be considered as the only true expositor of God's mind. Conscience is not, according to Mr. Fox, an expostulation with man, but an impulse in him, and its efficiency and strength in God can of course be estimated only by its results: so that the only means we could have of estimating the nature of the divine ruler would be to strike a kind of average of the various impulses of which He is the source, at the same time taking into account the indications of increasing force in this, the highest impulse. The miserable vagueness in the treatment of this primary revelation of God's nature, the speed with which it is dismissed and the suspicion with which it is treated rather as a rendezvous for impositions, than as our highest oracle of truth, is the most melancholy indication in this book. It is a consequence of this theory of the moral sense, that Mr. Fox pushes aside all retributive punishment as a superstition: he even calls it *vindictive*, a term that ought only to be applied to the anger excited by personal feeling; and as a natural consequence, the attribute of justice is nowhere given to God. Repentance becomes, of course, a mere discontent with an unsatisfactory and inharmonious position in creation:—

"Repentance is the opening of the heart to the mild and benignant influences of nature—an impatience of being any longer a discordant atom in that great system of things—a longing to be entirely at one with the life that is, and the life that is manifesting itself in progressive development."

One might have thought that an atom sufficiently humble when placed in such a position would rest contented with the great work to which it was instrumental, the development of more perfect harmony elsewhere, till it were swept along in the increasing stream of progress. But in this way must every system distort and caricature the moral nature of man, which takes the analogies of material science into the region of the spiritual life.

One sees clearly, indeed, in the chapter on Creation and Providence, that this *is* the side from which Mr. Fox has approached the solution of the religious problems of this book. The difficulties involved in the conception of Creation being, however, totally unreligious, so long, at least, as a divine power is not changed into a mechanical force, I pass them by with the remark that Mr. Fox, whilst ridiculing unmercifully the theory which makes distinct volition the creative power, has nothing better to substitute himself, but the dark phrases, "the infinite evolving the finite,"—and "the one infinite, universal, and eternal, the great Original," giving out " modifications and manifestations."

But the theory of Providence is one which, unless harmonized with general moral and physical laws, can assuredly stand no longer, and yet it is one which has exerted so profound an influence over every Christian mind from the earliest Christian ages to our own, that to part with it would be to give up the very life of religion. Mr. Fox dismisses the difficulty by giving up all particular providence,—*i.e.*, resigning Providence entirely,—in favour of general laws, and stating his belief that the whole series of objects and events are only complex results of a number of different and general laws. There are laws, he says, of the material, the mental, and the moral world, and no one class ever interferes with any other; the material result is the consequence of material laws, the moral of moral laws; and physical consequences are no more varied for moral reasons, than moral consequences for the sake of physical results. Now putting aside entirely at present the question of miracles (which of course would be assumed impossible by one who admitted the truth of this assumption), I am quite willing to admit this rule ; as, for example, to use Mr. Fox's illustrations, "The ship not sea-worthy will founder, whatever cargo it may bear of knowledge or benevolence ;"—" The careful will accumulate, though his heart be as hard as the nether mill-stone." It is quite certain that in the ordinary course of Providence, neither the physical effects ever fail to follow their appropriate causes, nor do the moral effects of a man's own moral actions ever fail in their moral results on the mind. Yet to admit this is not to banish Providence from the lives of individuals any more than from the life of classes. One may even admit that of which there is at present no proof, that the *first* moral as well as physical constitution of every one, results as certainly from the moral and physical constitutions of his ancestors, as physical effects from their causes. Yet there is opening wide enough for the action of particular providential agencies, without the necessity of assuming that in the construction of the general laws of the universe, God chose such as in His infinite wisdom He knew should be the best suited to the moral wants of *every* individual case.

Such an assumption would be impossible to prove, and sometimes seems to be untrue, as instances of strong seeming exception to the beneficial operation of these laws are constantly forcing themselves upon us. The true assumption with respect to these general laws, I am inclined to suggest, may be this ; that they have been so contrived as to be the best possible for the diffusion and strengthening of good in every individual case, *did* men always act with God and on the side of right. The human introduction of moral evil has introduced a confusion however into their operation, so that they often tend to give force and diffusion to evil by the very means originally intended to aid and cherish good. An example of such a case might be taken from that well-known law of association, that the most vividly interesting thoughts gather closely round them all the dress of objects and events in which they were first clothed, so that the least of these last will recall the former to the mind. In the minds of those who regulate their thoughts by the highest law, never allowing themselves to dwell passionately on any but noble objects, this is a law of transmutation which changes at a touch the dross of physical sensations to the pure gold of the highest feeling. On the other hand, where the rule of conscience becomes a cypher in the heart, this law intended to transmit agencies of good becomes powerful for evil. Other cases might be adduced.

But this is not all: not only is there providence in the *general* laws of God; but there is philosophical room also for its introduction into the destinies of particular lives, as all Christians have always held. Clearly we must look for that introduction at the points where all the analogies of physical law fail,—in the free decisions of the human will. Here it is that higher suggestions are so constantly *felt* to occur, and to be so strangely beneficent in their results. Here it is that a thought or feeling darting into the mind, which were it not for God's providence would have never entered, changes the whole course of duty and the whole destiny of life. From such moments of decision as these, go forth not only the immediate volitions, but the issues of life and death, and God, who knows the fates that await us, may often save us from the operation even of physical laws, not by suspending *them*, but by *leading us* from their sphere of action through the suggestion of an act that the will is prompt to do, or of a thought that detains us for a time from some eager pursuit. And thus, though it may be always true that no providential interference shall come *between* the care of the miser and the accumulation of his gold, yet it may, perhaps, intrude *behind* the sordid passion. At least, if the passion of avarice be not wholly rooted in him, but still be submitted sometimes to the deliberation of conscience, it may happen that a higher motive may for a time charm his heart into an hour's carelessness, and so cause the loss of all his hoarded gain: for the Providence who always *carries out* our volitions to their consequences, yet often interferes to prevent them, wherever that may be possible without a compulsion that He will not use. And so, too, though "the ship not sea-worthy will founder, whatever cargo it may bear of knowledge or benevolence," yet if God saw that such benevolence ought not to perish, He might turn aside its course by a suggestion of other duties in the moral deliberations *preceding* the decision to sail.

There is one consequence of this view of Providence,

which is worthy of notice, and may, perhaps, be thought in some measure a verification of it. It has often been noticed that in very rude and very low states of society, individuals seem cheap, and that no visible Providence guides their lives at all. On the other hand, the higher the mind, the more it seems to glide into the region of providential control, and not only to be filled inwardly with a finer spirit, but guided outwardly through the ways where God's influence will be greatest. Now the reason of this is plain on the supposition that the inlet for Providential care is through those moments of deliberation when a higher suggestion will avail. For in any society where men have not yet reached the stage of moral deliberation, this sphere is closed; they are like physical atoms borne about by forces which they never stop to control or direct; there is no space left between motion and action, desire and volition, where a suggestion may be interposed that could change their course. Animals who are blind slaves of impulse, driven about by forces from within, have, so to say, fewer *valves* in their moral constitution for the entrance of divine guidance; and evil men who would not follow any thought but the fixed self-willed purposes of their selfish hearts, shut the door on Providence, and imprison their fate in a darkness where comparatively little of this special guidance can reach. On the other hand, the minds that are alive to every word from God, give *constant* opportunity for His divine interference with a suggestion that may alter the courses of their lives; and like the ships which turn when the steersman's hand but touches the wheel, God can steer them through the worst dangers by the faintest breath of feeling, or the lightest touch of thought. Will not this reconcile the universal faith in a Providence watching ever over our lives, with the most strenuous doctrine of immutable law, physical and moral, to any one, at least, who holds the liberty of the human will? I have given some little space to it, because Mr. Fox's remarks on the modern scientific notions of law, as exploding the old notions of Providence, are not only likely to be generally impressive, but lie at the very root of his system, and colour his views throughout. For Mr. Fox obviously writes in constant dread of being supposed to believe anything superstitious, especially anything that could come into collision with the discoveries of physical science.

What, then, I have attempted to prove in this essay is, that free will is the very centre of human personality, and that as, without it, it is impossible to distinguish between the agency of man and the agency of God, so it is equally impossible to distinguish between human impulses and divine inspiration :—finally, that without free will, special divine guidance and special Providence could mean nothing except either a miracle (a suspension of law), or such an eternally pre-established harmony as had made universal law to fit absolutely every particular case of human difficulty—a conception only consistent with the denial of free will : whereas, granting a limited free will to man, there is room for Providential guidance in the life of every man who is capable of guidance by spiritual influence. It would be useless to follow Mr. Fox into the discussion of his reasons for believing in immortality, or into his conception of the Christian religion, with these vast differences as to the very foundations of religion in the rear. The only useful discussion that is possible between those who differ so widely, is discussion of the fundamental differences from which their other differences diverge.

V.

WHAT IS REVELATION?[1]

AS there is a substance, I believe, which not only burns in water, but actually kindles at the very touch of water, so there certainly are insatiable doubts, which not only resist the power, but seem to kindle at the very centre of Christian faith. There is one question which I should have supposed set at rest for ever in the mind of any man who believes either in the revelations of conscience or those of Scripture,—the question whether or not it is permitted to man to *know*, and grow in the knowledge of, God. If that be not possible, I, for my part, should have assumed that religion was a name

---

[1] 'What is Revelation? A Series of Sermons on the Epiphany; to which are added "Letters to a Student of Theology on the Bampton Lectures of Mr. Mansel."' By the Rev. F. D. Maurice, M.A. Cambridge. Macmillan, 1859.

'Preface to the Third Edition of Mr. Mansel's Bampton Lectures on the Limits of Religious Thought.' London. Murray, 1857.

for unwise, because useless, yearnings in the heart of man; and that the revelation—whether natural or supernatural—which professes to satisfy those yearnings, was simply a delusion. Yet so closely twined are the threads of human faith and scepticism, that probably half the Christian world scarcely knows whether to think God Himself the subject of revelation, or only some fragment of His purposes for man; while professed apologists for Christianity are often, like Dean Mansel, far firmer believers in the irremovable veil which covers the face of God, than in the faint gleams of light which manage to penetrate what they hold to be its almost opaque texture.

And, as I have intimated, this doubt is not only not extinguished by the Christian revelation, but it seems in some cases even to feed on the very essence of revelation. Dr. Mansel, for one, seems to regard the Christian revelation almost as express evidence that God is inscrutable to man, in that it only provides for us a "finite" type of the infinite mystery, and presents to us in Christ not, he thinks, the truth of God, but the best approximation to that truth—though possibly infinitely removed from it—of which "finite" minds are capable. In other words, he believes in the veil even more intensely than in the revelation: nay, he seems to think this conviction of his—that the veil is inherent in the very essence of our human nature, and indissoluble even by death itself, unless death can dissever the formal laws of human and finite thought—likely to enhance our reverence for the voices, so mysteriously "adapted" to finite intelligence, which float to us from behind it. "In this impotence of Reason," he says, "we are compelled to take refuge in faith, and to believe that an Infinite Being exists, though we know not how; and that He is the same with that Being who is made known in consciousness as our Sustainer and our Lawgiver." And again, in the preface to his third edition :—

"It has been objected by reviewers of very opposite schools, that to deny to man a knowledge of the Infinite, is to make Revelation itself impossible, and to leave no room for evidences on which reason can be legitimately employed. The objection would be pertinent, if I had ever maintained that Revelation is, or can be, a direct manifestation of the Infinite nature of God. But I have constantly asserted the very reverse. In Revelation, as in Natural Religion, God is represented under finite conceptions, adapted to finite minds; and the evidences on which the authority of Revelation rests are finite and comprehensible also. It is true that in Revelation, no less than in the exercise of our natural faculties, there is indirectly indicated the existence of a higher truth, which, as it cannot be grasped by any effort of human thought, cannot be made the vehicle of any valid philosophical criticism. But the comprehension of this higher truth is no more necessary either to a belief in the contents of Revelation, or to a reasonable examination of its evidences, than a conception of the infinite divisibility of matter is necessary to the child before it can learn to walk."

Thus, Revelation, as it is conceived by Dr. Mansel, is a mere adaptation of Truth to human forms of thought, whether it come through conscience or through Scripture; in both cases alike it is the formation in our minds of a "representative idea," or type, of God, not the direct presentation of the Divine Life to our spirits, which he holds that we could not receive and live. By conscience the vision of a holy but finite Judge, Lawgiver, Father, is borne in upon our hearts, namely, through the consciousness of our dependence and of moral obligation; by Scripture the historical picture of a finite law, a Providence adapted to finite minds, and lastly, a finite but perfect Son, are presented to our eyes. That is, certain messages have issued from the depths of the infinite mystery, which have been mercifully translated for us into the meagre forms of human thought: some of them are spontaneously welcomed by human consciences; others, attested as they are by superhuman marvels, and not inconsistent with the revelations of the conscience, are accepted as convincing by human reason; and both alike help to teach us,—not what God is,—but how we may think of Him with least risk of unspeakable error.

By these necessarily indirect hints,—the truest of which our nature is capable,—Dr. Mansel entreats us to hold, and to guide our footsteps; calling them "regulative truths," by which he means the best *working hypotheses* we are able to attain of the character and purposes of God. They are the only palliatives of that darkness, to which the blinding veil of a human nature inevitably dooms us. Revelation, we are told, cannot unloose the "cramping" laws of a limited consciousness; it cannot help the finite to apprehend the infinite; but it can do something to guide us in our blindness, so that we may not, in our ignorance, fall foul of the forces and laws of that infinite world which we are unable to know; it can give us a "conception" of God, which is quite true enough as a practical manual for human conduct. But, to use Dr. Mansel's own words, "how far that knowledge represents God as He is, we know not, and have no need to know."

This theory of Dr. Mansel's called forth from Mr. Maurice a reply, which was not merely an embodiment of a completely opposite conviction, but the insurrection of an outraged faith, the protest of a powerful character against a doctrine which pronounces that all the springs of its life have been delusions, and which tries to pass off human notions of God in the place of God. The somewhat thin and triumphant logic of Dr. Mansel,—the evident preference for analysing the notions of man rather than returning to the study of the realities from which those notions were first derived,—the dogmatic condemnation of human Reason to be imprisoned as long as it remains human in "the *Finite*,"—and finally, and most of all, the gospel of God's inaccessibility,— might in any case probably have drawn from Mr. Maurice a strong protest; but when all these instruments were used avowedly in defence of Christianity, and Christ was put forward, not as the perfect revelation, but as the least inadequate symbol of the divine nature, I do not wonder that the tone of Mr. Maurice's reply was, if always charitable, often almost austere. Dr. Mansel had preached that the sphere of Reason is the field of human things; Mr. Maurice holds that every fruitful study of human things implies a real insight into things divine. Dr. Mansel taught that the human mind is "cramped by its own laws;" and that divine realities, therefore, so far as they can be the subject of its thoughts at all, must be stunted, or, as the phrase is, "accommodated" to the unfortunately dwarfed dimensions of the recipient: Mr. Maurice holds that the mind of man is "adapted" to lay a gradual hold of the divine truth it is to apprehend, and to grow into its immensity; instead of the divine truth being "adapted" to the litttle capacities of the human mind. Dr. Mansel conceived that Christianity tells us just enough to keep us right with a God whom we cannot really know; Mr. Maurice, that the only way we can be so kept right is by a direct and, in its highest form, *conscious* participation in the very life of God.

On what, then, did Dr. Mansel profess to base his assumptions? Mainly on this, that if we really do hold direct and conscious converse with God, we should find the results of that converse, and of aptitude for it, inscribed on our mental constitution. "A presentative revelation implies faculties in man which can receive the presentation; and such faculties will also furnish the conditions of constructing a philosophical theory of the object presented." With the first part of this sentence every one must agree; if God can be present, as I believe, to the human mind, there must be faculties in us which enable us to discern that presence. But the latter assertion, that such faculties will also enable us to construct "a philosophical theory of the object presented," seems to me a most amazing and gratuitous assertion. A philosophical theory is possible when we stand above our object, not when we stand beneath it. The learner has faculties by which to learn; but if what he studies is inexhaustible, he will never have a "philosophical theory" of it. Principles, no doubt, he will reach; certain truths to mark his progress he will discover; he will know that he *understands* better and better that which he can never *comprehend;* but a theory of the whole he can never attain unless the whole be within the limited range of his powers.

Hence I entirely deny Dr. Mansel's assumption, that direct converse with God implies faculties for constructing "a theory" of God. This was the fundamental error of his work. He admits no knowledge except that which is on a level with its object. Nothing is easier than to prove that no plummet of human Reason can measure the depths of the divine mind; nothing falser than to suppose that this incapacity shuts us out entirely from that mind, and proves it to be the painted veil of "representative notions" of God, and not God Himself, who has filled our spirits in the act of worship.

I hold, then, that this was Dr. Mansel's first, and perhaps deepest, error. He saw that we have no "theory" of God which is not presumptuous and self-contradictory, and he argued therefrom that we have no knowledge. Surely he might have learned better from the simplest facts of human life. Have we any "theory" of any human being that will bear a moment's examination? Yet is our communion with our fellow men limited to a consciousness of our own notions of them? Are not "fixed ideas" of human things a sign of a proud and meagre intellect? Yet Dr. Mansel practically denies all knowledge of divine things, except knowledge through "fixed ideas." He mistakes that which hides God from us for that which reveals Him. "Notions," "fixed ideas," of God, no doubt, and very poor ones too, we have in abundance; but instead of being the media of our knowledge, they are more often the veil which every true moral experience has to tear aside. When we turn to Him with heart and conscience, we find half the crystallised and petrified ideas professing to represent His attributes, dissipated like mists before the sun. To know is not to have a notion which stands in the place of the true object, but to be in direct communion with the true object. And this is exactly most possible, where theory, or complete knowledge, is least possible. We know the "abysmal deeps" of personality, but have no theory of them. We know love and hatred, but have no theory of them. We know God better than we know ourselves, better than we know any other human being, better than we know either love or hatred; but have no theory of, simply because we stand under, and not above, Him. We can recognise and learn, but never comprehend. It is therefore idle to argue that knowing faculties imply the means of "constructing a philosophical theory," when every case in which living beings share their life and experience with us adds to our knowledge and to our grasp of principles; whereas we can construct adequate "theories" about only the most abstract subjects.

But this point granted, Dr. Mansel took his next stand in favour of a merely "notional" theology on the *infinite* nature of God. Admit, he said, that we cannot adequately comprehend our relations with finite realities, still such knowledge as we have of them may be direct, because our knowing power bears some definite proportion to the object known. But knowledge of an infinite being should either imply or generate,—so he reasoned, —infinite ideas in your own intellect. Have you such ideas? If so, produce them. If not, admit at once that what knowledge you have of such beings is not direct, not first-hand at all, but at best only by representative ideas—miniature copies of the reality on an infinitely reduced scale. The object to be known is unlimited; the intellectual receptacle a very narrow cell. There can be no room there for that which it professes to hold; if therefore, anything which gives a real notion of that object actually has managed to squeeze in, it can only be a minute image, a faint symbol, an "adaptation" to the poverty of human nature. Only a finite fraction of the infinite Reality could be apprehended by a finite intelligence at best; and that, of course, would give far less conception of the whole than a representative idea, reduced proportionately in all its parts to suit "the apprehensive powers of the recipient."

Such was, as far as I understand it, the nature of Dr. Mansel's objection. "In whatever affection," he said, "we become conscious of our relation with the Supreme Being, *we can discern that consciousness only by reflecting on it under its proper notion.*" Dr. Mansel did reflect on it, through many lectures, under several "notions," which he at least conceived to be "proper;" and finding them all what he terms finite, he ended by telling us that the human mind can only apprehend a finite type of God, and yet is compelled to believe that God is infinite: whence he argues we can have no direct knowledge of God at all, but can only study a limited symbol of Him, which He Himself has mercifully introduced into our minds, and reproduced in an objective and more perfect form in the incarnation of Christ. And if, still dissatisfied, any one suggests to Dr. Mansel that knowledge of God, like knowledge of human things, may be partial, but yet direct, and progressive, in short, a real and growing union of our mind with His,—he replies:—

"The supposition refutes itself: to have a partial knowledge of an object is to know a part of it, but not the whole. But the part of the infinite which is supposed to be known, must be itself either infinite or finite. If it is infinite, it presents the same difficulties as before; if it is finite, the point in question is conceded, and our consciousness is allowed to be limited to finite objects. But in truth it is obvious, on a moment's reflection, that neither the Absolute nor the Infinite can be represented in the form of a Whole composed of parts. Not the Absolute, for the existence of the Whole is dependent on the existence of its parts; not the Infinite, for if any part is Infinite, it cannot be distinguished from the Whole; and if each part is finite, no number of such parts can constitute the infinite."

Now what does all this prove? This, and this only: that if we take the words "Absolute" and "Infinite"

WHAT IS REVELATION?

to mean that He to whom they are applicable *chokes up* the universe, mental and physical, and prevents the existence of every one else, then it is nonsense and clear contradiction for any one else, who is conscious of his own existence, to use these words of God at all. Surely this might have been said without so much circumlocution. And what would Dr. Mansel thereby gain? Simply, as far as I can see, that he had established the certain non-existence of any Being *in this sense* "absolute" or "infinite." Dr. Mansel denied this, and said, 'No, I have only proved that a *philosophy* of the Absolute and Infinite is impossible to man.' But if asked, Why not to God also, and to all rational beings who do not believe in any philosophy of self-contradictions and chimeras? he would immediately turn upon me and say, 'Because, after all, you must admit that there is an "Absolute" and an "Infinite," and that these terms ought to apply to God. It is our incompetence to conceive, that involves us in all these self-contradictions. If you are going to deny the existence of the "Absolute" and "Infinite," you will get into as much trouble in another direction as if you admit and try to reason upon them. Suppose there is no Infinite and Absolute, and then we must assume the universe to be made up of finites, and to be itself finite. Which is the more inexplicable alternative of the two?'

Now, such reasoning seems to me a mere playing fast and loose with words. Dr. Mansel first wanted the words "Infinite" and "Absolute" to exclude all limitation or order of all sorts. Every thing like essential laws of mind or character,—every mental or moral condition or constitution, self-imposed or otherwise, under which the Divine mind could act,—he called a limitation, and excluded from the meaning of the words. When he had proved, what is exceedingly easy to prove on such an hypothesis, that we can only speak of the Infinite in self-contradictions, he added, 'Well, then, here is an end of the Absolute and Infinite. Clearly we are unable to grasp this; but the only alternative is the "relative" and "finite;" an alternative still more inexplicable.' And here by "finite," remember, he means, not that which acts under given conditions,—under the limitations, say, of a Perfect Nature, infinitely rich in creative power, though of *ordered* Creative Power, issuing from the depths of an Eternal Holiness and Eternal Reason,—but limited in every direction; conditioned everywhere, not by the life-giving order of Character, but by the helplessness of external bonds. I have no hesitation in saying that between unlimited Infinitude, understood in that sense in which Dr. Mansel thinks that less imbecile mental constitutions than ours would find no contradiction in it, and the absolutely cramped and fettered Finitude, understood in the sense in which there is no realm of unlimited development and free creation at all,—between these extremes, I say, the whole universe of mind, from the Divine to the human, is necessarily comprehended.

The one alternative, which Dr. Mansel did not deign

to admit into his religious dilemma even hypothetically, —that of unlimited energy, conditioned by definite laws, moral and spiritual,—is that which the revelation of conscience and the revelation of history alike offer to us as the actual standard of perfection. The sense in which the "Absolute" and "Infinite" are really self-contradictory terms is the sense in which we try to make them proof against every limitation; and they are so in that case for the very simple reason, that the *absence* of all positive characteristics is, as Dr. Mansel himself admitted, not only as great, but really a far greater limitation than the presence of those characteristics would be. A vacuum is certainly not limited, like a human being, by any specific mode of life; but it must be said to be still more limited by the absence of all modes of life whatever. On the other hand, the sense in which the conscience and reason of man eagerly assert the reality of an "Infinite" and "Absolute" Being, is not in the least the sense in which they are self-contradictory terms. We are forced to believe in a being whose moral and intellectual constitution is, not vaguer and less orderly, but infinitely distincter and more rich in definite qualities and characteristics than our own: but whose free Creative energies, as determined by those characteristics, are infinitely greater also. The mental constitution which impresses Order on the operation of Power is not, we are taught alike by conscience and inspiration, a true *limitation* on life, in the sense of a fetter; but is rather in itself a proper fountain of fresh life, and an enhancement of Power which would otherwise neutralise itself. Our incapacity to conceive the "Infinite" and "Absolute," in the sense in which they repudiate all conditions, turns out to be a positive qualification for conceiving them as names of God. We want them as describing attributes in which we can *trust*, and we can only trust in the attributes of a perfectly holy, and therefore, in some sense, defined Nature.

We may be fully satisfied, then, as the lesson of all experience, that the real fulness and perfection of character which we vainly strive to express by the word "infinite" is not gained by the absence, but by the expansion and deepening, of those defined moral qualities which Dr. Mansel wants to persuade us are to be considered mere *limitations* of nature. When, for instance, he applies the word "infinite," in its physical sense, to the divine personality, and asks if it does not exclude all other beings, because any other really free will must impose a limit on the operation of the divine will,—I ask if there would not be far deeper limitation in the denial to God of the possibility of that divine love which can exercise itself only on free wills. That only can be considered a real limitation which chokes the springs of spiritual life; and all self-imposed limitation on absolute power which is the condition of a real exercise of the spiritual or higher springs of life, is the reverse of real limitation. This is the lesson of every human responsibility. Is not every new duty, social or moral, a limitation of some kind—an obligation to others which at least in some direction appears to impose a limit on us, and yet which enlarges the whole scope of our nature? And is it not equally clear that a divine solitude would be more limited by the necessity of solitude, than by the freedom of the beings who are learning to share the divine life?

Dr. Mansel would say that all this is playing into his hands. He desired to persuade us that all direct knowledge of God is impossible, because we cannot tell what is limitation and what is not; in other words, we can form no adequate "conception" of fulness or perfection of life. What seems to us limitation, may be, not limitation, but a mode of divine power; what we reverently think of as belonging to God because it is included in our notion of power, may not really belong to Him, but be, in fact, a human limitation. Assuredly this is so. I have already admitted that if adequate or exhaustive notions, not of God only, but of any living being, were needful to us for direct knowledge, we should have no direct knowledge of life at all. But I have been protesting against Dr. Mansel's theory, not for saying that we have no *adequate* conception of God, but for saying that we cannot be conscious of His presence with us, conscious of the life we do receive from Him, conscious of what He really is, and in the same, indeed even in a far higher, sense than that in which we are conscious of what human beings are. We cannot tell whether this or that would be a limitation on the divine essence; but we can tell whether love and righteousness and power flow from Him into us. Does this give us no *knowledge* of God? Does this give us no communion with Him? 'No,' said Dr. Mansel; 'for "love," and "righteousness," and "power," can be received into your minds only in *finite* parcels, which give no approximation to a knowledge of their infinite fountain.' Here, again, we come upon that delusive and positive use of the word "infinite" which, in spite of Dr. Mansel's protest that "infinite" has only a negative meaning, ran through his whole book. He says we do not know what "infinite" means, and therefore cannot know that the "finite" is like the "infinite." We know God's love, and are obliged to believe that it is immeasurably deeper than we can know; and Dr. Mansel would persuade us that this last faith may change the whole meaning of the first, that the very depth and truth which we assert ourselves unable to gauge, ought to be a source of doubt whether we know the reality at all. A life comes into a man, the depths of which he cannot sound; and his very conviction that he has not the capacity to comprehend its fulness is to empty it of all defined meaning!

Surely Dr. Mansel must see that "infinite" is a mere hollow word when used in this way. The conviction we express by that word is simply that what we know to be restraints on our own highest and fullest life do not exist in God; but this conviction, instead of leading us to fear that righteousness and love change their nature in Him because He is "infinite," fills us with certainty that they do not. In short, righteousness and love are qualities which, if we are competent to know them really in any single act of God's, we know to be the same in all acts; and all that we mean by calling them infinite is, that we have more and more to learn about them for ever, which will not change and weaken, but confirm and deepen, the truth gained in every previous act of our knowledge. Dr. Mansel's notion, that because our knowing capacity is limited and God inexhaustible, we can never know directly more than such a fraction of His nature as would be rather a mockery than a personal revelation, is a mere physical metaphor. Our capacity for knowing may be limited either so that partial knowledge is *delusive* (as of one corner of a triangle) if taken for the whole; or so only that it is true in kind, and extends to the whole, but is utterly inadequate in depth. The latter is of course true of all direct knowledge of a *personality*, which we know to be one and indivisible. What we do not know is, then, mainly, the immeasurable range and inexhaustible depth of that which in a single act we do know. Or if there be other characteristics as yet wholly unknown, we know them to be in harmony, because belonging to the same perfect personality with those we do know.

In brief, I may sum up my differences with Dr. Mansel on this head by saying, that if "infinite" is to mean the exclusion of all definiteness of nature and character,—then we do know, and he himself admits, that infinitude has no application to God, if only because it would itself be a far greater limitation than that which it excluded; that if, on the other hand, it be admitted to be consistent with a defined character, and to mean rather "perfection,"—then that though we certainly have no abstract idea of what this is, we yet have positive faculties for conscious recognition of such a Perfect being when manifested to our conscience and reason, and an inextinguishable faith in His perfection even as unmanifested. Finally, if it be maintained that what we can thus recognise is as nothing when compared with what is beyond our vision, we may admit it, provided only that what we do know is direct knowledge, and knowledge of God, not of a part of God; and that it carries with it not merely a hope, but a *certainty*, that the inexhaustible depths still unrevealed will only deepen and extend, instead of falsifying, that knowledge at which we have arrived.

I have dwelt somewhat long on what seems to me a most transparent sophism, because it is on it that Dr. Mansel relies for his assertion that our knowledge of God cannot be direct; that Revelation cannot reveal Him, but only a finite type of Him, more or less different from the reality—how different no one can dare to say. Such a position destroys all interest in the revelation when it comes. If it be only a working hypothesis, to keep us, while confined in the human, from blindly and unconsciously dashing ourselves against the laws of the divine; if it merely says, 'Take this chart, which necessarily alters the infinite infinitely to make it finite;

but nevertheless, if you steer by it, it will save you as much from the rocks as if it were true,"—I do not believe any of us would care much for Revelation at all. We should say, 'Show us fresh realities, and whether they be finite or infinite, we will attend; but as for these magical clues, which only promise to keep us right, without showing us how or why, we would rather be wrecked against one really discovered rock, we would rather founder in the attempt to sound our own "dim and perilous way," than be constantly obeying directions which are mere accommodations to our ignorance, and which will leave us, even if we obey them strictly and reach the end of our voyage in safety, as ignorant of the real world around us as when we began it.' Yet Dr. Mansel's great plea for Revelation, as he understands it, is, that it provides us with *regulative* though not with *speculative* truth,—that it gives us wise advice, the wisdom of which we can test by experience; though furnishing nothing but guesses at the true grounds of that advice.

Now if any one is disposed to admire the apparent modesty of this conclusion, and to acquiesce in it as the true humility of mature wisdom, he will do well to study in Mr. Maurice's profound volume the evidence that every living movement of human thought, *religious or otherwise*, cries out against it. All regulative truth,— all truth, that is, which has a deep influence on human action, all truth in which men trust,—is founded in the discovery of ultimate causes, not of empirical rules. The distrust of empirical rules in science, in art, in morals, in theology, is all of the same root. It may be safest to act on probabilities where there is no certainty; to act by empirical rule where the principle of the rule is undiscovered; to follow a plausible authority where there is no satisfying truth; and by such rules, no doubt, *in the absence of all temptation to disregard them*, men are occasionally guided when they cannot reach any basis of fact. But, as Mr. Maurice very powerfully insists, there is no single region of life in which these "regulative" and approximate generalities exercise any *transforming* influence on the mind. The smallest probability will outweigh the greatest if it fall in with our wishes; the empirical rule suddenly appears specially inapplicable to the exceptional case in which it becomes inconvenient. The plausible authority is disputable where its recommendations are irritating or painful.

It is quite different where we have reached a fresh certainty, a new cause, a new force, a new and self-sustaining truth, a new fountain of actual life. Actual things and persons we cannot ignore; we may struggle with or defy them, but we cannot forget to take them into account. For the lottery-prize we will pay far more than it is worth, the number of blanks scarcely affecting the imagination; the danger of detection never checks the *bond-fide* impulse to crime; a single certain suffering which will be independent of success or failure, —the anguish of conscience, which success rather intensifies,—will outweigh it all. Exactly in proportion to the exclusion of hypothetical and the presence of known and tested elements is the really "regulative" influence exerted on the human will. Believe with Dr. Mansel that Revelation gives us a more or less true notion of God, and it will cease to kindle us at all. Recognise in it with Mr. Maurice the direct manifestation of God to the conscience, and the life thus manifested will haunt us into war, if it do not fill us with its peace.

If faith give no certainty, it is not "regulative," but itself speculative; if it does not satisfy the reason, it cannot overawe the will. Dr. Mansel appears to regard the phrase "satisfying to the reason" as applying to that sort of knowledge which can answer every query of human curiosity. He tells us that the influence of mind on matter is a regulative truth, of which we cannot give the least account,—and not, therefore, satisfying to the reason. In this sense, clearly, no living influence in the universe is satisfying to the reason; for we cannot reason anything into life. But this is a totally different sense from that in which he invites us to surrender our desire for a reasonable knowledge of God, as distinguished from a regulative message from Him. Reason in the highest sense does not pursue its questions beyond the point of discriminating between a real and permanent cause or substance, and a dependent consequence or a variable phenomenon. It asks, "why" only till it has reached something which can justify its own existence, and there it stops. True reason *is satisfied* when it has traced the stream of effect up to a living Origin, and discriminated the nature of that Origin.

It is not the impulse of Reason, but, as Mr. Maurice has finely said, the disease of Rationalism, which continues to make us restless questioners in the presence of those living objects which ought to fill and satisfy the reason,—inducing us to ask for a reason deeper than Beauty before we can admire, for a reason deeper than Truth before we can believe, for a reason deeper than Holiness before we can love, trust, and obey. But no true reason is, or ought to be, satisfied with an echo, a type, a symbol, of something higher which it cannot reach. If it find transitory beauty in the type, it turns by its own law to gaze on the Eternal beauty beneath; if it find broken music in the echo, it yearns after the perfect harmony which roused the echo. Reason might be defined to be that which leads us to distinguish the sign from the thing signified,—which leads us back from the rule to the principle, from the principle to the purpose, from the purpose to the living character in which it originated,—which, in short, will *not* be satisfied with any image, but cries after the Original.

If this be Reason, then to satisfy Reason is to find out truly regulative truth: for what is it which, in the passion and fever of life, truly transforms and chastens human purposes? Surely nothing but the *knowledge* of realities,—sensible realities more than spiritual abstractions,—spiritual realities most of all; mere *things* painful or delightful far more than any abstract ideas; men far more than things; men present more than men absent; but men absent more than the dream of an absent God, because we have lost our faith in God altogether when we have lost our faith in His direct presence with us. I need scarcely take more than one example of what Dr. Mansel calls regulative moral truth. It will be quite sufficient to test the utterly hollow and unregulative character of the gospel which he can alone deliver to his disciples. He tells us that our human morality, like our human objects of faith, is an adaptation to our condition; though it may resemble, with nevertheless inconceivable differences, the divine morality from which it has been epitomised for us. What is his illustration? One so extraordinary, that it is difficult to believe he was not trying to prove that such reduced and "adapted" rules and types can have *no* regulative influence on the human will. He is arguing that there is not, and cannot be, "a perfect identity," or even "exact resemblances" between the morality of God and man,—that actions may be "compatible with the boundless goodness of God which are incompatible with the little goodness of which man may be conscious in himself." The case he takes is the duty of human forgiveness. It is the duty of man, he says, to forgive unconditionally a repented sin. People who argue that God cannot be less good than man, assume that God must do likewise. The fallacy lies, he maintains, in forgetting that the finite form of human duty essentially alters the moral standard in the mind of God. This he proves as follows :—

"It is obvious, indeed, on a moment's reflection, that the duty of man to forgive the trespasses of his neighbour rests precisely upon those features of human nature which cannot by any analogy be regarded as representing an image of God. Man is not the author of the moral law; he is not, as man, the moral governor of his fellows; he has no authority, merely as man, to punish moral transgressions as such. *It is not as sin, but as injury, that vice is a transgression against man; it is not that his holiness is outraged, but that his rights or his interests are impaired.* The duty of forgiveness is imposed as a check, not upon the justice, but upon the selfishness of man; it is not designed to extinguish his indignation against vice, but to restrain his tendency to exaggerate his own personal injuries. The reasoner who maintains 'it is a duty in man to forgive sins, therefore it must be morally fitting for God to forgive them also,' *overlooks the fact that this duty is binding on man on account of the weakness, and ignorance, and sinfulness of his nature:* that he is bound to forgive as one who himself needs forgiveness; as one whose weakness renders him liable to suffering; as one whose self-love is ever ready to arouse his passions and pervert his judgment."

I scarcely ever met with a passage in any thoughtful writer which seemed to contain deeper and more disastrous misreadings of moral, to say nothing of Christian truth, than this. To me the profound and fatal falsehood lies exactly in that which constituted its value to Dr. Mansel—the assumption that man's duty to forgive is not grounded in his likeness, but in his unlikeness, to God. But it is not to this point I wish to call attention, but to the *worth* of such a truth as regards its power to *regulate* human conduct. If there be anywhere a duty hard of performance, it is the duty of human forgiveness. If there be one which the ordinary nature of man spurns as humiliating, and almost as a wrong to his whole mind, it is that duty. Ground it in the very nature of God, in the holy living will which, ever close to us, ever able to crush, is ever receiving fresh injury, and yet, even in inflicting the supernatural anguish of divine judgment, is ever offering anew both the invitation and the power to repent,—and you open the spirit to a reality which cannot but awe and may melt it, in the hour of trial. But ground it with Dr. Mansel on the old, worn-out, lax sort of charity which is indulgent to others because it is weak itself, and it will be the least regulative, I suspect, of regulative duties. Mr. Maurice's exposure of the hollowness of this foundation is too fine to omit :—

" 'The duty of forgiveness is binding upon man on account of the weakness and ignorance and sinfulness of his nature.' But what if the weakness, ignorance, and sinfulness of my nature dispose me *not* to forgive? What if one principal sign of this weakness, ignorance, sinfulness of my nature is, that I am unforgiving? What if the more weak, ignorant, and sinful my nature is, the more impossible forgiveness becomes to me, the more disposed I am to resent every injury, and to take the most violent means for avenging it? It is my duty to forgive, because I am 'one whose self-will is ever ready to arouse his passions and pervert his judgment.' To arouse my passions; to what? To any thing so much as to acts of revenge? To pervert my judgment; how? In any way so much as by making me think that I am right and other men wrong, and that I may vindicate my right against their wrong? And this is the basis of the duty of forgiveness! The temper which inclines me at every moment to trample upon that duty, to do what it forbids! The obvious conclusion, then, has some obvious difficulties. Obvious indeed! They meet us at every step of our way; they are *the* difficulties in our moral progress. Forgiveness is 'to be a check on the selfishness of man.' Where does he get the check? From his selfishness. It is the old, miserable, hopeless circle. I am to persuade myself by certain arguments not to do the thing which I am inclined to do. But the inclination remains as strong as ever: bursts down all the mud fortifications that are built to confine it; or else remains within the heart, a worm destroying it, a fire consuming it. Whence, O whence, is this forgiveness from the heart to come, which I cry for? Is it impossible? Am I to check my selfishness by certain rules about the propriety of abstaining from *acts* of unforgiving ferocity? God have mercy upon those who have only such rules, in a siege or a shipwreck, when social bonds are dissolved, when they are left to themselves! All men have declared that forgiveness, real forgiveness, is *not* impossible. And we have felt that it is not impossible, because it dwells somewhere in beings above man, and is shown by them, and comes down as the highest gift from them upon man. . . . . And whenever the idea of Forgiveness has been severed from this root,—whenever the strong conviction that we are warring against the nature of God and assuming the nature of the Devil by an unforgiving temper has given place to a sentimental feeling that we are all sinners, and should be tolerant of each other,—then has come that weakness and effeminacy over Christian society, that dread of punishing, that unwillingness to exercise the severe functions of the Ruler and the King, which has driven the wise back upon older and sterner lessons, has made them think the vigour of the Jew in putting down abominations, the self-assertions of the Greek in behalf of freedom, were manlier than the endurance and compassion of the Christians. Which I should think too, if, referring the endurance and compassion to a divine standard, I did not find in that stardard a justification of all which was brave and noble in the Jewish protest against evil, in the Greek protest against tyranny. Submission or Compassion, turned into mere qualities which we are to exalt and boast of as characteristic of our religion, become little else than the negations of Courage and Justice. Contemplated as the reflections of that Eternal Goodness and Truth which were manifested in Christ, as energies proceeding from him and called forth by his Spirit,—submission to personal slights and injuries, the compassion for every one who is out of the way,—become instruments in the vindication of Justice and Right, and of that Love in the fires of which all selfishness is to be consumed."

I have done my best to explain why I utterly disavow

Dr. Mansel's interpretation of Revelation, as a message intended to regulate human practice without unfolding the realities of the divine mind. It is a less easy task, but not less the proper task of those who are gravely sensible of the emptiness of such an interpretation, to give some exposition to the deeper meaning which the fact of revelation assumes to their own minds. I hold that it is an unveiling of the very character and life of the eternal God; and an unveiling, of course, to a nature which is capable of beholding Him. It is not, in my belief, an overclouding of divine light to suit it for the dimness of human vision, but a purification of human vision from the weakness and disease which render it liable to be dazzled and blinded by the divine light. It is, in short, the history of the awakening, purifying, and answering, of the yearnings of the human spirit, for a direct knowledge of Him. It proceeds from God, and not from man. The cloud which is on the human heart and reason can only be gradually dispersed by the divine love; no restless straining of turbid human aspiration can wring from the silent skies that knowledge which yet every human being is formed to attain.

Coming from God, this method, this "education of the human race," as Lessing truly termed Revelation, has been unfolded with the unfolding capacity of the creatures He was educating to know Him. Its significance cannot be *confined* to any special series of historical facts; but it is clear that the Divine government of the Jewish race was meant to bring out, and did bring out, more distinctly the personality of God, while the history of other races brings out more clearly the divine capacities of man. Hence the coöperation of different nations was requisite for the efficiency of the revelation. Centuries were required for the complete evolution even of that special Jewish history that was selected to testify to the righteous will and defined spiritual character of the Creator. Centuries on centuries will be required to discipline fully the human faculties that are to grow into the faith thus prepared for them. The blindness of the greatest men, of the highest races, of wide continents, cannot shake one's faith that this purpose will be fulfilled; for the term of an earthly life is adequate at best only for an immortal life's conscious commencement, and only under special conditions even for that; nor are there wanting indications that both in the case of men and nations the longest training, and the dreariest periods of abeyance of spiritual life, are often preparations for its fullest growth. By tedious discipline, by slow Providence, by inspirations addressed to the seeking intellect of the philosopher, to the yearning imagination of the poet, to the ardent piety of the prophet, to the common reason and conscience of all men, and by the fulfilment of all wisdom in the Son of God's life on earth, has the Divine Spirit sought to drive away the mists that dim our human vision. Alike through its wants and powers has human nature been taught to know God. Its every power has been haunted by a want till the power was referred to its divine source ; its very wants have become powers when they have turned to their divine object. If this, then, and nothing short of this, be Revelation, a living and direct unfolding of that divine mind in which, whether we recognise it or not, we "live and move, and have our being,"—an eternal growth in our knowledge of the eternal Life,—one ought not to rest satisfied with showing that Dr. Mansel's reasons for disputing the possibility of such a wonderful truth are unsound,—one ought also to show by what criteria we judge that this is the actual fact, the great reality, on which all our love of truth and knowledge rests.

The first stage in any revelation must be, one would suppose, the dawning knowledge that there is a veil "on the heart" of man, and that there is a life unmanifested behind it. In Dr. Mansel's, as in my view, this is a knowledge which can be gained by man ; but he makes it the final triumph of human faith and philosophy to recognise and *acquiesce* in it ; while I hold it to be the very first lesson of the personal conscience, the very first purpose of that external discipline which was intended to engrave the Divine personality on Jewish history, to teach that though such a cloud will ever threaten the mind and conscience, it *can be dispersed.*

What, indeed, is the first lesson of the human conscience, the first truth impressed upon the Jewish nation, but this, that a presence besets man behind and before, which he cannot evade, and which is ever giving new meanings to his thoughts, new direction to his aims, new depth to his hopes, new terror to his sins? Where, then, if this haunting presence be so overpowering, if it follow us as it followed the deepest minds among the Jewish people, till it seem almost intolerable,—where is the darkness and the veil which Revelation implies? Just in the fact that this presence does seem intolerable; that it is so far apart from that of man, that, like a dividing sword, it makes his spirit start; that he seeks to escape, and is, in fact, really able to resist it; that he can so easily case-harden his spirit against the supernatural pain; that instead of opening his mind to receive this painfully-tasking life that is not his own, he can so easily, for a time at least, set up in its place an idol carved out of his own nature, or something even more passive than his own nature, and therefore not likely to disturb his dream of rest.

This, I take it, is the first stage or act of revelation, whether in the individual conscience, or in that special history which is intended to reveal the conflicts between the heart of a nation and the God who rules it. It is the discovery of a presence too pure, too great, too piercing for the natural life of man,—the effort of the mind, on one pretence or another, to be allowed to stay on its own level and disregard this presence,—the knowledge that this must end in sinking below its own level,—the actual trial and experience that it is so,—the reiterated pain and awe of a new intrusion of the supernatural light,— the reiterated effort to "adapt" that light to human forms and likings,—the reiterated idolatry which all such adaptations imply, whether physical, as in the Jewish times, or intellectual, as in our own,—and the reiterated shame of fresh degradation. If this be,—as, I believe, the human conscience testifies,—whether as embodied in the typical history of the Jews, or in the individual mind, the first stage in that discovery which we call Revelation, what becomes of Dr. Mansel's theory, that Revelation is the "adaptation" of the "infinite" to the "finite," of the perfect to the imperfect, of the absolute morality to the poor capacities of a sinful being? If so, why this craving of the nature to be let alone,—this starting as at the touch of a flame too vivid for it,—this comfort in circumscribing, or fancying that we can circumscribe, the living God in some human image or form of thought, and worshipping that by way of evading the reality? Does the human spirit ever quail thus before a mere notion? If God Himself is inaccessible to knowledge, should not we find it extremely easy to adapt ourselves to any abstract or ideal conception of Him? It is the living touch of righteousness, even though human only, that makes us shrink; not the idea of righteousness, which, as all theologies testify, is found pliant enough. But if it be a righteous life and will, not merely the idea or idol of a righteous life and will, that stirs human nature thus deeply, and finds us, as it found the Jews, afraid to welcome it, awestruck at the chasm which divides us from it, fearful to surrender ourselves to its guidance, ready to adapt it in any way to us, unready to adapt ourselves to it,—if, I say, we know it to be a *living* will that thus checks, urges, and besets us, Dr. Mansel's theory as to the narrow limits of human knowledge would scarcely induce him to deny that it is God Himself; for there is nothing in his theory which is not almost as much contradicted by *any* living spiritual converse between the human spirit and a spirit of perfect holiness as by direct converse with God.

This first stage of Revelation, which I have called the Jewish, may be said to discriminate the divine personality of God *more* sharply from His own works and creatures than is possible or true in any subsequent and maturer stage of His unfolding purpose. It is, in fact, the first stage in the divine "education" of the individual conscience, as well as of the human race; and is so vividly reflected in the national history of Israel, only because that is the only history in which the appeals of God to the corporate conscience of a whole nation are recorded as fully as the actual national deeds in which those appeals were complied with or defied. In the history of other nations the divine will for the nation has been at once far less vividly interpreted, and, even when adequately interpreted, far less carefully recorded; it has been allowed to gleam forth only fitfully through the often uneducated consciences of national heroes; while in the case of the Jews, we find a succession of great men, whose spirits were more or less filled with the divine light, in order that the world might see in at least one national chronicle some continuous record of the better purposes of God for the nation, as well as of the actual history by which those purposes were partially frustrated or fulfilled.

This, I believe, is the only peculiarity of Jewish history, that a race of prophets was permitted to proclaim, with varying truth of insight, no doubt, but still with far clearer and more continuous vision of the divine purpose than any other nation has witnessed,— what God would have had the people do and abstain from. To the nation itself this was not always a gain; probably that which was evil in it would not have grown into so stiff and hard a subsistence but for the power inherent in divine light to divide the evil from the good, (for the vision of a purpose too holy for the life of a people issues in greater guilt as well as greater goodness); but for the world at large no doubt it has been and is an immeasurable blessing,—strictly speaking, a revelation,—to see written out, parallel with the national life of a single people, the life to which God, speaking through the purest consciences of each age of their history, had called them. But the phase of revelation which we see in Jewish history is simply, on the scale of national life, what the first discovery of God by the individual conscience is in individual life. In both cases there is a contrast presented between God and Man, between God and Nature, sharper than belongs to any other stage of His unfolding purposes. The separate personality of God is engraved on Jewish history with an emphasis which indicates that to the Jew there seemed scarce any common life between God and man,—any bridge between the supernatural will and the easy flow of Nature. And is it not thus engraven on the individual conscience when first men become aware that the natural veins and currents of their characters tend to a thousand different ends, whither the Spirit of God forbids them to go,—or whither if they do go, it haunts them with stings of supernatural anguish till they turn again? Is it not simply the discovery that the actual bent of our whole inward constitution is not divine, —the despair of seeing how it is ever to become so,— which makes us, like the Jew, separate the divine Spirit so sharply from God's living works and creatures, that for a time we doubt whether the nature within us can be used by God at all—whether, much rather, its forces must not be wholly cancelled, before the will can be set free?

But this sharp contrast between the personality of God and the nature of man, and in lesser degree of the external universe, is not and cannot be final. And if the Jewish history witnesses that the Will of God is the starting-point of a new order, that the forces of human nature must be brought into subjection to that, if they can be used by God at all,—then the history of a hundred other nations, more especially of the Greeks, and in later centuries of the Teutonic races, does testify with equal explicitness that natural life is essentially divine, and requires at most remoulding by the Eternal Spirit,—a remoulding which is so far from cancelling, that it brings out the true nature in all its freshness,— in order to become the fitting organ of a Supernatural

Righteousness. In other words, so long as man takes his stand on the level of his own motives and affections, and shrinks from the transforming influence of the Spirit of God, these motives and affections are the veil which needs taking away; but if he will permit himself to be raised above that level, and will open his heart freely to the supernatural influence at which he trembles, then it will not be *against* the voice, but *by* the voice of his own spiritualised motives and affections, that God Himself speaks. The veil itself becomes transparent; the glass that was dark, illumined.

Accordingly the revelation to conscience, which is more or less Jewish, and sets all the fibres of the natural life quivering like an aspen-leaf in the wind, is necessarily partial and temporary. Even in the highest of the prophetic strains there is perhaps an undervaluing of Nature, and of human nature in its natural manifestations,—a disposition to anticipate something like a revolution rather than a regeneration in its constitution, to represent direct praise of God as better and more worthy than the indirect praise implied in a perfect natural development. Could God's Self-Revelation have been stayed at that point, I doubt whether Gentile nations,—the Greek for instance,—could ever have embraced it. Deep sensibility to the divine beauty of all human faculty and life was so deeply wrought into the very heart of Greece, that the Greek only recoiled at the Hebrew vision of a God before whose presence human faculty seemed to pale away like starlight in the dawn. Nor could the Hebrew faith itself have lived on permanently in that phase. Already, before the Jewish era came to a close, the danger of idolatry with which Jewish faith was first threatened,—the danger that God would be confounded with His works,—had been exchanged for the danger that He would not be recognised as living at all in His works. There is an exactly parallel movement in the history of the revelation of God to the individual conscience. When first

> "Those high instincts before which our mortal nature
> Doth tremble like a guilty thing surprised"

come upon us, we feel that man is nothing, and God every thing; but soon human nature re-asserts its dominion; and if there be no full reconciliation between the two, either the "high instincts" become ossified into dogma, and the "mortal nature" runs a fouler course in their presence than it would in their absence, or they fade away again altogether.

There is a natural and legitimate revolt in man against any Supernaturalism which does not do full justice to Nature: and the opposite risk of a deification of Nature, such as Greece and the Gentile nations were prone to, produces perhaps less fearful, certainly less unlovely results than the error which divorces Nature from God, and by disclaiming in the name of piety any trace in Him of the life of the world, strips that world bare of all trace of God. Judaism taught us that Nature must always be interpreted by our knowledge of God, not God by our knowledge of Nature; but it was only the perversion of Judaism which completely dissolved the tie between the two. The Greek shuddered, and with reason, at the sacrilege of ignoring the breath of divine life in the harmony of the world; but it was but a perversion of Hellenism when the Pantheist sought to identify the two,—to multiply his delight in natural organisms until their influences fell into a kind of musical harmony in his mind, which he called the Divine Whole. Both of these opposite tendencies are equally perversions. And both alike witness to the expectation in the human mind of some revelation of the true tie between the life of God and the life of His creatures,—the yearning to know, not only what God is in His essential character, but what seed of His own life He has given to us, and what power it is by which that seed may be guarded through its germination from the extinction or corruption with which it is threatened. Accept with the Greek the capacity for a divine order in man and the universe; accept with the Jew the reality of the "Lord's Controversy" with man; and how are the two to be reconciled? how is the supernatural righteousness to avail itself of the perverted growths of human capacity? how is the "Lord's Controversy" to be set at rest?

This was a question which the Jewish revelation never solved for the questioner,—except so far as it taught him that God could *conquer* the most rebellious nature. But even then he recognised the Supernatural will as *triumphing over* the poverty of human and natural life, rather than as revealing itself actually *through and in* the divine springs of that life. The "Controversy" was solved for him rather by the power of God over Nature than by the power of God in Nature. But what was it that the Gentile nations craved? Some new conviction that the Supernatural was not at war with the constitution of Nature, but the eternal source of it; that the gradual growth, the seasonal bloom, the germinating loveliness of the natural and visible universe, culminating in the wonderful life of man, is itself not a veil but a revelation, a harmony of voices addressing us from the Divine life, and claiming our allegiance to One higher than themselves. They too saw, what the Jew had been taught, that in fact this was not really so, that there was a jar, a discord somewhere; but if they saw far less clearly whence came the power which could command the discord to cease, they saw far more clearly that, if it could cease, the *true* Nature would be restored and not conquered, vindicated and not extinguished, strengthened and not exhaled.

The human condition of this revelation, as of all other revelation, is born with the human mind. The Supernatural and Righteous Will, who besets and confronts on every side the unruly impulses of our lower self, is revealed to the Conscience, and without the Conscience could not be revealed at all. But besides this, there is another experience of man's which renders him capable of another revelation. Quite apart from the conscience and the sense of guilt and of the law,—quite apart from the living Will, who looks into our hearts and searches out their evil,—there is, I suppose, in every man a more natural and genial experience of the spontaneous growth and unfolding, or it may be only the *effort* to unfold, of the true nature as it ought to grow,—a gentle spontaneous resistance to the shapes into which our faults and imperfections force or try to force it,—the effort of the true man within us to grow into his right and perfect state in spite of the resistance of frailty, incapacity, and sin. What I am now speaking of is not an experience merely of the moral life, but of the whole nature. Does not every man feel that there are unused capacities of all kinds within him, gently pressing for their natural development?—that a living tendency urges us to grow, not merely in moral but in physical and intellectual constitution, towards the individual type for which we were made?—that the various frictions of evil, moral or merely circumstantial, which prevent this, distort the true divine growth, and leave us less than what we might have been? It was this experience which the religion of Greece has preserved so vividly,—the faith that, beneath the deformity of real life, there is a formative plastic power that is ever urging us towards our truest life; beneath ungainliness, a growth, or effort to grow, of something more harmonious; beneath ignorance, a growth, or effort to grow, of the true understanding; beneath impurity and evil, the growth, or effort to grow, of the true moral beauty.

It was, I believe, to this experience in every man's mind,—an experience which cannot be called moral so much as the true instinct of *life*,—that the unveiling of God in Christ appealed, and which fitted the Christian revelation to include the Greek as well as the Jew. There at last was the harmony of the Supernatural and the Natural,—the divine effort at harmonious growth which seemed to be in every man, unfolding from the germ to the full fruit without the canker or the blight, and yet at the same time revealing to all of us exactly what the supernatural vision reveals to the conscience, the absolute will of good, the divine anger against sin, the infinite chasm between evil and good, the power and holiness of God. What was this life, in which the unity of God and man was at length vindicated? Did it not utter in clearer accents the awful Will which had spoken within the Jew? Did it not image in living colours the perfect Nature which had stirred so gently and breathed so deep a sense of divinity into the finer folds of Grecian life? Was it not at once the answer to that craving for a true vision of the moral nature of God which had haunted the Hebrew conscience, and the answer to that craving for a true vision of the undistorted life of man which had haunted the Grecian imagination? True, it was a vision of the Father only as He is seen in the Son, of the filial and submissive Will, not of the original and underived Will; but as it is the perfection of the filial Will to rest in the Will of the Father, the spiritual image is perfect, though the personal life is distinct.

And this was, in fact, exactly what answered the yearning of the Greek for an explanation of that living.

germ of divine life within him. Was it not a perfect *nature*, filial like his own,—the very nature into which he was capable of growing,—that had thus been pushing against the weight of deformity, stirring the sources of *natural* perfection, and warning him that his mind was growing in wrong directions, and not blossoming into the beauty for which it was designed? He was ready to recognise as the divine Word, which had grown into perfect humanity in Christ, the very same higher nature which had been in him but not of him; which had filled his mind with those faint longings after something that he might have been and was not; which was still stirring within him whenever a new blight, or a new failure, or a new sin, threatened to divert him still further from the destiny to which he knew he was capable to attain. The secret Will of God was, according to the longing of the Jews, first fully manifest in Christ; the secret hopes of man were, according to the "desire of all nations," there first fulfilled.

If Christ, then, was to the Jew mainly the revelation of the Absolute Will as reflected in the perfect filial will; to the Greek mainly the revelation of that perfect human nature which had been so long stirring within him, we might expect to find acts in which Christ especially revealed the living ruler of the Universe, and acts in which Christ especially revealed the inward influences which were to restore order to the human heart;—acts in which He manifested the Father, and acts in which He unsealed the eternal fountains of purity in human life. Mr. Maurice, in answering Dr. Mansel's assertion that the Absolute is beyond human vision, called attention especially to the former class. He intimated that in the miracles and the parables, for instance, we have revelations of the spiritual source of the physical world. There had been ever in man an awe at the mighty powers of the physical universe, and the apparent recklessness with which these powers acted. The Jew, who loved to see in God the source of all power, still hardly dared to refer these crushing forces to the same national Providence which had guarded and governed his race with a personal care so express. The Greek thought them in their awful undeviating order far more sublime than he could have done had he held them to be exercises of a mere supreme Will. But yet he would willingly have connected them with an order, spiritual as well as physical, such as he recognised in the destinies of men. Christ, by manifesting the power which controlled and upheld them, and yet manifesting it with a healing and life-giving purpose, answered both these cravings. 'These powers,' His miracles said, 'which seem so physical, so arbitrary, sometimes so destructive,—which sometimes appear to be wielded by an evil spirit, are all in the hands of one who would heal men's miseries, restore their life, moral and physical, purify them from disease, and hush the storm into a calm : if it ever seem otherwise, be sure that the seeming destruction has a life-giving purpose, the physical disease a deeper healing influence ; that the tempest is a bringer of serener peace, the blindness a preparation for diviner light. The order of the universe has a spiritual root; the purpose of love which changes is also the purpose of love which directs it. He who can bind and loose the forces of nature, has thus revealed the eternal purposes in which they originate.'

So again, Mr. Maurice, in a sermon of great beauty, claimed for the parables that they were intended to reveal the spiritual significance which had been from the first embodied in the physical processes of the universe, —that the analogy between the light of the body and the light of the spirit, the sowing and reaping of the external and of the spiritual world, and the other analogies in what we usually call Christ's "figurative" language, are not really metaphorical, but exhibit the perfect insight of the divine mind of the Son into the creative purposes of the Father. If it be true that the creator of our spirits is the creator of our bodies also, we might only expect that He who revealed the true life of the one, would know and exhibit its close natural affinities with the life of the other. Is not the physical universe as a whole meant to be for man the vesture of the spiritual universe? Is not all the truest language, therefore, necessarily what we call figurative; and only false when the spiritual is interpreted by the physical, instead of the physical by the spiritual?

"But if there is this correspondence between the organs of the spirit and the organs of sense, if experience assures there is, does not that explain to us the meaning and power of the parables? May not all sensible things by a necessity of their nature, be testifying to us of that which is nearest to us, of that which it most concerns us to know, of the mysteries of our own life, and of God's relation to us? May it not be impossible for us to escape from these witnesses? They may become insignificant to us from our very familiarity with them; nay, we may utterly forget that there is any wonder in them. The transformation of the seed into the full corn in the ear may appear to us the dullest of all phenomena, not worthy to be noted or thought of. The difference in the returns from different soils, or from the same soils under different cultivation,—the difference in the quality of the produce, and the relations which it bears to the quality of the seeds, —may be interesting to us from the effect such varieties have upon the market, from the more or less money we derive from the sale; not the least as facts in nature, facts for meditation. The relation between a landholder or farmer and those who work for him, between a shepherd and his sheep, all in like manner may be tried by the same pecuniary standard; apart from that, they may suggest nothing to us. Thus the universe becomes actually 'as is a landscape to a dead man's eye;' the business in which we are ourselves engaged, a routine which must be got through in some way or another, that we may have leisure to eat, drink, and sleep. Can any language describe this state so accurately and vividly as that of our Lord in the text? Seeing we see and do not perceive; hearing we hear, and do not understand."

This revelation, however, through Christ,—by His life, by His miracles, by His parables, by His resurrection and ascension,—of the supreme Will, would not have fulfilled as it did the "desire of all nations," had it not also revealed that living power in man by which human nature is wrought into His likeness. To know God has been, in all ages, but an awful knowledge, until the formative influence which is able to communicate to us His nature is revealed also.

And accordingly, Christ no sooner disappears from earth than all the Christian writings begin to dwell far more on the new strength He had revealed within them than on His outward life. The interior growth of divine nature thus revealed might be called new, because now first it was recognised as a divine power, as a power inspiring *trust*, as a life that would grow by its own might within men if only they did not smother it and were content to restrain their own lower self from any voluntary inroads of evil. This power had been there, no doubt, in all men and all times; the germinating life of an inward spirit of involuntary good had never been a stranger to man; it had always pushed with gentle pressure against the limits of narrow minds and narrow hearts and of positive evil,—not, indeed, with the keen and piercing thrusts of divine judgment, but with the spontaneous movement of better life striving to cast off the scale of long-worn habit. But now this power was not only felt, but its origin was revealed. It was that same divinely human nature which had been embodied in the earthly Christ, that was stirring in the hearts of all men. It was He, whose life had been so strange and brief a miracle of beauty, to whom they might trust to mould afresh the twisted shapes of human imperfection, to push forward the growth of the good seed and the eradication of the tares within them. The same life which had shed its healing influence over the sick and the sinful in Galilee and Judea, was but the human form of that which fostered the true nature beneath the falsehoods of all actual life, and worked within the disciples as they preached their risen Lord. It was not they, but

"Christ that worked in them." Here was the true explanation of the unity of the human race, the common life which was the source of all that was deep and good; as separative influences grew out of all that was profoundly evil. They were all members of Christ; His nature was in them all, drawing out the beauty and chastening the deformity, breathing the breath of universal charity, and kindling the flame of inextinguishable hope. This was a power to trust in, the image of the Father's will, because breathing the very spirit of that will; and fuller of hope than any vision of a holy king commanding an allegiance which men could not bend their stiff hearts to pay, or conquering their moral freedom without acting on the secret springs of their humanity. They had known this power in themselves before; but they had not read it aright, because they had not estimated aright its source and the certainty and universality of its operation. They had not before known it as directly manifested in Him who opened the eyes of the blind, and cleansed the leper, and stilled the storm; who forgave sins, and wrestled with temptation; and finally passed through the grave, and trouble deeper than the grave, without being "holden" of it, because His will was freely surrendered to His Father's.

Here, then, was a revelation not simply of the Absolute nature of God, but of the formative power of Christ that is at work to cancel distorted growths, and even mere natural deficiency in every human heart. But it was to do more than this,—it was to take away sin itself from those who could bring themselves to trust their hearts freely to His influence;—to reveal to them, in short, the great divine law that, as through the unity of human nature "if one member suffers, all the members suffer with it," so through the same unity a new life may spread into even the weakest and corruptest member. It was to reveal it as the highest privilege of this great central human life to purify others when once their will begins to turn towards Him, by entering into the very heart of their evil and reaching the very core of their inward misery; so that while new life returns to *them*, the shadow of pain inseparable from the perfect knowledge of human guilt falls back on the spirit of the great Purifier. This was the revelation of the true nature in man; a nature that not only, as the Gentile nations felt, asserted the primitive truth and goodness properly belonging to every human creature, but that is capable of restoring that truth and goodness, cancelling the sinful habit, melting the rigid heart, emancipating the sullen temper, by the mere exertion of its spontaneous fascination over any spirit which once surrenders to its control.

And this, accordingly, is the great subject of Christian writers after once Christ had left the earth. It was to them a new discovery that the restorative power in every heart was *not* the power of their own wills, which they knew to be limited at most to a rejection of evil acts, but the very same power which had grown up into a perfect humanity in Christ, and only required an act of continuous trust to claim them for its own. To trust in such a power was not hard. To stifle the active rebellion of their own wills was possible; but to purge the turbid fountain of their human life, had that also been required of them, as both Jew and Gentile had often fancied, was mere impossibility. To *know* who it was who was working in them, was to multiply infinitely the regenerating power of His life.

Such, then, I hold to be the essence of the divine Self-Revelation of God. Into the question of its exact relation to the historical narrative in the Bible I cannot here enter. I feel little doubt that true criticism shows a large admixture of untrustworthy elements in the narrative of the Old, and some also in that of the New Testament; and that when this is admitted, the emancipation of the intellect from what seems a purely literary superstition as to the infallibility of the Bible narratives, will probably bring far more gain to the spiritual freedom of man, and do more to direct attention to the spiritual evidences of truth, than any belief in verbal inspiration could educe. Bibliolatry has been, and is likely long to be, the bane of Protestant Christianity. Spiritual realities would indeed be recognised *as* spiritual realities by few, had they had no perfect manifestation in the actual works and Providence of God,—had not the desire of the heart been embodied in the desire of the eyes. But that no minute history was needful of the earthly life of Him who can interpret His own meaning, and who came that He might draw the veil from eternal power and truth, and not to fascinate men's eyes and hearts to one single illuminated point of space and time,—is sufficiently proved by the absence of all records of His life which can be called minute, or which do not rely on the faithfulness of memory even for their outlines. Human vanity, eager to guarantee its own immortality, carries laboriously about all the paraphernalia for setting down every word and action before its transient life is spent. He who is solving the agonizing problems of ages, speaking to the depths of the human spirit in generations on generations yet unborn, and uttering "the things which have been kept secret from the foundation of the world," can afford to dispense with the minute history of His life, when He has power to turn every human conscience into a new witness of His truth, and every heart into a new evangelist of His glory.

VI.

THE HISTORICAL PROBLEMS OF THE FOURTH GOSPEL.[1]

FOR many years back there have appeared, from time to time, one-sided and negative historical criticisms on Christian and Jewish records which have far exceeded in practical interest and power, books of what seem to me much sounder judgment. These criticisms have recognised the fact, that history must lead to a conviction much deeper than history itself can give, if it would have a religious significance. They usually deny that history does do this, it is true; but they echo the genuine feeling

---

[1] 'Kritische Untersuchungen über die kanonischen Evangelien, ihr Verhältniss zu einander, ihren Charakter und Ursprung.' Von Dr. Ferdinand Christian Baur. Tübingen, 1847.

'Beitrage zur Evangelien-kritik.' Von Dr. Fried. Bleek. Berlin, 1846.

'The Gospel of St. John.' By Frederick Denison Maurice, M.A. Note I. On Baur's Theory of the Gospels. Macmillan, 1857.

of men about historical criticism, in making the assertion. They say boldly: 'Historical criticism has an intense interest, if it is only one stage in the education of men's spirits into truths lying far beneath it: but better clear it away altogether than mistake the title-deeds for the title, —the hold on the mere medium of revelation for the hold on the reality revealed. If you find that an imperfect history and literature is the introduction to a living and perfect trust—that as you pierce beneath the surface you get hold of far clearer and deeper certainties than the mere authority of the history or literature could bring with it—then historical criticism has a living significance, and we will follow it with you that it may lead us to something better than itself. But if you find that the thing revealed can only stand by the mere external force of its historical credentials, then you have got hold of no religion, but a mere piece of antiquarianism; and we will show you how baseless your confidence is.' And I believe that such destructive criticism has done a great and most needful work. Why, indeed, is the sacred literature so complex in character, and the sacred history so entirely on a level in authority with all other ancient history, unless for this very purpose, to prevent us from holding religious faith by the wrong, *i.e.*, the external, side,—to teach us to hold our trust in God by the same tenure as our trust in man, that of living and growing *personal* impression; beginning, it may be, in outward historical evidence, but quite unable to hold and extend its influence on that evidence *alone?*

To my mind, the genuine and candid portion (for no doubt there is much both ungenuine and uncandid) of the destructive criticism of the last half-century has far more tendency to open the real issues of religious questions, and indirectly, therefore, even to *quicken* faith, than the "apologetic" criticism by which it has generally been met. The former has, at least, often delineated a real crisis in the history of individual lives—the first conflict between the groping intellect and the yearning heart —the fixed resolve to find something deeper than historical records on which to rest—the unshrinking scrutiny into the uneasy corners of intellectual profession ; while the latter has been emphatically " apologetic "—seldom courageous enough to face the inward crisis at all— dealing with its enemies in detail—wounding one, disabling another, slightly hampering a third—making the most of each separate triumph, but seldom daring to confront with its whole force the whole force of the foe— seldom asking itself: 'Are these "reasons" that I assign, *the* roots of my own faith ? Have I any deep inexhaustible springs of conviction, which no "difficulties" could choke up ? And if so, would not the clearest and sincerest proof of the depth of those springs be attained by admitting eagerly and heartily the whole force of all opposite considerations, and convincing myself how powerless they are to undermine inward trust ?' As a rule, the most depressing and disheartening of all religious literature is the apologetic literature. If I wished to doubt the possibility of a revelation, I should take a course of reading in defence of it. The works of professional assailants are often, indeed, of exactly the same description; but I know no books so valuable to probe the sources and show the real depth and realities of the Christian revelation as the books of profound-minded, honest, reluctant sceptics, if only, instead of being scared by them, we would allow them to sink quietly into the mind, and be there fairly tested as "working hypotheses," by involuntary judgments, thought, and reading. No doubt, at first, they often produce a strong and painful, and purely negative impression—an impression partly due to their strength, partly to their weakness; but, if they prove true, the pain is wholesome pain; and if not, the quiet and unshrinking study of them draws out latent truths and new aspects of truth, such as sadly few "apologies" bring to light. All delineations of real and eager mental conflict, of minds in honest transition, open fresh realities to the mind; and if tranquilly laid to heart, for every new difficulty there is generally found more than one new spring of faith.

A very remarkable instance of this effect of genuine, even when most negative, criticism, is to be found in the influence which Bretschneider's and Baur's assaults on the Fourth Gospel are likely to produce on the present condition of Christian faith. Baur's book shows remarkably how a genuine historical investigation, conducted on broad and courageous principles, will lead us beyond itself, and suggest issues of a deeper and more instructive class. Every learned English theological critic of the present day is acquainted with Baur's able researches, and occasionally mentions points therein in order to refute them; but only one has ventured to face, in its original strength, the general tenor of Baur's argument, and he was precluded by the nature of his work from giving it more than a general consideration. I propose to condense the combination of converging evidences by which Baur demonstrates, to his own satisfaction, the historical incredibility of St. John's Gospel; and to use the aspects of the subject, that will be thus brought out, as a guide in estimating the most plausible views of it. Theologians certainly miss more instruction by their timidity and negligent appreciation of hostile arguments, than, by any diligence and enthusiasm of advocacy, they can contrive to make up for.

Baur maintains and, I may safely say, proves that the unity of the Fourth Gospel is a theological unity; that the whole of the narrative is threaded together, by the single intention to unfold the relation of the Father to the Son or Divine Word, as *the* divine relation through a living participation in which all men may be transfigured and set free. But it is not the theology of the fourth gospel which I intend to consider in the present essay; it is the bearing of that theology on the *narrative* of the Evangelist to which I must, for the present, limit myself. Baur's view is briefly this. The theology it contains is the theology of the second century. The Christian Gnosis or unfolding of the relation between the Father and the Son or Word, in the fourth gospel, presupposes the coarser Gnosis of the Syrian and Alexandrian schools; and is set out partly at least, in answer to them. The great superiority it has is mainly in this—that, while the false Gnostics represented the Light and Darkness as contending in an external and semi-physical conflict, the Christian writer limits the arena to the soul of man. But not the less, as Baur holds, does he fall into the Gnostic error of subordinating the moral freedom of man to the overruling metaphysical necessity he delineates. Only those who are virtually God's *already*, "come to the light, that their deeds may be made manifest that they are wrought in God:" while all whom the Father has *not* "drawn" to the Son, seem to remain helpless organs of the Darkness; and "hate the Light, neither come to the Light, lest their deeds should be reproved."

To the delineation of the conflict between the "Word made flesh," and the power of darkness or unbelief in the Jews, and their leaders the Pharisees, the whole narrative of the fourth gospel is, according to Baur, subordinated—and not merely subordinated, but completely accommodated—sometimes by the skilful use of traditional material, sometimes by the invention of symbolic miracles, everywhere by the free composition of appropriate discourse. It is to bring out more markedly the metaphysical opposition between the Divine Light and the Darkness of Jewish unbelief, that the scene is so often shifted from Galilee—almost uniformly the scene of Christ's ministry, up to the last crisis, in the other three gospels—to Jerusalem and its neighbourhood, where that unbelief was at once most intense and most culpable. It is to deepen the dark colouring of this unbelief, that most of the new facts, and new aspects of fact, are drawn up by the Evangelist. It is because it does not bear directly on this strife between the self-manifested Light and human Darkness, that so much of the traditional history is left unused. But there was one other theological controversy in the second century, besides the Gnostic controversies as to the divine emanations issuing from the Godhead—the Paschal controversy. The Jewish passover had, by its connection with the crucifixion of Christ, acquired in the minds of Christians an association with spiritual deliverance from the power of sin and death, which almost absorbed its old association with the deliverance from political degradation and the Egyptian bondage. The paschal lamb was a sign of that mighty hand of God, which had been put forth to rescue the Jews from the rapidly multiplying sins of slaves; and now, at the same season, they celebrated another sacrifice, a sign of a still mightier power, put forth to rescue them from the growing slavery of sin. The deliverance was greater; for, in the former case, their sins had been in some measure a result of their degraded political condition; in the latter, their degraded condition was the simple result of their sins. Hence the Jewish passover early obtained a Christian interpretation; and even St. Paul exclaims, " Christ our passover was sacrificed for us."

Gradually, the minutely superstitious mind of the second century wanted, says Baur, to verify this broad and true insight by the minutest correspondences in times and observances; and it became a matter of importance to prove, that Christ was slain exactly on the day and at the hour when the paschal lamb was slain, so fulfilling and exhausting the meaning of the Jewish rite. The three first gospels, however, represent Him as *eating* the paschal lamb with His disciples, at the usual Jewish season, on the evening before His death. It became necessary, therefore, for an evangelist, who, in Baur's view, certainly belonged to the Alexandrian school, to defend the views of that school, by altering the date of the crucifixion by a day, and so bringing every thing into accordance with that view of the Jewish passover which regarded it as a typical anticipation of the Christian Easter.

It was with constant reference, then, to these two leading theological controversies of the second century —the Gnostic and the Paschal controversy—that Baur conceives that the primitive gospel was intentionally and consciously remodelled by the fourth Evangelist. But, before I give in detail the evidence by which he defends his view, I must clear away two intermediate hypotheses, which might be, and have been, put forward in regard to this gospel. The differences between the facts of the fourth gospel and the others, and the preponderance in it of the theological element, may be explained on four distinct suppositions :—

1. That the theology, brooding in the minds of successive generations, has gradually modified, where it has not actually *produced*, the facts: the mythic theory.

2. That though the facts are, probably, *less* reliable than those of the other gospels, because they are preserved by a less primitive stream of tradition, their peculiar character may yet be explained, on the assumption that they were preserved by the Hellenistic Christian tradition, as distinguished from the Hebrew Christian, — each selecting, and perhaps exaggerating, those aspects of Christ's ministry which were most suitable to its own cast of thought: this may be called the theory of Hellenistic tradition.

3. That the facts are consciously dressed up, and modified to meet the thoughts and wants of the Alexandrian Christianity in the second century: Baur's theory.

4. That the facts were selected for special illustration of certain religious Truths; but are more reliable and closer to such events as this gospel touches at all, than even those of the other gospels, being more certainly the recollections of a personal disciple of Christ.

Now, the first assumption may be very quickly disposed of. Baur's own answer to it is quite sufficient; and Baur does not put anything like the whole strength of the case. He maintains, justly, I think, that there is no single portion of Scripture where there is so complete an absence of any indication of the gradual condensation of belief into fact as in the fourth gospel. Distinct theological purpose is not only everywhere present, but everywhere conscious; and the boundary between it and the facts narrated is remarkably sharp and clear. Narrative and theological principles are both there, no doubt, and both in organic connection; but they are as separable as the principles and purposes of the hero of any modern biography are from the practical steps by which he illustrates them. For example, the gift of sight to the man born blind is clearly meant by the Evangelist to be taken in close connection with Christ's words: "I am the Light of the world," and with His rebuke to the Pharisees: "For judgment am I come into this world, that those who see not may see, and those who see may be made blind;" nor can it well be doubted that both the miracle and the sayings are strictly an illustration of the Evangelist's own prologue, where he speaks of the Light as shining in Darkness,— of the Darkness as comprehending it not, while "as many as received" it therewith received power, like the man whose eyes were opened simultaneously to the physical and spiritual personality of Christ, to become "sons of God." There can be little doubt that in such instances as these discourses of Christ, the narrative of His actions and the introductory theology of the Evangelist are intended to form an organic whole; but clearly one in which there is a conscious discrimination of the different elements of fact and doctrine. The procedure of Christ, the debate in the Sanhedrim, the examination of the blind man's parents,—none of these things have either a symbolic or a mythic character: they are at least put forth as straightforward incident: nor is there any single circumstance treated as narrative in the whole gospel, which has any appearance of being intended to bear an allegorical or merely symbolic interpretation, nor anything like an imaginative representation of a popular faith.

Even Baur has not noted the whole strength of this case. The temptation, the transfiguration, the supernatural birth, are none of them to be found in this gospel. The darkness which brooded over the earth when the Son of God expired,—the sudden rending of the veil of the Temple,—the visible ascension of the Saviour from the earth,—all of them events which *necessarily* have symbolic aspects, and are therefore especially liable to symbolic modes of interpretation,—are wanting in the fourth gospel. In fact, though the miracles of this gospel may possibly bear classification on a theological principle, in regard, namely, to the particular aspect of the Divine Word that each may illustrate,—as the restorer of health and strength to the physically and morally paralysed,—as the "Bread of Life" to the common labourer in the fulness of his strength,—as the "Light of the World" both to the seeing and the blind,—as the "Resurrection and the Life" to the dead; —yet in the account of the miracles themselves there is no disappearance of those small physical details and incidental facts which seem to distract the mind from the ideal element. On the contrary, the only great miracle which the fourth gospel and the other three have in common, — the multiplication of the loaves (which in this gospel, we must recollect, immediately precedes the discourse on " I am the Bread of Life"),—is related in a way even less ideal than in the synoptic narrative. A narrative which was merely the imaginative embodiment of the discourse, would certainly not have specialised the loaves as "barley loaves." Yet this is peculiar to this gospel's account. And not only here, but everywhere, the fact and the engrafted teaching are kept sedulously apart. There are few matters of fact in the other gospels which it is so impossible to analyse hypothetically into purely ideal elements as those of the fourth ; simply because the ideal and the real side both exist here in their fullest strength, so that there is no pretence for saying that either of the two gave birth to the other.

(2). The second or traditional hypothesis, which regards the gospel as the result of a less primitive but *bonâ-fide* tradition of the Hellenistic Christians, is hardly more tenable. In the first place, if a genuine tradition, its germ or historical nucleus must have been the personal testimony of one of Christ's apostles, who can have been no other than St. John. The gospel introduces us to the most private intercourse held by Christ with his disciples ; it contains in the last chapters the reported testimony of one specially connected with Peter (as we find John to be in the opening of the Acts of the Apostles) ; and it has domestic elements of Christ's history recorded by no other Evangelist. In short, if it be a genuine tradition at all, it can only have originated in the reports of one of the three apostles everywhere spoken of in the synoptic gospels as the special friends and followers of Christ,—Peter, James, and John. Peter is excluded by the narrative itself. James was early put to death by Herod; nor has any tradition ever connected the gospel with his name. Moreover, as has often been remarked, on the assumption either that this gospel is written in simplicity, or otherwise, the habitual absence in it of the description of John the forerunner of Christ as "the Baptist"—a description universal in the other three gospels—rather points (unconsciously or fraudulently, as the case may, be) to a writer who, being himself the other John to be distinguished, could not possibly have got into the habit of thus distinguishing John the Baptist from the well-known disciple of the same name.

But be this as it may, the last chapters of the fourth gospel certainly profess to record much of the personal testimony of our Lord's most intimate friend among the twelve apostles; and Baur freely admits that they intentionally indicate John. But when we add to this certainty, which bears, no doubt, only on a portion of the gospel,—a portion which may therefore have been the mere germ or nucleus of the rest,—the unanimous inference of all great critics,—Baur being the single exception, —from the mere styles of the gospel and the first epistle of John, that these, as wholes, are the compositions of one and the same author; and find, moreover, at the very outset of the epistle an assertion of the author's direct personal intercourse with Christ exactly similar both in tone and substance to an assertion in one of the later chapters of the gospel,[2]—it is almost impossible to avoid the conclusion that the fourth gospel was not merely originated, but written as a whole, by one who professed to be a personal—and most intimate personal —follower of Christ.

But is it not possible to conceive the elements of the narrative properly *traditional*, in case the implied authorship by an apostle is a mistake or a fraud? I think not. Taking the broadest view of the contents of the gospel, I can find nothing less in it than a traditional character if by tradition we are to understand that which has passed from mind to mind, and gradually taken the proportions and colouring in which it most powerfully affects the imagination either of a people or of a school. This traditional hypothesis, we must remember, is an attempt to account for the *new* aspects of Christ's character, and

---

[2] In the gospel, chap. xix. ver. 35, we read, "And he that hath seen it hath borne witness, and his witness is true; and he knoweth that he saith true, that ye may believe." And again, chap. xx. ver. 31, "But these are written that ye may believe that Jesus is the Christ, the Son of God, and that believing ye might have life in his name." In the epistle, the words are, "And the life was manifested and we have seen, and bear witness and declare unto you that eternal life that was with the Father and was manifested to us: that which we have seen and heard declare we unto you, that ye also may have fellowship with us; and our fellowship is with the Father and with his Son Jesus Christ."

the new—nay, to some extent inconsistent—account of his career, which this gospel, when compared with the three synoptic accounts, brings out. There is, it is remarked, a haze of mystic glory brooding over the character and purposes of Christ in the last narrative, which clears away in the three first, showing the delicate and majestic outline of a distinct human personality. Again, the miraculous power, which in St. Matthew, St. Mark, and St. Luke is mainly the organ of a Divine compassion for human misery and pain, is in this gospel—primarily, at least—the revealing medium of a mighty spiritual Presence, and intended more as a solemn parting in the clouds of Providence, to enable man to gaze up into the light of Divine mystery, than as a grateful temporary shower of blessing to a parched and blighted earth. And further, the religious love which in the synoptic gospels confines itself to the children of the kingdom, in this embraces at the very outset a village of the alien Samaria, and solemnly anticipates at the close not only the coming welcome of the Greeks, but the assembling of all men at the foot of the cross. And all these differences, together with that subordinate difference as to the ordinary theatre of Christ's ministry which was needful to give the requisite solemnity of antithesis to the narrow notions of the Jewish teachers, it is proposed to explain by the colouring influence of a Hellenistic stream of tradition, which strove to see in Christ its own dream of supersensual brightness and self-revealing power.

Now it is quite a different question whether or not

this gospel contains a refracted and unfaithful image of the ministry of Christ, and whether or not that unfaithfulness looks like the unconscious modification of tradition. For many reasons it is desirable to keep the discussion of these questions as far as possible distinct, and it is the latter which I am just now discussing. The fourth Gospel is much too remarkably peculiar and individual in its whole tenor to be the result of tradition. It is not simply that the selected thoughts and discourses of Christ are so entirely of one cast and tone, but the narratives themselves are all taken from the same point of view,—that of showing how the Son came into the world, not in His own name but His Father's, how the world would not receive Him, and how yet as many as received Him were, in proportion to the simplicity and fulness of their trust, justified by the issue. Now tradition does not take up single truths, or single aspects of truth, and illustrate them throughout a series of facts. If it takes hold of character, it sketches the same character from a number of different points of view, till the essence is engraved upon your mind by the variety of aspects in which you have seen it. If, on the other hand, it takes hold of narrative, as narrative, it brings out in clear colours the popular emotions,—the fear, the hope, the anguish, the triumph,—on which the interest of the story turns. Thus Elijah's character is brought out with marvellous clearness and sublimity by the traditions of his people, in its various attitudes towards God and man,—towards the king and the widow,—in the hour of awe-struck inspiration, and in the hour of blank despair. But all these scenes are threaded together in the imagination of the people simply by the distinct personality they express, not by the illustration of any single aspect of Divine truth. And in the pastoral traditions of the Jews,—the narratives of Jacob and Esau,—of Joseph and his brethren,—of the Shunamite woman whose son was restored to her by Elisha,—we find, on the other hand, the vivid colouring of popular sympathy with the broad human emotions of parental love and anxiety, of brethren's jealousy, of awe at the loneliness of Nature, and of trust in God.

In short, the effect of tradition is to reduce the human narrative to its effective elements,—to pare away the small discrepancies and unrealities of a great character, which only mar the spectacle of it as a whole,—to omit those portions of a narrative which have no special fascination for the simple and universal feeling of the national heart. No doubt, in the case of an intellectual people like the Hellenistic Jews the tendency might be something different—namely, to reduce the memory of facts to their ideal essence,—their intellectual significance as thoughts. But of this too there is no trace in the fourth gospel. The facts remain presented not as distinct ideal wholes, but as accumulated illustrations of a single truth. It is not the varying and characteristic essence of *each* individual act and sign which the fourth Evangelist brings out, but a single permanent theological meaning, which he traces through all of them: and this, too, is so remarkably the case, that if we stripped the narratives peculiar to this gospel of all the details recorded with special reference to this permanent theological design, we should leave little for the share of "tradition" except the naked assertion that such or such an event had once happened during the ministry of Christ.

The only new details, indeed, which are not of this kind—namely, of illustrative theological significance—are details of personal and private affections, such as Christ's last recommendation of His mother to His disciple, the request of Peter at the Last Supper, "Lord, not my feet only, but also my hands and my head," the grief of Mary Magdalene at finding the body of Christ removed from the sepulchre, the imputation of treachery to Judas in relation to his anxiety at the waste of the ointment, the demeanour of Martha and Mary after their brother's death, and at the feast in Bethany, and the little by-play at the marriage feast of Cana in Galilee. Indeed, where the narrative of the fourth gospel seems confused at all, it is from the *absence*, even where you most expect them, of those broad general effects which tradition always preserves. It is almost impossible that the story of the marriage at Cana, for example, should in its present form have been preserved by either a Jewish or a Hellenistic tradition; there is none of that broad feeling of the sacredness of family life which would have endeared it to the Jew, and no clear ideal element which might have fixed it in the memory of the Greek. It does not catch the tone of sacredness and joy with which the popular imagination,—especially amongst the Jews—always invests the threshold of family life; it does not even mention the wonder of the rustic guests at the greatness of the miracle. And it has puzzled rationalistic criticism ever since by the absence of any clear suggestion for an allegoric interpretation, such as might have suited the Greek taste for symbol. Yet it glances at the private background of the scene, indicating the familiar terms on which the mother of Jesus stood in the household, both by the interest she feels for the hospitable treatment of the guests and by her freedom in addressing the servants; it asserts emphatically, in the little dialogue between Jesus and His mother as to His "time being not yet come," a truth which is repeated again and again throughout this gospel, that there was a higher law for Christ's actions than could be derived from mere external circumstance—the law of a being whose guiding impulses were from within and from above; and it draws careful attention to the circumstances proving the greatness and the reality of the miracle—the magnitude of the water-pots, and the attestation by the governor of the feast. And lastly, it tells the effect of the sign;—that His disciples "saw his glory, and believed on him." Now this may be theological invention *for a purpose;* or it may be personal recollection or hearsay, modified by a special aim in recording; but it surely is not proper tradition. There is a disproportion in the parts of the narrative, a want of *wholeness* and distinctness, whether imaginative or rational, in the effect, which is extremely unlike the filtering and colouring results of a slow straining through the minds of men.

I doubt especially if any tradition—properly so called—concentrates the attention on *points of evidence.* These are, indeed, always prominent in the first narration of marvellous events, and in the immediate rehearsal of them; but while the links of proof gradually fall out of the popular mind, and are absorbed into the ultimate effect which they were meant to accredit, the imaginative or intellectual influence which the event was calculated to put forth is developed and brought out into clearer outline. Thus, among all the proper Hebrew traditions, there is none in which any special stress is laid on the points which a lawyer would value as establishing the truth of his case. And indeed this is one remarkable point in which most of the miracles peculiar to the fourth gospel differ from those in the other three, which approach more closely to traditions. The nobleman whose son is healed by Christ in Cana, goes down to Capernaum (John iv. 52, 53), and finds that the child had begun to recover at the *exact* hour at which Christ said to him, "Thy son liveth." In the accounts of the miracle on the man born blind, and of the resurrection of Lazarus, there is very much of the same character,—a predominance, namely, of that view of the narrative in which its testimony to the higher nature of Christ, and its adaptation to awaken belief in the beholders, are the two points regarded.

The concluding assertion of the Evangelist, "These are written *that ye may believe that Jesus is the Christ, the Son of God*," is verified through every narrative he gives. Everywhere attention is fixed on the indications of a nature obeying higher and more mysterious laws than the common nature of man; everywhere attention is fixed on the indications that Christ's divine acts were real, and not fictitious. In the account of the miracle on the man born blind, this is remarkably the case. The narrative is introduced with an emphasis on the former point, in the recorded saying of Christ, that "neither did this man sin nor his parents, but that the works of God should be made manifest in him. I must work the works of him that sent me while it is day .... as long as I am in the world, I am the light of the world." And then, throughout the narrative, the emphasis is laid on all the points which bring out the evidence of the fact most irresistibly, and which make the unbelief of the Pharisees seem most obstinate and culpable. But what we may call the general graphic effect, the *spectacle* of the divine act, is scarcely painted at all: the surprise of the neighbours, the emotion of his parents, the dawning of a new sense on the man himself, are not touched at all, or only touched in relation to the no-result produced on the minds of the obstinate Pharisees : " We know that God spake unto Moses, but as for this man we know not whence he is." We are not told, as St. Mark tells us in in a similar case, that the blind man's sight came gradually, that he first saw "men as trees walking." We are not told even of the man's own joy. These are the sides of a miracle that take hold of the popular imagination. But we are told of the beggar's immediate *inference* that Jesus was a prophet, and how, in spite of all evidence, the Pharisees remained blind though saying "we see," and cast him out of the synagogue. Every winding of the story that bears on its strength of reality as against sceptics, and on the certain inference it yields with regard to the nature of Christ, is anxiously followed out; but no others. And as a whole, it is a living representation of the petty doubtings of Pharisaic pride and disbelief, but certainly not the *popular* vision of a mighty act of power.

The same remark may be made of the account given us of the resurrection of Lazarus. It begins as before with Christ's teaching: "This sickness is not unto death, but for the glory of God, that the Son of God might be glorified thereby." It then tells us that Christ, after hearing of the illness of Lazarus, staid two days without moving. And later on He tells His disciples: "I am glad for your sakes that I was not there, to the intent ye may believe." Here, as elsewhere, the Evangelist not only takes pains to bring out the glory of God *in the belief* of the disciples as the end of the miracle, but lays stress on the circumstances that show the law of Christ's nature to be mysterious and given from above, and not determined by the small occasional motives which make sport with human wills. He does not go on the first news; but when, afterwards, the disciples object to Him the great danger of going into Judea again, Christ intimates that there can be no danger in doing anything where there is clear light from Heaven. As all men can walk safely during the twelve hours of the day,— so could He go safely whenever His mind was clearly illuminated from above, as to the duty before Him. His light of life was, not like other men's, reflected back from the mere visible circumstances of His earthly lot, but shone directly on the earthly lot from the Heaven in which His spirit dwelt. Then, if we omit the personal traits of Thomas's courageous affection and the sisters' grief and trust, the principal stress of the narrative falls on the great words to Martha, "I am the resurrection and the life;" and on the thanksgiving to which He gives utterance, "for the sake of the bystanders," that the Father had heard Him. This precedes the act of power itself; and the Evangelist clearly means to draw attention to this, as bringing out Christ's *conscious* unity with God more strikingly than if it had been offered afterwards.[3] Even the words "Loose him and let him go"—strikingly as they close the scene— are the *natural* ending rather to a mind riveted intensely on the manifestations of Christ's personal glory, than to one painting the startling awfulness of the event itself.

---

[3] A parallel incident in the other gospels is the healing of the man whose sins have been *first* forgiven by Christ, when He asks "Whether is it easier to say, 'Thy sins be forgiven thee,' or 'Arise and walk'? but that ye may know that the Son of Man hath power on earth to forgive sins, he saith to the sick of the palsy, 'Arise, take up thy bed and walk.'"

It is the calmness of Christ's majesty, not the awe of the grave giving up its dead, which these words express.

And as the evidences of His miracles, and the higher law of His heavenly nature, are the points on which the Evangelist always fixes attention in regard to Christ,—so the *sincerity* of other persons' belief, and the depth to which their belief in Him went, are the points on which he always fixes attention in regard to other men. They are all classified or measured by the kind and amount of their belief. The Galileans are marked as believing only because they had seen the signs He did at the feast; His mother believes, but not implicitly enough to forego prompting Him; the nobleman at Capernaum cannot at first leave to Christ the *mode* of His divine help, but prescribes to Him "to come down" ere his child die, yet afterwards believes with his whole household; Nicodemus can assent to the convincing power of outward marvels, but cannot believe in the freedom of the spirit; Nathanael, and afterwards the Samaritans, believe on Him on the testimony of their own inward experience to His divine power; the Pharisees reject Him, because their own nature and deeds are evil; the Jews of Capernaum are staggered by the first "hard saying,"—with whom Peter is contrasted, asking, "Lord, to whom shall we go? thou hast the words of eternal life, and we have believed and know that thou art the Christ, the Son of the living God;"[4] the brethren of Jesus tauntingly say

---

[4] I adopt here and generally a translation of this gospel by five clergymen after the authorized version (London, J. W. Parker,

to Him, "'If thou be the Christ, manifest thyself to the world;' for even his brethren did not believe on him;" Thomas,—bold and enthusiastic, who would follow Christ into danger that "he may die with him"—who yet tells His master, "We know not whither thou goest, and how can we know the way?" and who after the resurrection will not believe except he see the "print of the nails,"—is finally classified by Christ in regard to the nature of his faith, in the words, "Thomas, because thou hast seen, thou hast believed; blessed are they who have not seen, and yet have believed;" and in briefer hints, the apostles at the last supper, Peter and the "other disciple" who "saw and believed" in the empty sepulchre, and, in a word, all the actors, from the beginning to the end of the Evangelist's narrative, are described, compared, and delineated by their various symptoms of belief or unbelief.

All this continuity of purpose is not, it will be observed, limited to the mere doctrinal application of the narrative, but is impressed on all the details of fact selected for narration. It cannot have arisen in traditional materials. Tradition might bring out or impress an ideal unity, but could not thread together narratives marked throughout by the mention of small circumstan-

---

1857): a translation which, is, however, by no means adequately corrected. For example, it is a very great mistake to continue to translate σημεῖα "miracles." I do not think that the word necessarily implies the miraculous element; I am sure that it always implies much more. And clearly the version ought to have been made from the purest text.

tial evidences, of frequent indications of the supersensual law of Christ's nature, and of the special kinds and degrees of belief that nature met with in men. This implies unity of *design* or *purpose*, not the vague ideal unity which tradition delights in. And when we observe also the fact noticed above, that the only incidents which are in any way beside the express aims of the narrative, are incidents of *intimate* personal relations with Christ, the evidence of individuality in the narrative is still more striking.

Nor does the hypothesis of a Hellenistic tradition seem to me at all to suit the intellectual tone of this gospel. No doubt there is a religious universalism in it which is scarcely rivalled elsewhere in the New Testament; but it is not an intellectual and Greek universalism founded on the universality of human nature and moral law, but a divine and theological universalism, taking its point of departure from the personal self-revelation of God. The fourth gospel is essentially a universalised *Judaism*. The Greeks are mentioned far more slightly than the Samaritans, and the Samaritans with far less theological favour than the Jews. "Ye worship that which ye know not," says Christ to the Samaritan woman; "we worship that which we know, because salvation is of the Jews." The emotion which the Evangelist tells us was displayed by our Lord when He heard of the desire of the Greeks to see Him, has no special relation to them as Greeks, but to the "much fruit" His death should bear in "drawing *all men*" unto him. As has often been observed, the desire of the Evangelist to show the minute fulfilment of Jewish prophecies (which are frequently quoted by the writer directly from the Hebrew version, and not from the Greek) is uniform and anxious.

But besides these subordinate indications,—the theology is essentially Hebrew *in character*—too Hebrew by far even for the Alexandrian school of Judaism. If there is one point more than another that distinguishes the strictly *natural* element in Hebrew religion from the natural element in the Greek, it is its Oriental disposition to subordinate entirely human ideas of right to the fiat of an unquestioned omnipotence. The Jewish *revelation* struggles, sometimes successfully, sometimes almost vainly, with this disposition in the minds of the national kings and teachers and prophets. God was trying to teach them that He did not ask for worship because He was all-powerful, but because He was all-holy. The Jews constantly forgot the latter in remembering the former, and were ever gravitating towards a kind of worship in which the arbitrary appointments were superstitiously and pharisaically observed, while the moral order which those appointments represented was utterly effaced from the mind of the people. No Oriental people, least of all the Jews, had any difficulty in prostrating themselves before the personal Majesty of God; but they had difficulty in learning, what even Isaiah's inspiration strove, with very unequal success, to make manifest, that the divine commands were nothing but the practical expression of God's living and personal holiness, and worthless in letter unless their spirit also were drunk in. The Jews could hardly realise that the human virtues were both the truest obedience and truest sacrifice. They were ever straying into the conception that God was to be propitiated as an irresponsible king. They were in danger of losing morality in self-obeisance. God was *over* them, not in them. The human atom was too small to be of value before the throne of Deity. This was the evil tendency with which the self-revealing Spirit of God struggles throughout the history of the Jewish nation.

With the Greeks it was very different. Whatever was noble in their religion was an assertion of the divine element *in* man. They humanised all things, and truly felt that thought, love, human purity, and righteousness, were the divinest realities in life. To them, no Will could supersede right. The highest being was rather "the essential good" than a holy Will. They lost the personality of man in losing the personality of God. Spiritual obedience disappeared in the reverence for a mere natural goodness of disposition; but at the point where their religion was highest and truest, it consisted in the assertion that right and good are eternal and immutable, liable to no personal control at all,—not even to a god's,—but necessarily secure of the allegiance of all godlike natures. The Jew said, "As the heavens are higher than the earth, so are thy ways higher than our ways, and thy thoughts than our thoughts;" while the Greeks were most effectively appealed to in the exhortation "to seek the Lord, if haply they might feel after him and find him, though he be not far from every one of us; for in him we live, and move, and have our being; as certain also of your own poets have said: 'For we are also his offspring.'"

Now, with reference to this cardinal distinction between the starting point of the Hebrew and Greek religions— a distinction unquestionably most real and striking—let me ask to which side of religious character does the fourth gospel most remarkably lean? Does it start from God or from man? Does it assume, like Plato, the human ground of immutable moral distinctions, and argue to the divine holiness; or does it try to unfold the nature of God as the key to the highest life of man? No one can hesitate for a moment in replying, that the latter is the aim of the whole gospel. It is in order to indicate in the mind of Christ a "way higher than our ways," a mode of thought "higher than our thoughts," that almost every detail concerning Him is inserted. It is in order to show that men's holiness is almost inseparably connected with their *belief;* that some deep belief in a power above, though close to them, is absolutely essential to holiness, that almost every detail of human character is inserted. It is that men may "believe and have life through Christ's name," that the whole gospel is composed.

Again, what I may call the weaker side of the gospel, as compared with the other gospels, in its delineation of Christ, is a certain exclusive sense of His personal majesty and mystery, which overshadows the human and moral features of His character. There is the indistinctness of an almost feminine view of His life, which brings out more clearly than any other gospel, at once the mystery and the tenderness of His acts, as well as the devoted affection of His personal followers; but which omits much that was needful to develop the stronger and more definite characteristics of His ministry. It dwells almost exclusively on Christ's personal *title* to authority as the son of God, and on the personal relations between the Father and the Son,—not trying to delineate, except indeed as regards the infinite depth of *love* and *patience* in Him, how the character of the Son contrasted, in general traits and results, with that of the men amongst whom He lived and taught. The morality of the gospel is *based* upon the personal relations in which Christ stands to the spiritual world. I do not mean, of course, that it falls into the Old Hebrew disposition to regard righteousness as merely subordinate to the will of God, instead of as constituting the essence of His nature, but that it does not delineate or describe what this righteousness practically was, except on the side of love. It neglects the picture of Christ's character as a whole, to insist on His personal union with God, on the overflowing love in which that union consisted, and in which again it issued towards the lower world. The insight into special virtues and sins, the warnings against special temptations, the parables illustrative of the *details* of the Christian character, find no place here: the whole gospel is occupied in declaring the spiritual relation between men and Christ, as branches of one vine, or the sheep of one shepherd, and the eternal union between Christ and God. Need one ask, for a moment, whether this is characteristic of a Greek or Hebrew authorship?

Once more, I cannot even think it like the production of Alexandrian Judaism. For though theological, the writer of this gospel is far less *metaphysical* than St. Paul, and *à fortiori* than Philo. Metaphysicians analyse the relations of thoughts, as even St. Paul does at times; but here there are no relations of thoughts which are not relations between persons, and that of the very simplest kind. "The Father worketh hitherto, and I work."—"The Father beareth witness of me."—"I am come in my Father's name, and ye receive me not; if another shall come in his own name, him ye will receive."—"As my Father hath loved me, so have I loved you; abide ye in my love." Such, and such only, are the metaphysics of the gospel. Indeed, it betrays no intellectual interest in ideas or definitions as such, apart from personal *influences*. No one who has read Mr. Jowett's essay on Philo and St. Paul will disagree with me when I say that, far apart as are St. Paul's Epistles from the manner and matter of Philo, the style of this gospel, notwithstanding the Logos doctrine it contains, is much farther. "If, from time to time," says Mr. Jowett, speaking of the first Alexandrian school of Christian fathers, "they are found making extravagant suppositions to support a favourite theory, playing with words, numbers, or colours; reading the Old Testament backwards, that they may absolutely identify it with the New; we may compare them first with Philo; . . . . . they occasionally allegorise numbers; he, it may be said, never misses the opportunity. They, in a very few instances, supersede the historical meaning; he can scarcely be said to allow the historical meaning to stand at all."

Nothing can be more totally different than this from the manner and thought of our Evangelist. Neither allegory nor metaphysics appear in his theology. Even ethical ideas are absorbed into personal influences. To me there seems to be something not merely Oriental, but, as I have said, almost feminine in the exclusive importance attached to the personal origin and *derivation* of divine or evil influence, as distinguished from the *character* of that influence considered purely in itself. Christ's saying that "the tree is known by its fruits," does not seem to take strong hold of the Evangelist. His method seems to me to be the method of one who cared more to know that he drew his spiritual life from the individual Master he had loved, than he even cared to know exactly what the character of that spiritual life in itself was; and who, as a natural consequence, loved to call to memory all Christ's assertions of His own like dependence on the Father, even more than to delineate in what sort of general character that dependence issued. This manner seems better adapted to the parting hours than to any other part of Christ's ministry, because then the consciousness of the personal relation between Christ and His disciples naturally assumes more depth and pathos. Indeed, if, as some philosophers say, "the sense of dependence" were the only essence of religion,—a definition which almost entirely excludes the Greek type of religion,—then the fourth gospel would be at once more essentially religious and less Hellenistic than any other book of the New Testament.

(3.) Having thus cleared away, at least to my own satisfaction, the mythic and traditional hypothesis of the fourth gospel, and given my reasons for thinking its religious universalism of strictly Hebrew, not Gentile origin, I come to the theory of Baur, which represents the peculiar historical elements of this gospel as consciously-invented fiction, prepared in the interests of special theological purposes. I believe this to be a much more plausible and, intellectually speaking, tenable critical hypothesis than either of those with which I have been dealing. In other words, if assumed as a base of explanation, there is more that it would seem to account for, and less that is absolutely unintelligible on that supposition, than there would be on either of the former suppositions. I am trying, it must be remembered, to look at the facts peculiar to this gospel purely critically, and understand with what origin of the gospel they seem most consistent; and I will venture to say that, apart from all previous hypothesis, the most repulsive theory of all, which regards them as purposely modified or invented by theological design, is far more plausible than any except the view which regards them as more directly attested by personal experience than those with which they most seem to clash in the three synoptic gospels. Baur is a theorist, and has the German passion for a complete "view." He pushes his supposed discovery into some absurd extremes; but, taking his book as a whole, notwithstanding the shock it may give on a first perusal, or rather, perhaps, very much in consequence of this shock, it has done more to promote the true understanding of the gospel,—nay, is written, on the whole, with more eager desire truly to understand it, whatever it might cost,—than most of those shy and timid apologies which seem to owe to mere theological caution what I hold to be their truer and certainly far more orthodox explanation. I will try and do justice to Baur's view.

Baur supposes, then, that the writer of the fourth gospel had access to the other three, and probably, also, to the Acts of the Apostles. His object was to delineate Christ as the impersonated Logos, or Word of God, and to represent him as expecting from the first to be glorified through suffering and death, simply because the Darkness of human evil, being in deadly contest with him from the beginning, could not be persuaded to recognise the true Light on any easier terms than those of seeing how undiminished was the glory with which it had passed through apparent annihilation. Hence Christ was not only the Divine Word, he was also the

Paschal Lamb offered to celebrate the deliverance of his people from spiritual bondage; and thus it became important to record his death as occurring contemporaneously with its sacrifice. The gospel begins, says Baur, with a radically different assumption from that of the other Evangelists. With *them* the personal subject of the biography first came into existence at the birth of Christ; according to this gospel, its subject had not merely existed eternally, but even eternally as the Light of man, and only its distinctive personal self-manifestation in a human form was to be treated of in the gospel of Jesus Christ. Hence the supernatural birth is not only not mentioned, but would be out of place. It would be impossible to conceive of the Eternal Word in growth or progress; therefore the Evangelist passes at once and abruptly from the Word or Son in the bosom of the Father, to Jesus Christ's maturity and public ministry.

Again, in the other gospels, the baptism by John the Baptist is the consecrating act which officially inagurates his Messiahship,—without which he could not have "fulfilled all righteousness," *i.e.*, have been completely qualified for his public office. But in this gospel he cannot *become* any thing which he is not already; it is only "*manifestation* to Israel" which is in question; consequently the act of baptism is intentionally omitted,[5] and

---

[5] This is certainly false criticism. The baptism by John is assumed. The Baptist, according to this gospel, says, "*That he should be made manifest to Israel*, therefore am I come, *baptising*

instead of it his forerunner, John, merely relates the vision by which God has satisfied his mind that Jesus is the Word or the Divine Son. Christ is thus introduced by the solemn testimony of his forerunner to the people of Israel as the promised Messiah. That the Jews may have no excuse for rejecting the explicit testimony of John, the Evangelist expands the vague words of Luke (iii. 15), "All men mused in their hearts whether he (John) were the Christ or not," into a formal embassy of "Priests and Levites" from the sacerdotal authorities at Jerusalem, to whom John expressly disavows all claim to be the Messiah, and announces his merely preparatory functions as a "voice crying in the wilderness" (John i. 19). By a testimony as formal,—"Behold the Lamb of God,"—Jesus is introduced by John to the two first of his disciples, Andrew and one other, by whom again he is made acquainted with Simon, when Christ's divine insight into character is at once proved by giving him the surname of Cephas, or Peter. This name, Baur assumes, is not conferred, according to St. Matthew's account, till the date of the confession of Peter (xvi. 18); but, clearly, Christ's answer there implies that Peter is

---

with water." "He that sent me to baptise with water, the same said unto me, Upon whom thou shalt see the Spirit descending, &c." It is perfectly clear that the Evangelist describes John as implying that it was *in the official act* of baptising with water that that greater Baptist, who should baptise with the Holy Spirit, should be manifested to him. That the vision of the dove was subjective, both St. Matthew and St. Mark's account would seem to imply. In *their* narrative, it seems to be subjective to Christ; in this, subjective to the Baptist.

already so called, and that Christ is merely laying a new and special emphasis on the appropriateness of the name.[6] A greater exercise of insight into Nathanael's nature secures him at once the full belief of Nathanael.

From miraculous insight he passes to miraculous power, and "manifests his glory" by the sign at Cana in Galilee, and "his disciples believe in him." This Baur takes in its close and obviously-intentional connection with John's baptism by water. He thinks the miraculous change of water into wine was meant to attest the wonderful transition from the weak human ministry of John, which could not give new strength, but only wash away old stains, to the "new wine" of the spirit, which poured fresh and divine life into the heart. Wine, like fire, is the symbol of the Holy Spirit. Shortly afterwards (iii. 29), the Baptist calls Christ the bridegroom, and himself only the friend of the bridegroom. Surely, then, this wedding-feast,—at which, as we see (ii. 9, 10), the bridegroom himself ought to provide the wine,—is meant to symbolise the mystic Messianic wedding-feast, at which the Messiah entertains his guests with the overflow of his divine gifts? Here Baur cannot quite make up his mind between the literal and symbolic interpretation, but regards the fact as certainly an invented one, whichever be taken. He thinks the

---

[6] "κἀγὼ δέ σοι λέγω, ὅτι σὺ εἶ Πέτρος." "And I say to thee that thou *art* Peter"—the "art" being emphatic; otherwise it would run, ὅτι σὺ Πέτρος. Just so a Roman Catholic might say to Pio Nono, "Thou art indeed Pius."

wine may be an allusion also to the sacramental wine.

The manifestation of Christ to his personal disciples being thus completed, his contest with the greater darkness of the outer world is to begin. He goes to Jerusalem, the great scene of that conflict; and as it would not do to let him at any time seem to tolerate, from want of desire or power to remove them, abuses in the Temple, against which, in his later ministry, he so indignantly protests, the Evangelist narrates at once the cleansing of the Temple, which the other gospels also narrate on occasion of Christ's public visit to Jerusalem, but not till the close of his career in their account; his first visit being also, in their account, the last and only visit of his ministerial life. The other Evangelists directly assert that Christ's official career began when John was cast into prison. The fourth Evangelist gives him a preliminary career both in Galilee and at Jerusalem before that event. In fact, he contrasts graphically the waxing and the waning light, by bringing Jesus and the Baptist into a kind of competition in baptising in Judea (iii. 22), at a time when the former was only beginning to be great, and the latter had not yet ceased to be so; but only in order to make the Baptist prophesy his own decrease, and the increasing power of the Messiah.

Nicodemus is then sketched as a type of that kind of belief which, resting only on marvel, was closest to absolute unbelief. On bringing Christ back to Galilee, the Evangelist takes occasion to show that even the capacity to draw conviction from the most marvellous of all Christ's works necessarily involves some deeper belief in him personally as the Word of God. This he does by the example of the Capernaum nobleman, whose sick son Jesus heals from a distance by a spoken word. The nobleman believes the word, and so proves that a tentative belief which precedes the test of the miracle,—*i.e.*, a preliminary willingness to trust Christ's personal character,—is the condition of the fullest subsequent conviction by means of miracle. Baur sees in this tale a clearly-intentional modification of the centurion's servant's[7] cure in the other Evangelists. In both cases the ready belief on the *mere word* of Christ is the point of the story; only there is this difference: in the fourth gospel the nobleman is anxious that Jesus should "come down," and is rather reproached for insisting on it as want of faith. In the others, he himself begs Christ not to trouble himself, as he is sure that a word from a distance will do as well, and receives the warm eulogy of Christ for his great faith. This change, Baur thinks, accords with the theology of John, which usually elevates Christ's nature so infinitely above the capacity of others to understand, that it would not allow an ordinary man to anticipate the greatness of his signs,

---

[7] The word being παῖς in Matthew, and δοῦλος in Luke, Baur thinks John has taken his υἱός from the former, but the scheme of a person returning to the house and finding the cure already effected during his absence, from the latter.

but would prefer to make them proceed, unsuggested, from Christ alone.[8]

The next-recorded miracle is that of the man at the pool of Bethesda, illustrating the doctrine that "the Son hath life in himself." It is the only one selected of the ordinary kind of miracles of healing so common in the other gospels, and seems taken, says Baur, from Mark (ii. 9-11) (with which the language, in one or two sentences, verbally agrees), only it is transferred to Jerusalem, and magnified in kind by the mention of the man's thirty-eight years' paralysis, in order to render it more appropriate as the subject of the discourse on the Son of God as the Life of man. Then comes the only great miracle which this gospel has clearly in common with the others,—the foundation of the discourse on the "Bread of Life." It differs, however, thus, that Christ is represented here as putting forth the miracle as the beginning of, and conscious preparation for, his teaching to the multitude; while in the other gospels it finishes a day of protracted teaching, and is a mere measure of compassion for a fasting crowd. "Jesus then lifting up his eyes, and seeing that a great multitude cometh to him, saith unto Philip, Whence are we to buy bread that these may eat? But this he said proving him; for he himself knew what he was about to do." This, Baur argues, is clearly a theological transformation of the miracle from an act of divine compassion

---

[8] This latter remark is, I believe, Strauss's, not Baur's.

into one of conscious didactic purpose. Reluctant to send them away fasting, after long fatigue, he, feeds them by miracle in the one case; anxious to manifest forth his glory in such a way that it may illustrate his discourse, he *begins*[9] by a physical and needless sign in the other. The miracles of this gospel all have their first purpose in manifesting the glory of God,—only their secondary aim in blessing men. Then comes the single miracle on the blind,—a type of its class, and greater (inasmuch as the man had been "*born*" blind) than in the other gospels,—but in the mode of healing borrowed from Mark's account of the healing of the deaf-and-dumb man (Mark vii. 33; compare John ix. 6). It is meant to be the practical commentary on "I am the light of the world."

And finally, when the Evangelist wants to bring the Pharisaic hatred felt for Christ to a crisis, having exhausted most of his resources already in those frequent contests with Pharisees in which the "stoning" was only delayed because Christ's "hour was not yet come," he substitutes for the irritation created according to the synoptic gospels by Christ's first appearance and bold teaching in Jerusalem, the excitement caused by the

---

[9] The supposed difference is by no means candidly stated, nor is it what Baur assumes. The Evangelist (John vi. 2) states first that "a great multitude followed him, because they saw the miracles which he did on them that were sick;" *then*, that Jesus withdraws to a mountain; and lastly, that the multitude still follow him, and he puts the above-mentioned question to Philip. The day's work, by implication, *preceded* the withdrawal to the mountain.

resurrection of Lazarus, which *they* do not mention. Of the mode in which this miracle was invented Baur gives a very ingenious account. Luke's gospel, he thinks, suggested the elements of the narrative, and this in two distinct divisions. First, Luke mentions "a certain village" where dwelt a woman named Martha and her sister Mary (Luke x. 38); and the characters of the sisters, the one practical and restless, the other quiet and contemplative, are suggested. Again, Luke (xvi.' 19-31) gives the parable of the rich man, in which Christ teaches that those who do not already rightly use Moses and the Prophets, would not be likely to repent though one rose from the dead; and the man whom it is there proposed to send as a messenger from the dead is called Lazarus. This suggested to the fourth Evangelist to conclude his narrative of the strife with the Pharisees, by showing that such a one did actually rise from the dead, and that the Pharisees were not the less obdurate. He introduces Lazarus therefore, as the brother of Martha and Mary, —declares the "certain village" to have been Bethany, in order that he may afterwards reintroduce Mary at the supper in Bethany as pouring the spikenard over her master's feet in gratitude for his miracle, and makes Christ claim to be "the resurrection and the life;" ending his series of great miracles by this the greatest of all.

The resurrection of Lazarus answers the purpose in this gospel, of thoroughly frightening the Sanhedrim, and accounting for that final measure of hostility which *needs* no new motive in the three synoptic gospels, since Christ's severe tone of preaching was, according to them, now new at Jerusalem, and quite cause enough for a criminal prosecution. In the fourth gospel this motive had been long exhausted; a new one was wanting. But Baur maintains that if the resurrection of Lazarus had really had this great importance in its bearing on the last crisis, it could never have dropped out of the synoptic narrative. Again, the supper at Bethany, in the house of "Simon the leper," at which "a woman" comes to anoint Christ, is seized hold of by the fourth Evangelist as affording a final motive to Judas's treachery. He introduces Lazarus to the supper, tells us that "Martha served," and that Mary is "the woman" who (mentioned without name in Matthew and Mark) brought the precious ointment. He, and he alone, also tells us that it was Judas whom Christ checked for his suggestion that the ointment should have been sold for the poor; and he alone speaks of the bad motive in Judas which caused that suggestion. Again, the triumphal entry is quite differently conceived by this Evangelist. It begins only from Bethany, where Christ was then staying. In the other gospels, he was only passing Bethany in going from Jericho straight to Jerusalem. The crowds which accompany him, in the three first gospels, are a Galilean band of friends going up to the passover in the same caravan. In the fourth gospel, the procession comes out *from Jerusalem* to meet him, because they had heard of the resurrection of Lazarus.[1]

---

[1] Again, the difference is not what is stated. Even in the synoptic gospels, Jesus is not coming direct from Galilee with the

Then there is the great difference as to the time of the last supper, the fourth gospel explaining that it was not the passover supper, but took place on the evening before the passover; the others assuming that it was an ordinary passover. Moreover, when Jesus leaves the room with his disciples, he is, in this gospel, tranquilly comforting and strengthening them, not in any anguish for himself.[2] The conflict in Gethsemane is passed over entirely by this Evangelist; and when Judas comes with the priests and guard, instead of his active aid being needed to betray Christ "by a kiss," Christ is not passive, but voluntarily comes forth to give himself up, and strikes so much awe into his enemies, that they "go backwards and fall to the ground." Here again we see, says Baur, the theological modifications made to enhance the dignity of Christ. The scene of quiet expostulation with Pilate is peculiar to this gospel; and Pilate's reluctance to deliver him to death is delineated much more anxiously than by the others, in order to enhance the guilt of the Jews.[3]

Galilean caravan, but from a residence *beyond Jordan*, by way of Jericho (a town not on the Galilean road). In the fourth gospel, he had also just been staying in the wilderness of Judea, which is in the same direction. Also, it is not the *Jerusalem* crowd which, according to this gospel, goes out from Jerusalem to welcome him, but "much people *that had come to the feast*,"—probably, therefore, Galilean friends.

[2] Yet Luke *alone* records the words of calm pity addressed by Christ to the women who follow him when he is bearing his cross, "Daughters of Jerusalem, weep not for me but weep for yourselves and for your children."

[3] Yet Matthew *alone* records the saying, "His blood be upon us, and upon our children."

And at his death, the narrator, Baur thinks, lays the greatest stress on the fact, peculiar to this gospel, that while the soldiers broke the legs of the two malefactors crucified with Christ, they only pierced the side of Christ, in fulfilment of the prophecy, "a bone of him shall not be broken,"—a sentence which Baur takes to be a quotation from Exodus (xii. 46) in reference to the paschal lamb, thus proving the writer's anxiety to identify Christ with the paschal lamb, and suggesting a motive why he took care to put back the day of his death to that (14th Nisan) on which the paschal lamb ought to be killed, from the great day of the feast (15th Nisan), on which, according to the three synoptic writers, Christ really died. Finally, taking from the Acts of the Apostles the hint of Peter's intimacy with John, the Evangelist exalts into a position of something like equality with Peter "the other disciple" (who is clearly intended for John), by introducing the new facts, that he went along with Peter into the palace of Caiaphas; that he was the only disciple of Christ who stood beneath the cross; that he there received in trust from his dying master the care of his mother; and that, running with Peter to the empty sepulchre on the morning of the resurrection, he even outran him, and, though Peter was eventually the first to enter, was the first to believe.

Such is, in brief, Baur's account of this gospel. He adds an argument, of much ingenuity and apparent weight, directed against the special authorship of the Apostle John. Of course it goes further than to subvert that special authorship. The whole carefully prepared internal evidence, as well as tradition, points so clearly to John, that, if the authorship be not his, it very much increases the probability that the work was altogether a pious fraud, by a later hand. Baur's argument is briefly this: It was long the Apostle John's practice to celebrate the day of the Jewish passover (14th Nisan), as the anniversary of the Lord's last supper; this is inferred from the most explicit testimony of the Ephesian church, which specially cited his authority as their apology for adhering to the day of the Jewish festival, at a time when the Church of the West enjoined on them to celebrate the last supper of Christ on the Thursday night preceding the movable feast of Easter Sunday. Now the fourth gospel was certainly the great authority of the Western Church in *opposing* the doctrine of the Asia-Minor Christians,—the Quartodecimans as they were called,—that the last supper of Christ had taken place on the evening of the passover feast—that is, on the 14th Nisan. How is it possible, then, that the Apostle John should have been the author of a gospel, which was the main authority against his own traditional practice?

Again, the earliest attestation we have for the authorship of any New Testament book, is that for the authorship of the Apocalypse by the apostle John. Most critics now, however, agree that the books are too completely different in style to be the production of one author; and everything, Baur thinks, should induce us to choose the Apocalypse as the work of the apostle. It is more narrowly Jewish, which agrees with John's association with Cephas and James, in Paul's account to the Galatians of the quarrel about circumcision. It is more vehement, which agrees with the title given by Christ to James and John, of "Sons of thunder;" and with the question addressed to Christ, whether they should call down fire from heaven on the Samaritan village, which did not receive him; and, again, with the circumstance told by John to his Master: "We found one casting out demons in thy name, and we forbade him" (Mark ix. 38): and lastly, with the tradition of John's fleeing out of the bath in which the heretic Cerinthus was bathing, lest it should fall and destroy the enemy of the truth. Moreover, the contents show that the Apocalypse was written by one familiar with the churches of Ephesus and its neighbourhood, to which universal tradition assigned the last years of John. If, then, the Apocalypse and the Gospel cannot be the work of one mind, Baur has no doubt that the Apocalypse is the genuine work of the apostle, and the Gospel a spurious history of later date. These considerations, together with the general improbability that three, in some measure, distinct gospels should all be in error on such cardinal points as the principal theatre of Christ's ministry — the day of his crucifixion — the proximate cause of his arrest and condemnation — make out assuredly a strong *primâ facie* case for Baur's view.

Nevertheless, after a long and careful examination, I feel confident that Baur is wrong; and that, as regards such facts as it registers at all, the fourth Gospel is better and more personal testimony than the collected and often fragmentary narratives of the other gospels, which seem to me to bear distinct marks of being different recensions of a purely Galilean tradition; except indeed, that Luke embodies in his narrative additions from a Judean source. It is impossible to disagree with Baur, about the individual theological purpose of the fourth gospel. It is to be read clearly in every chapter. It is even probable that John, looking back on the events of Christ's ministry from a new stage of conviction, discerned, often too exclusively, in his Master's miracles the purpose of "manifesting forth the divine glory," as distinguished from the human and temporary purpose of conferring blessing on private lives. The transient human pain relieved, the transient human joy produced, had passed away from the earth for ever. The only purpose of the miracles that *still remained*, was the revelation they had given of the nature of God; and it was natural that the disciple should merge the immediate and temporary aspect of the signs, in that which was now the permanent root of all his religious convictions. That Christ's discourses had real elements, similar, both in subject and manner, to those which the fourth Evangelist alone has preserved, there are distinct enough traces, even in the other gospels;[4] but, being little suited to

---

[4] Matt. xi. 25—27, and xv. 13; Luke x. 22; and compare also the remarkable parallel in Mr. Maurice's eighth note to his *Gospel of St. John*, between the style and teaching of the Sermon on the Mount and that in the eighth chapter of St. John.

the character of a popular tradition, they seem to have been specifically retained only—and probably also (looking to the style of St. John's first epistle) to have been rendered *more* diffuse and special in manner—in the report of the fourth Evangelist.

I will speak first of Baur's last arguments, those which refer to the special authorship by the apostle. I am inclined to agree with him, and most modern critics, that, notwithstanding some essential harmonies in substance between the Apocalypse and the Gospel, they are too remarkably distinct in general character, to be the writings of the same man. It seems certain, however, that there were, at the end of the first century, two Johns resident in Ephesus, both of them immediate disciples of Christ—one of them his apostle; and Bleek has shown several reasons, to which some others may be added, why we should *not* ascribe the Apocalypse to the apostle.[5] Papias, the bishop of Hierapolis in Phrygia, in the beginning of the second century, quoted by Eusebius (iii. 39), tells us, he did not attend much to mere books, but "if anyone came who had been a personal follower of the elders (πρεσβύτεροι), I questioned them about the words of the elders (πρεσβύτεροι); what Andrew or Peter had said, or what Philip, or Thomas, or James, or what *John or Matthew*, or any other of the disciples (μαθηταί) of the Lord; and what Aristion and

---

[5] See pp. 182—200 of Professor Bleek's able work, noted above. He seems to me nearly the only opponent of Baur I have met with, worthy, both from his candour and his ability, to cope with him.

John the elder (πρεσβύτερος), *the disciples of the Lord*, say? for I did not suppose that the accounts of books would be of so much use to me, as that which came from a living and still existing voice;" on which Eusebius remarks, that there are still said to be shown in Ephesus two tombs, each the tomb of a John, who had been a disciple of Christ; and that Papias often speaks of having been a personal hearer of the second John (not the apostle). Now the writer of the Apocalypse, we must notice, lays great stress on the privileges of the apostles, as such, saying: "Thou hast tried them which say they are apostles and are not, and found them liars" (Revelations ii. 2; see also xxi. 14); and yet does not anywhere give any indication of claiming for himself such a title (i. 2, 4, 9; xxii. 8).

Again, there are many indications, both in the Acts of the Apostles and in the Gospels, and also even in St. Paul's Epistle to the Galatians, that John the apostle was a man who took no *leading*, though he took a *remarkable* part among the disciples of Christ. He accompanies Peter in the Acts, but leaves all the acting and speaking to him. John's *name* only is mentioned, while the special influence, both of Peter and James, is alluded to by St. Paul in his Galatian letter. The tradition that he "leaned on the breast of Christ" at the last supper, which is separately and early attested (*before* the fourth gospel seems to have been in universal use), in the letter of Polycrates, bishop of Ephesus (quoted by Eusebius, v. 24), leads to the same conception of his character;

and the tradition of his latest addresses, in extreme old age, to his Ephesian flock, as consisting merely of the exhortation, "Little children, love one another," entirely agrees with the tone of the gospel and epistle. But it is difficult to believe, on the other hand, that one so full of imaginative power, and apparently so strongly inclined to exercise a stern pastoral authority, as the author of the Apocalypse seems to be in his letters to the Seven Churches, should not, if really one of the twelve apostles of Christ, have taken a much more active position in the early church than seems to have been his. Especially in the controversy of which St. Paul speaks in Galatians (ii. 9), it is not very easy to imagine that the author of the Apocalypse, if it had been he who is there referred to, would not have had something sharp and individual of his own to say to one who did not object to eat "things sacrificed to idols." (Compare Rev. ii. 20.)

There are, I think, two Johns round whom tradition has clustered its characteristic rumours; one, he who followed Peter's lead in practical matters—passive, affectionate, severe only where his jealous affection for his Master was excited—a reader of the Jewish Scriptures—in short, a theologian, qualities which would agree well with the tradition of him, as "he who lay on the bosom of the Lord, who became a priest (ὃς ἐγενήθη ἱερεύς), who bore a plate on his forehead, a confessor and teacher;"[6] and which would agree completely with the whole tone

---

[6] The letter of Polycrates, bishop of Ephesus, above referred to (Eusebius, v. 24).

and character of this gospel—full as it is of knowledge of the Old Testament, and of applications of that knowledge to Christ; another John, not contemplative, but passionately imaginative; in temperament like an old prophet, and a vehement Jew; an authoritative pastor, rather than a theological thinker,· who stamped all the rich colours of his mind on the book of Revelations. Now, James the apostle, John's brother, who if one may judge by Herod's singling him out as the first martyr, had certainly taken a more fiery and prominent part in the early church than John, may well have gained for both the brothers the title of Boanerges; nor can I suppose, from the fourth gospel, that the author of it would at all have been one to *object* to summoning fire from heaven in his Master's cause, had his brother proposed it (Luke ix. 54). His wish to forbid one teaching in Christ's name, "because he followeth not us" (Mark ix. 38), is completely in keeping with the gospel, which, though not fiery, betrays extreme jealousy for his Master's honour; as, for example, in the severity of its tone concerning Judas (xii. 6), and elsewhere. The difficulty of supposing the Gospel and the Apocalypse the productions of the same mind, is the extraordinary difference of intellectual character therein displayed,—the one, full of deep and quiet colourless thought; the other, of a vehemently disciplinarian temperament and highly-coloured imagination; the latter qualities being exactly those which would have most certainly given the author prominence amongst the apostles, had he belonged to their number. I can scarcely imagine such a man a quiet follower or companion of Peter.

No one who knows the state of the external testimony to the authorship of the Apocalypse and Gospel will hold that it adds much, in any way, to the elucidation of the question. Neither of them receives any explicit testimony till the time of Justin Martyr, about the middle of the second century, when the two Johns, having been both disciples of Christ, probably enough would be already confused. Within another ten years both books are explicitly acknowledged.

The second argument of Baur's against the apostolic authorship of the gospel is still more plausible. There can be no doubt that the apostle had handed down to his Christian successors in Ephesus the practice of celebrating with a feast the evening of the Jewish passover on the 14th Nisan, the evening on which, according to the synoptic gospels, Christ eat his last passover; but according to the fourth gospel, was buried. There can be no doubt but that sooner or later this Jewish festival took a purely Christian character, and included a celebration of the Eucharist. But it seems to be a double mistake to suppose that this was an anniversary celebration of Christ's last supper with His apostles. In the first place, before the destruction of Jerusalem, the Apostles, including St. Paul, held themselves bound to celebrate the ordinary Jewish passover,[7] and this would have been

---

[7] Acts xviii. 21; xx. 6. Even St. Paul regarded it as sacred;

the origin of the practice of having a feast on the evening of the 14th Nisan. St. Paul's account of the celebrations of the Lord's Supper in these early times, implies that it was not an annual anniversary at all, but a rite that was often repeated, that *might* be observed at any time. The idea of an *annual* celebration of this memorial service had not entered into the mind of the church. "When ye come together therefore into one place," says St. Paul, "this is not to eat the Lord's Supper." "For *as often as* ye eat this bread, and drink this cup, ye do show forth the Lord's death till He come" (1 Corinth. xi. 20, 26).

In the next place, even when the Easter dispute broke out, about A.D. 160, the question was as to when the passion fast should cease, and the redemption-feast begin. It was the practice to fast during the time of our Lord's sufferings, but the Western Church continued this practice up to Easter morning, the Church of Asia Minor only up to the evening of the 14th Nisan. The authority adduced for keeping 14th Nisan is, that Philip, John, and other immediate disciples, " all kept the 14th day of the passover (*i.e.* 14th Nisan) according to the Gospel, transgressing in nothing, but following strictly the rule of faith." Again, " Neither was Anicetus [Bishop of Rome] able to persuade Polycarp [Bishop of Smyrna] not to observe it [14th Nisan], since he had always observed it

---

and Christ expressed a feeling that must have been strong in his apostles, when he said, "With desire I have desired to eat this passover with you before I suffer."

along with John, the Lord's disciple, and the other apostles with whom he lived; nor was Polycarp able to persuade Anicetus to observe it," the whole dispute turning on whether the 14th Nisan should be "kept" or not, the "keeping" it implying, as Professor Milligan has, I think, entirely demonstrated ('Contemporary Review,' vol. vi., article on the Easter Controversies), a strict fast on the day itself, followed by an eucharistic feast in the evening. The fast was probably held in commemoration of the death of Christ, the feast in commemoration of the finished redemption, which the Asiatics (no doubt, partly from their feeling for the old Jewish festival of redemption) celebrated on the same evening as the Jewish passover, alleging that the redemption was then finished by the offering of the great sacrifice. This explanation of the observation of the 14th Nisan, so far from being inconsistent with the narrative of the fourth gospel, strikingly confirms it.

The great question still remains. On the assumption that St. John is the author of the fourth gospel, can we explain its great deviations from the traditions of the other three? Have we any grounds for regarding its narrative details as more historical than those of the Galilean gospels, or are Baur's grounds for suspecting fraud legitimate? There are two main points on which the last gospel is at issue with the others—the day of the crucifixion, and the length of Christ's ministry; the latter involving the question of His frequent attendance on the feasts at Jerusalem. Can we explain these differences best on the fictitious or historical hypothesis with regard to the last and most independent account? These will be two testing points, by which, if we could clearly decide upon them, we might fairly estimate the accuracy of the gospel as a whole.

1. As to the day of the crucifixion, the discrepancy no doubt *exists*. The more I see of attempts to reconcile the account of the fourth gospel with that of the other evangelists, the more uncandid and futile they appear. But Baur assumes, as I have said, that he can not only detect the falsehood, but the ground of the falsehood in the last account. It had become, he says, an object to represent Christ as the "Christian passover,"—according to St. Paul's expression "Christ our passover was sacrificed for us." To carry out the analogy, it began to be asserted [not, however, as far as anybody knows, before 160 A.D., when the fourth gospel was almost certainly in circulation] that the paschal feast which Christ is described as *eating* in the three first gospels, was merely an anticipatory rite, while He Himself was sacrificed at the time of the sacrifice of the paschal lamb. A fourth gospel therefore was wanted in order distinctly to declare this, and to show that the real feast took place after, not before, the slaying of the new passover lamb. To this end the later chapters were modified. The secret purpose is marked, according to Baur, clearly enough in chap. xix. 36, where the apostle, so solemnly testifying to the piercing of Christ's side, adds "These things were done that the Scripture should be fulfilled: 'A bone of him shall not

be broken;' and again, another Scripture saith, 'They shall look on him whom they pierced;'"—the reference being, as Baur maintains, to Exodus xii. 46, or Numbers ix. 12, where it is said of the paschal lamb, "Neither shall ye break a bone thereof." I believe the answer I can give to this ingenious criticism is complete. The chapter on the crucifixion has several references to minute fulfilments of prophecy from the books of Psalms and Prophets—those Psalms, namely, which describe suffering and disgrace. From Psalm xxii. 18, the passage is quoted, "They parted my raiment among them, and for my vesture they did cast lots;" from Psalm lxix. 21, the words of Christ on the cross, "I thirst," are expressly cited. From Zechariah xii. 10, a passage is taken in immediate connection with the one in dispute, "They shall look on him whom they pierced." None of these passages has any reference at all to the paschal rite; all of them but the last seem to be quoted as anticipations of the pain and shame to which Christ was exposed, while the last refers to the remorse which the Jews must suffer.[8] Now, in Psalm xxxiv. 19, 20, occurs the passage, "Many are the afflictions of the righteous, but the Lord delivereth him out of them all. *He keepeth all his bones, not one of them is broken.*" Taken in such close connection with the passage from Zechariah, which

---

[8] Zechariah xii. 10. "They shall look on me whom they have pierced, and they shall mourn for him as one mourneth for his only son, and shall be in bitterness for him as one is in bitterness for his firstborn."

cannot refer to the paschal lamb, and which does refer to a people's repentance after ingratitude to a righteous shepherd, it seems incredible that the verse in question should be intended as a reference to the chapter in Exodus, rather than to Psalm xxxiv., which is also speaking of the sufferings of the righteous, and God's providence over him.[9] But if this be so, the whole of Baur's *motive* for the theological reconstruction of the narrative fails; since the Evangelist could not have omitted even to hint to his readers the analogy for the sake of which he is supposed to have modified and falsified the traditional facts.

But though Baur's theory of the theological ground of the misrepresentation is broken down, can it be shown that the narrative itself is not misrepresentation—contradicting, as it does, the concurrent testimony of three other gospels? One can only deal with historical probabilities, but these seem to be very strong indeed. We must remember that the fourth gospel is the only one that can, in its present form, pretend to come from the

---

[9] Here are the three passages possibly quoted, compared with the quotation itself:—
John xix. 36. ἵνα ἡ γραφὴ πληρωθῇ· ὀστοῦν οὐ συντριβήσεται αὐτοῦ.
Psalm xxxiv. 20. φυλάσσει πάντα τὰ ὀστᾶ αὐτῶν, ἐν ἐξ αὐτῶν οὐ συντριβήσεται· (no reference to the paschal lamb).
Exodus xii. 46. καὶ ὀστοῦν οὐ συντρίψετε ἀπ' αὐτοῦ. } References to
Numbers ix. 12. καὶ ὀστοῦν οὐ συντρίψουσιν ἀπ' αὐτοῦ. } the paschal lamb.

Looking at the mere form of the quotation, it seems to me perfectly obvious that the reference is to the Psalm, and not to Exodus or Numbers.

hand of a single writer. Whatever the extremely curious phenomena of the constant verbal agreements, and yet frequently wide divergencies, in the three first gospels may indicate, they at least indicate *common sources for some elements of the narrative, and distinct sources for others.* Hence we cannot take the truth or falsehood of one historical portion as supporting or invalidating the history of another portion, at least not to the extent that is certainly justifiable in a homogeneous work. Now the *only* fragment which asserts or implies that the last supper of Christ was the ordinary passover meal, is one of about three or four verses in length. It is found, with variations, in all the three synoptic gospels, and states that, "on the first day of unleavened bread, when the passover must be killed," Christ directed two of His disciples to go into the city and ask a specified person there for the use of his room, that He might eat the passover there on the same evening with the twelve. Nothing else throughout the narrative either of the last supper or of the crucifixion, even *tends* to the supposition that Christ was crucified on the great day of the feast: but a good deal else that we find in the synoptic account itself, does tend to throw much doubt on that supposition. More than this, even in the three verses mentioned as the only authority for this belief, St. Matthew's version has one element which seems to point to Christ's having *anticipated* the ordinary passover-time; for He is made to say, "Go into the city to such a man, and say unto him, The Master saith, *my time is at hand;* I will keep the passover at thy house with my disciples;" as if he were assigning the short time now left Him as a reason for some unexpected arrangement.

Now remembering that after the account of the meal once begins, there is *no* allusion to its passover character, except St. Luke's report of Christ's opening words: "With desire I have desired to eat this passover with you before I suffer; for I say unto you, I shall eat no more thereof till it be fulfilled in the kingdom of God," words which, taken alone, admit an equally satisfactory or even better, interpretation, if we suppose the meal to have been in anticipation of the regular passover; and remembering, also, that when St. Paul recalls Christ's institution of the memorial service to the minds of the Corinthians, he does not describe it as instituted on the evening of the passover feast, but "on the night on which he was betrayed," it becomes really worth while to look carefully at the subsequent and previous narrative, to see whether or not it confirms or invalidates the few verses mentioned above, as the only authority for the statement that the meal was the ordinary Jewish passover. Nothing seems to me so clear as that the separate elements of the synoptic gospels must have existed long in separation before they were consolidated by any single mind into a continuous whole. The short passage as to the appointment with the owner of the "upper chamber" is just such a separate element, not closely connected either with the foregoing or subsequent narrative. Though incorporated into all three gospels, its authority can scarcely be much greater than if it stood only in one. And, no doubt, any indication in the original tradition that the house to which the apostles were sent was the place where Christ *had intended* to eat the passover, had not His fate been too near,—and such an indication we find in Matthew's version of the message,—would easily pass into the explicit error which the passage now, I believe, contains.

There is another slight confirmation of this suggestion. In the account of the priestly council, in which it is determined to put Christ to death, the priests say: "Not on the feast-day, lest there be an uproar of the people" (Matt. xxvi. 5; Mark xiv. 2). Now had this report come to our Lord's ears, He would of course have understood that they would try to apprehend Him *before* the feast-day, and would therefore naturally send a message to hasten the last supper which He had so much wished to celebrate with His disciples, on the ground that His "time was at hand." But if the account as it at present stands were correct, the priests would have changed their prudent determinations without apparent ground, and waited till the last day for the crucifixion of Christ. There are, however, other stronger indications that the remainder of the narrative in the synoptic gospels really assumes the order of things we find explicitly given in this gospel. It is scarcely credible that the very evening and night on which was celebrated the great religious ceremonial of the year, and on which by the strict law the celebrants might not leave the house, should have been chosen by the priests for arresting, examining, and condemning Christ. Moreover, the 15th Nisan had all the character of a sabbath;[1] and as, even according to the synoptic gospels, every care is taken to observe the sabbath, it cannot be imagined that the Jewish laws had fallen so much into disuse as to render it no longer a necessity to observe in like manner the still more sacred great day of the passover. Yet not only does the trial, the whole transaction with Pilate, the crucifixion, and the release to the people of a prisoner (which last was an *annual* privilege, and would take place on a given day, not being an exceptional affair), occur, according to our present reading of the synoptic gospels, on this great day of the feast, but, by both St. Mark's and St. Luke's account, "fine linen" is "bought," and "spices and ointments" are prepared on the *evening of this same day;* although the women are obliged by the approach of the sabbath to wait to use them till after it is past, in order that they may "rest according to the commandment."

Again, all the three Evangelists call the day of crucifixion a mere "preparation-day" and "the day before the sabbath;" which is inconceivable if the original accounts regarded it as the great day of the feast, the 15th Nisan (Matt. xxvii. 62; Luke xxiii. 54; Mark xv. 42). The 15th Nisan was entitled, like a sabbath, to its *own* day of preparation; and to speak of it

---

[1] Exodus xii. 16, Levit. xxiii. 7, Numb. xxviii. 18, cited by Bleck.

thus, as the mere preparation-day for an ordinary sabbath would be quite unprecedented. It is sometimes said, that the Jewish nation was in a very irregular state, and that the old ceremonial laws may not have been at that time obeyed. Besides that this is quite conjectural, the gospels themselves give strong evidence that on sabbatical points the ceremonial law was over-strictly obeyed; and a decree of Augustus, which conceded that the Jews should not be required "to give security on the sabbath, or on the preparation-day before the sabbath, later than the ninth hour,"[2] shows that even the Romans respected this institution, and had no inclination to force on them any breach of their sabbatical law. When, now, we consider that the notes of time in the fourth gospel not merely agree, but agree in a minute and apparently undesigned way,[3] with this supposition,— and agree far better with every thing in the synoptic accounts except the three or four verses I have spoken of, than their own subsequent statements can be made to agree with the same passage,—the evidence seems to me irresistible that the account of the fourth gospel is the accurate one. I may add, that most of the Jewish authorities not only maintain that the proceedings

---

[2] Joseph. Ant. xvi. 6, 2, cited by Bleek, who states that in the edict the "sabbath" is taken in the larger sense to include all "sabbatical feast-days."

[3] As, for example, in the statement that the disciples supposed Judas had gone out to buy something "against the feast;" and again in the explanation that "that sabbath-day was a high day," which it would be if the 15th Nisan coincided with an ordinary sabbath.

against Christ *could* not take place on the great day of the passover feast, but that an old Jewish tradition specifies the 14th (not the 15th) Nisan as the actual day of Christ's crucifixion.[4]

2. The other great historical discrepancy between the fourth and three first evangelists has relation to the frequent presence of Christ, during His ministry, in Jerusalem. It cannot be denied that the three first gospels have, as we now read them, no direct assertions that Christ ever visited Jerusalem during His public ministry till immediately before His death, nor that they contain some passages which are rightly held, in their present position, to point the other way. Of these, by far the strongest is one of two verses which occurs only in St. Matthew, and which links together the account of the triumphal entry into Jerusalem with the account of the expulsion of the money-changers from the Temple. It is this: "And when he was come into Jerusalem, all the city was moved, saying, Who is this? And the multitude said, This is Jesus, the *prophet of Nazareth of Galilee*. And Jesus went into the Temple of God, and cast out all them that sold and bought in the Temple," &c. If this be in its right place, Jesus was evidently quite unknown to Jerusalem and its people. The passage therefore directly suggests the question, whether or not the last evangelist is correct in his date for the purification of the Temple, which he places at the very

---

[4] See tr. Sanhedr. fol. 43, 1. cited by Bleek, p. 148.

commencement of Christ's public ministry, while all the other evangelists place it at its very close. These two verses prefixed in St. Matthew, and which I believe really *belong* to the passage, speak strongly to my mind, for the date given by the fourth evangelist. For even supposing that Christ were now, at the close of a lengthened ministry in Galilee, entering Jerusalem for the *first* time during His public career—a view against which I shall presently give what I believe to be strong reasons,—it is far from likely He would have been so completely unknown to the people as this graphic record of popular curiosity would seem to imply. The emphatic description of Him, as "Jesus the prophet of Nazareth of Galilee," would have been far less applicable after He had, according to St. Matthew's own account, long left Nazareth for Capernaum as His Galilean centre of operations, and for some time back left Galilee altogether, to work in the "parts beyond Jordan," whence He had come to Jerusalem, than it would have been at a time when the rumour was *fresh*, that something "good had come out of Nazareth," at a time when His only reputation was derived from the testimony given to Him by the Baptist, and the influence He had gained among Galilean disciples at Nazareth, Cana, and Capernaum.

But there is yet stronger ground than this. It seems to me clear that the cleansing of the Temple belongs naturally to the time when Christ was fresh from His association with John the Baptist. No one can read the discourse of the Baptist in St. Matthew without feeling that his teaching was a renewal of the prophetic Judaism; that it was against exactly such abuses as these in the Temple, that the Baptist's spirit would have burned. And doubtless his greater disciple, whose baptism was with fire, would know that He should appeal best to the noblest elements of His nation's mind by beginning with a reform, such as John himself might have initiated,—by claiming for the visible Temple the sacredness and purity which the Baptist would have claimed, and so leading the best among the Jews to feel more earnestly that no "Temple made with hands" could *limit* that worship of a Father which its impurity and unsacredness could nevertheless easily obstruct. The purification of the Temple was a "baptism with water" perhaps, but just such a one as would best teach the deeper meaning of a baptism with fire; and Christ ever avails Himself of a sympathy with what is noble but incomplete, to lay the foundation of a deeper perfection. It is very remarkable that placing this purification of the Temple where they do, all the synoptic gospels should yet bring the "baptism of John" into the closest connection with, and obvious reference to, this great act. Immediately after it, we read in all the synoptic gospels, —and this is the more remarkable because in the fourth gospel, where it would come in far more appropriately, the answer of Christ is omitted,—"And when he was come into the Temple, the chief priests and the elders of the people came unto him as he was teaching, and said, By what authority doest thou these things? and who gave thee this authority? And Jesus answered and said, I also will ask you one thing, which if ye tell me, I in like wise will tell you by what authority I do these things. The baptism of John, whence was it? from heaven or of men? And they reasoned with themselves, saying, If we shall say, From Heaven; he will say unto us, Why did ye not then believe him? But if we shall say, Of men; *we fear the people; for all hold John as a prophet.*[5] And they answered Jesus, We cannot tell. And he said unto them, Neither tell I you by what authority I do these things."

Now, no one, I should think, can read this without the strongest impression that John's prophetic influence was then fresh on the mind both of Christ and the people. The Pharisees would hardly have *feared the people* when John was no longer living, and when his great popular influence, almost as a consequence, had passed away along with the hope that his mission would issue in any great deliverance. Still less would Christ's first appeal have at *that* time been to John's authority. He had at the end of His career the right to claim "a greater witness than that of John;" nor could John's testimony to Christ justly have had much weight, if an interval long enough to verify that testimony by *His own* career had elapsed since it was given. It was known, too, that John him-

---

[5] The wording even seems rather more natural if used when John is still alive, though in prison, and deterred from his public ministry, for it is "for all men hold" (*not* 'held') "John as a prophet," πάντες γὰρ ἔχουσι τὸν Ἰωάννην ὡς προφήτην.

self had subsequently wavered as to the divine mission of the greater prophet whom he had announced; so that we may well feel clear that this appeal would have been in place, and would have had the effect which it obviously produced on the Pharisees, only if made very soon after the baptism of Christ. To my mind this almost demonstrates the falseness of the position into which the purification of the Temple has got in the synoptic gospels. Moreover, it is pretty clear that at the time of Christ's last passover, the proper population of Jerusalem, as distinguished from the country people "who came to the feast," was anything but favourable to him. His depreciation of the Pharisees, His religious universalism, His compassion for the "publicans and sinners," had undermined His influence with that ostentatiously religious party which was generally in immediate command of the mob. They cried out eagerly for Barabbas when Pilate was most anxious to release Christ; and at this period, therefore, I do not believe that they would have supported Him in any attempt at cleansing the Temple. When, as a disciple of John, He was a distinctly *Jewish* reformer, they supported Him with enthusiasm; but when He became the antagonist of all Jewish selfishness and ritual bigotry, they cried out, "Crucify him! crucify him!"

Nor do I think that at a time when Christ saw clearly how much deeper than any improprieties in the Temple service the canker had grown into the national life, this would have seemed to Him a reform important enough to attempt. His "hour was come." His spirit was nerved for the suffering before Him. He saw that the hope of the world lay, as much as it lay in anything human, in the little band of personal disciples, not in the services of the Temple; and I believe He was much more anxious then to sow an ineffaceable trust in the mind of His apostles than He could be to brush away the uppermost stratum of Pharasaic rottenness. The mood in which He wept over Jerusalem as past recovery, was not the mood in which He would have driven sellers of oxen and sheep out of the Gentiles' court. And when one remembers—if I may assume for a moment the genuineness of the gospel on which I am writing—how deeply the relation between the "baptism of water" and the "baptism of the spirit" enters into that conversation with Nicodemus which immediately follows this purification of the Temple, in the narrative of this evangelist: and how again the relation between the "Temples made with hands" on Mounts Zion and Gerizim, and the universal spiritual Temple, enters into that conversation on the "water of life" with the Samaritan woman, which follows next, I cannot doubt that the religious problem as to the *grounds* of spiritual purification suggested by the Baptist's ministry, was predominant in Christ's mind at this first period of His career, and that to that period we owe the event misplaced in the synoptic gospels.

In this last gospel also, it will be remembered, "the Jews" come to Christ after the purification, and ask Him, "What sign showest thou unto us, seeing that thou doest these things?" and Christ answers, "Destroy this Temple, and in three days I will raise it up;" a remark apparently misinterpreted into a symbolic prophecy of His resurrection by the Evangelist who looked back on it after that event, but the actual utterance of which is strictly confirmed by the evidence of the false witnesses at the trial of Christ, in St. Mark's gospel:— "There arose certain, and bare false witness against him, saying: We heard him say, I will destroy this Temple made with hands, and within three days I will build another made without hands: but neither so did their witness agree together" (Mark xiv. 57)—a statement of the more weight as agreeing with the fourth Evangelist's report, but *not* with his interpretation; and by the accusation brought against Stephen (Acts vi. 13)— "This man ceaseth not to speak blasphemous words against this holy place and the law; for we have heard him say, that this Jesus of Nazareth shall destroy this place, and shall change the customs which Moses delivered us." The real bearing of Christ's answer seems to me to have been, that One who would shortly enable them to dispense with the Temple altogether, One who, as He says, in St. Matthew's gospel, is "greater than the Temple"—could alone give the spiritual authority to *purify* it. But it is worth notice, that unless this remark had occurred at a *considerable interval* before the last scene of His life, there could not very well have been that hesitation and contradiction about the evidence of the "false witnesses," and the extreme difficulty in procuring it, which both St. Matthew's and St. Mark's accounts of the trial of Christ distinctly attest.

But if in two remarkable points—the date of the crucifixion and that of the purification of the Temple—the strongest probability exists that the fourth gospel has corrected the accounts of the others, we may feel no little confidence that in it we are on historic ground. Let us look at the other passages by which the purely or mainly Galilean view of the ministry of Christ seems most strongly supported, and see whether or not they are reconcilable with this last narrative. That the synoptic gospels quite *ignore* the Jerusalem ministry up to the last passover is obvious. The question is—does their positive information concerning Christ's career in any way tend to *exclude* it? The principal passages are the following: (Matt. xvi. 21) "*From that time forth* began Jesus to show unto his disciples, how that he must go unto Jerusalem, and suffer many things of the elders and chief priests," &c., as if this were a thoroughly *new* line of action. Again, the terror displayed by the disciples at the absolute resolve of Jesus to go up to Jerusalem is thus described by St. Mark (x. 32): "And they were in the way going up to Jerusalem, and Jesus went before them, and they were amazed, and as they followed they were afraid;"—while St. Luke (ix. 51) tells us, "And it came to pass when the time was come that he should be received up, he *steadfastly set his face* to go to Jerusalem." Now, no doubt, these passages in their present form seem to imply perfect unconsciousness on the part of the last compilers of the gospel-histories that Christ had exercised any public ministry in Jerusalem. But when we come to ask the reason of the great fear of the apostles on the one side, and the steadfast, compressed purpose manifested by their Master on the other, it becomes much more intelligible if we suppose, as we find it stated in the fourth gospel, that for a long interval before this time "Jesus walked in Galilee; for he would not walk in Judea, *because the Jews sought to kill him*" (John vii. 1). In fact, the fourth evangelist really presents just such a struggle in his Master's mind on His last departure from Galilee, as the other three, only giving the sufficient causes also, which the others do not. We find His brethren, who "did not believe on him," urging Him to depart and go into Judea, alleging that "no man doeth any thing in secret, and he himself seeketh to be known openly: if thou doest these things, *manifest thyself* to the world;"—and we find Christ declining at first, on the ground that His "hour was not yet full come," and that it would be certain destruction to Him, as the *world* "*hated*" Him; and then at last finally resolving to go, not in the public caravan, but privately: all which remarkably agrees with the state of mind indicated in St. Luke's gospel—"When the time was come that he should be received up, he *steadfastly set his face* to go to Jerusalem;" and with the passage in St. Mark's in relation to the terror of His disciples at His fixed resolve. True, this journey is not, as it is apparently, and only apparently, in the other three gospels, the *immediate* antecedent of His death, being at least six months earlier, and directed to the feast of Tabernacles which preceded the last passover; but it *is* His last farewell to Galilee.

Now all the evangelists agree in making Him devote a certain undefined portion of His latest ministry to the districts beyond Jordan: the only difference being, that while one evangelist directs His Master's course first to Jerusalem, and then twice takes Him away thence to the district beyond Jordan during the winter, the other narratives confusedly represent Him as at first going straight to Jerusalem, but without any explanation whether He really at that time went there or not, next speak of Him as in Perea beyond Jordan, and then *once more* represent Him as going up forebodingly to His death. Thus St. Luke, immediately after the passage I have quoted, speaks of a Samaritan village rejecting Christ, "because his face was set as though he would go to Jerusalem;" in the following chapter we have the account of Martha and Mary, and the parable of the good Samaritan plundered between Jericho and Jerusalem; all which points to a ministry in the neighbourhood of the city. Then comes a long period of ministry in perfectly undefined localities, but all with more or less reference to strifes with the Pharisees, in the middle of which occurs that remarkable indication of a ministry of some duration in Jerusalem—" O Jerusalem, Jerusalem, which killest the prophets, and stonest them which are sent unto thee, *how often* would I have gathered together thy children, as a hen doth gather her brood under her wings, and ye would not! Behold your house is left unto you desolate; and verily I say unto you, ye shall not see me [again][6] until the time come when ye shall say, Blessed is he that cometh in the name of the Lord." Then come a series of parables (*e. g.* that of the Pharisee and the publican in the Temple), which appear far more adapted to those familiar with Jerusalem, and more suited for the large and general questions of Jewish theology, than for the quieter atmosphere of a purely country audience; and then at last we learn again (xviii. 31), "Behold we go up to Jerusalem," on which occasion they pass through Jericho, which would be the natural road from "beyond Jordan," but not from Galilee.

St. Matthew's and St. Mark's accounts are simpler, but lead to the same result. Already, in the 19th chapter of St. Matthew and the 10th of St. Mark, Jesus leaves Galilee for ever, after telling His disciples of His fixed resolve to "go up to Jerusalem," and face the sufferings He there expected. In neither case, however, does He seem actually to go at this time to Jerusalem, but unto the "coasts of Judea beyond Jordan." While there, His ministry is scarcely related at all, two chapters being devoted to it in St. Matthew without any specification of localities, and one in St. Mark; and then again we find Him going up full of fresh foreboding to Jerusalem by way of Jericho. It is *after* His triumphal entry at this

---

[6] ἀπ' ἄρτι occurs here in St. Matthew's version of the same passage.

time that St. Matthew places the address to Jerusalem on its frequent rejection of His efforts to save it. In all these accounts there is not only room, but the distinct demand for an interval passed in Judea and the parts beyond Jordan, between the first setting of Christ's face towards Jerusalem and the last. In St. Luke's account the inference is almost inevitable, that He did visit Jerusalem on the first occasion, and returned to it from Judea on the last. In all accounts, the fourth included, He leaves Galilee for the last time, and leaves it statedly for Jerusalem, with a sad foreboding of His fate, at least *some time* before His death, as the admitted ministry beyond Jordan of course necessarily implies. The extreme vagueness and absence of all localisation from this period of the ministry in all the synoptic gospels shows that they had little definite information about Christ's movements,—Luke's suggesting, however, strongly that the intimacy with Martha and Mary, the neighbourhood of Jericho, and constant conflicts with the Pharisees on great questions, fall into this period of His career.

This is exactly the view that the fourth gospel confirms. It takes Christ first—after much hesitation—to Jerusalem to the feast of Tabernacles, after which occurs the restoration to sight of the man born blind, and a conflict with the Pharisees on their betrayal of their trust as religious shepherds of the people. Again, in the winter in the feast of Dedication, Christ is in Jerusalem,—no account being given of the interval. Then He goes away beyond Jordan, where John at first baptised. Thence He returns to raise Lazarus from the dead at the peril of His life. Then He again retires for a time to a town called Ephraim " near to the wilderness," until He finally comes up before the passover, and enters Jerusalem by way of Bethany, in the so-called triumphal procession. That these are the facts compressed into the very vague synoptic narrative of the interval between His first painful departure from Galilee for Jerusalem, and His *last* entrance thither, there is some incidental evidence in St. Luke's gospel, and no kind of disproof in the others.[7] The other passages usually regarded as proving the complete freshness of Christ to Jerusalem on his last visit, are of very trifling weight. They are those which seem to show that Jesus and His disciples looked at the Temple buildings with the admiration of complete strangers. (Mark xi. 11, xiii. 1 ; Luke xxi. 5 ; Matt. xxiv. 1). When we remember that the Temple was then *building*, not built (it was not completed till A.D. 64), it seems likely enough that at each new visit there might be room for fresh remark.

I have, I think, now shown some reason for affirming the last gospel's account, both of the first passover and of the last, as the correct one—and also for identifying the final (and private) departure of Christ from Galilee

---

[7] It is scarcely worth notice, perhaps, that the question and discussions with the Pharisees on adultery occur in all three synoptic gospels at the beginning of this interval that occurs after His Galilean ministry, while the disputed passage in the last gospel on Christ's treatment of a woman taken in adultery occurs just in the same place.

to the feast of Tabernacles (John vii. 10) with the *first* "setting of his face towards Jerusalem," which we find in all the synoptic narratives,[8] — after which comes a vague period (perfeetly indistinct in all the first three gospels, and only marked by a few single great events in the last), which extends to the last passover. The only visit to Jerusalem which cannot be connected in any way with the synoptic account, is the short one (John v.) in which Christ heals the man beside the pool of Bethesda.

I may end this discussion, already far too long, of the historical truth of the fourth gospel by briefly summing up my results, and a few minuter evidences not yet mentioned that the gospel is no pious fraud of a later age. I think I have shown ground for assuming that the synoptic narratives are collections—no doubt arranged on a *principle*, but still collections—of the traditional events in Christ's life, derived, almost exclusively in Matthew and Mark, principally in Luke, from *Galilean* sources; while the fourth gospel is at least the work of one single mind. The oldest evidence concerning St. Matthew's gospel—that of Papias—speaks of it expressly as a collection of Christ's *discourses* (λόγια). And I cannot but think that many of the narrative illustrations introduced are of far less authority and later collection. It has some narrative passages of a distinctly apocryphal

---

[8] In the fourth gospel, as in the synoptic gospels, this takes place almost immediately after Peter's confession, "We have believed and know that thou art the Christ, the Son of the living God."

character, while its discourses have every evidence of perfect genuineness. Especially all the portions of St. Matthew which refer to events *out of* Galilee (the earliest and latest) have far less internal evidence than the others. Its account of the resurrection is more confused than that of any gospel; and its account of the birth of Christ also. St. Mark's gospel only *professes* to begin with the Galilean ministry, and confessedly breaks off just at the resurrection, the rest being added by a later hand. In it, too, the non-Galilean part — the account of the crucifixion, especially—seems less trustworthy and more traditional than any other portion. St. Mark's gospel is a collection of Galilean records—the most faithful of any, I think, in registering the Galilean *events*, but careless about discourses.[9] St. Luke's gospel is less Galilean, but still principally so; probably embodying, also, much of the information to which St. Paul had access. His account of the resurrection approaches closely to that of

---

[9] Notwithstanding all the German criticism, I cannot but think St. Mark is—as to Galilean *events*—the most reliable and original of the three synoptic gospels. His occasional confusions as to Christ's words—as, *e. g.*, his evident interchange of the occasion of v. 37, c. ix. with that of v. 15, c. x.—only prove that he could not have copied from either St. Matthew or St. Luke. The abrupt beginning and close,—the non-occurrence of the technical word *apostle*, so common a little later in St. Luke and St. Paul, a word which, in this sense, also never occurs in the fourth gospel, but which does, by the way, frequently in the Apocalypse,—and a great many other small notes of antiquity and simplicity, pointed out by the Rev. John Kenrick in his Biblical Essays (Longman, 1863)—convince me that in the *Galilean* portion St. Mark is on historic ground.

the last gospel. The last Evangelist's history of the crucifixion and the resurrection stands, I believe, on much higher historical ground than any of the others, It entirely omits the rending of the veil of the Temple, and the darkness over the whole earth; and it gives us an exposition of Pilate's conversation with Christ, which is quite an essential link in the understanding of the narrative.

As I have tried to prove, this evangelist has set right for us two great errors as to time, into which a traditional fragment in the other gospels would have led us. He writes with a definite selective purpose,—which does not, however, I believe, distort the historical accuracy of those facts which we have any means of testing. His materials approach, often very nearly, the *special* materials of St. Luke, as in his account of the sisters of Bethany, and the intimate relation between Peter and John; but he adds many of which not even the germs can be found in any other gospel; and he sometimes agrees remarkably with St. Mark. In the mention of the "two hundred pennyworth of bread" at the feeding of the multitude,— and of the supposed value of the ointment at the supper in Bethany,—we have small points of agreement very curious in writers so distinct. But his own new minor details—all of those details implying personal intimacy with his Master—are those which inspire me with the most trust,—the demeanour of Martha and Mary at the tomb of Lazarus,—the characteristic declaration of Peter, when Christ would wash his feet,—the answer to

John at the last supper, which seems to direct *his* attention to Judas, and yet is not heard by any of the others, since they simply wonder at Christ's saying, "What thou doest, do quickly,"—the distress of Mary Magdalene in the garden of the sepulchre,—Christ's dying recommendation of His mother to the care of His disciple,—and the character of Thomas, sketched nowhere else, and here only incidentally touched, all are details that recommend *themselves*. When, in addition, we find a narrative wholly free from the mythical elements which had crept into the other gospels, and yet full of the *supernatural* elements, simply and naturally described; and discourses which, the more closely they are studied, exhibit—not withont a real modification from the apostle's own diffuseness and repetition of style—a type of religious teaching that appears more and more essentially similar to the greater discourses in St. Matthew's gospel,—I believe that no one who could accept the theological teaching here recorded as divine, will reject the *history* as spurious. On that the real credibility of St. John's gospel depends, and is no doubt intended to depend.

NOTE TO ESSAY VI.

The discussion as to the real length of our Lord's public ministry, *i. e.* as to the dates of his baptism and death, has received a good deal of light of late years from one or two sources, especially from Dr. A. W. Zumpt's learned treatise on the year of Christ's birth (Das Geburtsjahr Christi, von Dr. A. W. Zumpt. Leipsic, Teubner), and from Mr. Samuel Sharpe's investigations, the results of which he communicated some years ago in a letter to the

'Athenæum' newspaper. Both these learned men, whose general attitude towards the historical credibility of the supernatural elements of the New Testament is entirely different,—Dr. Zumpt being a conservative and Mr. Sharpe a rationalistic critic,—have alike come to the conclusion that the crucifixion took place in the year 29 A.D. (the year of the consulship of the two Gemini), to which tradition assigns it; and this seems, indeed, now to be a sufficiently well fixed point. Mr. Sharpe mentions that Origen, in his answer to Celsus, states that the destruction of the temple of Jerusalem by Titus took place *within* forty-two years of the crucifixion. The temple was destroyed in September, A.D. 70, which gives April, A.D. 29, for the date of the crucifixion, and confirms the other statement that it was in the year of the consulship of the two Gemini. The only difficulty is that this year, A.D. 29, would be, according to ordinary reckoning, the fifteenth of Tiberius, which is the date given by St. Luke for the baptism of Christ and for the *beginning*, instead of the end, of His ministry. Mr. Sharpe and Professor Zumpt resolve this difficulty quite differently, but both in a way which would give a longer ministry to our Lord than the synoptic gospels appear to give. Mr. Sharpe relies on the oriental mode of counting the civil year. Tiberius succeeded Augustus on the 19th August, A.D. 14. On "the New Year's Day"—the 29th August—though Tiberius had been reigning only ten days, the oriental calculation would have made the *second* year of Tiberius begin, consequently, on the 29th August, A.D. 27 (though Tiberius had then been emperor only 13 years and 10 days) the fifteenth year of Tiberius, according to the oriental mode of calculating, would begin; and soon after this, Mr. Sharpe places the baptism of our Lord, *i. e.* probably in September, A. D. 27. His further ministry would then last till April, A. D. 29, or a little more than a year and a half, covering one passover besides the passover of His death. Dr. Zumpt, on the other hand, believes that St. Luke reckoned the reign of Tiberius from the first elevation of Tiberius to imperial authority over the provinces, that is, from the association of Tiberius with Augustus in authority as co-regent of the provinces, and Imperator of the troops,—the proper reckoning for Syria, as Dr. Zumpt shows by very elaborate, and, as it seems to me, weighty historical evidence. He assigns this association of Tiberius with Augustus as co-regent of the provinces to the end of the year A. D. 11, which gives the year 26 A. D. for John the Baptist's first public appearance. As Christ's baptism and public ministry follows certainly in a few months, perhaps in a few weeks (we do not know precisely *how* soon) this gives between two and three full years at least for His public ministry, while Mr. Sharpe's reckoning gives only between one and two. Dr. Zumpt, also shows that the remark which the Jews are reported by the fourth evangelist as having made in answer to our Lord's assertion, " Destroy this Temple, and in three days I will raise it up " (John ii. 19), " Forty and six years was this temple in building, and wilt thou rear it up in three days?" would put the date of this conversation before the Easter of either 27 A. D., or 28 A. D., *i. e.* either two years or one before His crucifixion (Zumpt's 'Geburtsjahr Christi,' p. 252) ; the latter of which dates Mr. Sharpe would also accept as the date of a passover occuring during Christ's public ministry, and before the passover of the crucifixion. This is in itself a strong confirmation of the date given by the fourth evangelist to the cleansing of the Temple, and of his assertion that Christ taught publicly at Jerusalem before the year of His crucifixion. No reckoning will give the 46th year of the building of Herod's Temple to the date 29 A. D., which may be now taken pretty certainly as the date of the crucifixion.

Finally, Mr. Sharpe, who, as I said, is not at all predisposed to favour the fourth gospel, being one of the most learned critics of the rationalistic school, has satisfied himself by the help of Professor Adams, the Cambridge professor of astronomy, who has calculated the date of the first new moon after the Spring Equinox of A. D. 29, that in the year A. D. 29 the passover day occurred on a Saturday (Saturday, 16th April), concurring with the sabbath day, and making that day, as our evangelist says, " a high day ; " and that, therefore our Lord could not by any possibility have eaten the legal or Jewish passover with His disciples,—being, indeed, already dead before it was eaten. This curious concurrence of quite independent historical evidence to lengthen the time of Christ's public ministry, so as to include certainly either one or two passovers besides that of His crucifixion,—to confirm, in some degree, the fact of His presence at Jerusalem at one of them,—and to sustain the statement of the fourth evangelist in relation to the Last Supper,—seems to me to add very great weight to the historical character of this gospel. It is incredible that such a correction should have been made by a forger *by accident*, and still more incredible that such a one should then have detected the blunder which the early evangelists had made.

I must add, what I have hardly dwelt upon enough in the text, that I cannot conceive a gospel originating in the middle of the second century, either dwelling so much and so incidentally, as this gospel does, on the traits of private and personal character exhibited by the various apostles and disciples—especially by Peter, Thomas, Mary, Martha, and Mary Magdalene—or exhibiting so little trace of the ecclesiastical developments of Church authority during that period.* As I have pointed out, this gospel, and that of St. Mark, agree in never using the word 'apostle' in any technical sense, but adhering to the old phraseology of "the twelve." That hints as to personal character should have been developed, and so finely developed; nay, that one personal character, that of the ardent but doubting Thomas should have been invented and yet so *leniently* treated by an evangelist whose whole object was to prove the theological value of faith,*—and that the conceptions of ecclesiastical authority should *not* have been developed in a spurious gospel of the latter half of the second century, is to me quite incredible.

* See on this point a striking criticism by the Rev. Stanley Leathes in his 'Witness of St. John to Christ,' The Boyle Lectures, for 1870, p. 125. (Rivingtons.)

VII.

THE INCARNATION AND PRINCIPLES OF EVIDENCE.

THE secret panic which besets the faith of England just at present may be fairly described as hanging almost entirely on the following doubt:—'Is it possible to do full justice to the relative and wavering human element in religious history without throwing an impenetrable mist over the absolute and divine? Is there any fixed limit to the encroachments of human uncertainty on Divine Certainties? Can a man who honestly admits and fairly realizes the fluctuating character of the evidence of men, whether historical or spiritual, still enjoy without the slightest violence to his own intellectual sincerity any profound rest in the assurances of an Eternal voice?' Were there not a growing fear that these questions may be answered in the negative, that all Revelation proceeding from God will gradually be sublimated into the abstract idealities of man, recent criticisms, as in 'Essays and Reviews' and elsewhere, would have had no power to awaken the strife of the last few years. This is the real fear at the bottom of our uneasiness :—Theology, it is thought, the divine foundation of hope and rest for man, is in danger of being absorbed into a department of morbid psychology—into the mere higher aspirations of the *homo desideriorum* as he analyzes sadly what he *wishes* to believe. Not, indeed, that any large or increasing number of sincere men doubt as yet the existence of God, but that there is more and more disposition to speak of Him, as Dr. Mansel has indeed described Him, as the unknown and residual cause of a great number of undefined phenomena. Notice the great preference felt in the religious school of scepticism for the word and thought "Inspiration," as compared with the word and thought "Revelation." It is admitted that there are conceptions and feelings,—sometimes vague and shadowy—sometimes luminous and painfully intense,—which do not take their rise in our own finite natures, but indicate what is above and beyond us. 'We can speak with confidence,' it is said, 'of human phenomena; we can be sure that some of our thoughts come from a higher and a better than ourselves—from "what we *deem* is Lord of All"—but we would rather keep to the word which denotes only the vague influence breathed into the human spirit—the word which uses as its symbol 'the wind that bloweth as it listeth'—and abandon the word which forces upon us the other and absolute side of the same fact. We are sure that the flying lights and shadows which pass over our conscience come from some mysterious light beyond, but we do not know whether they be the result of direct or reflected rays, and we are warned by all the course of religious history that we must be content with these gleams of transient illumination as they are, without dogmatising as to the divine source from which they issue. The whole tendency of human thought and knowledge has been more and more to dissipate the fixity, and cloud with transient elements the extra-human origin—whatever it be—of the Divine oracles. Science and history have alike shown the inextricable fusion of human error and passion with higher thoughts; and hence a word like Revelation, which professes to lift our eyes from these strangely mixed phenomena of earth to the very processes of the Eternal mind, and to the very acts of the Eternal will, seem now to us almost an irony invented by some keen thinker in the bitterest anguish of speculative imbecility.'

If this train of thought represents the state of mind of the idealising school of religious doubters, the dogmatic confutations which are put forth in reply seem to me to be vitiated by the very same fundamental error—perhaps even in a more malignant form. Every step in the history of dogmatic Orthodoxy has been an effort to fortify some reliable human base for a Divine infallibility—to slide in a false bottom into the abyss of Eternal Truth—to justify the exchange of the arduous duty of discriminating what God has told us of Himself, for some such (apparently) easier duty as discriminating what a given Church or a given book *states* that He has told us. I believe that the latter task is only *apparently* easier, for the moment we propose to ourselves any human test as a final criterion of God's voice, we assume an unreality which deprives us of all power to accomplish even that task adequately. The man who will accept a secondary authority because it is more within his grasp, in fact accepts it because it is less true and divine, and so inevitably loses his insight even into the full significance of that secondary authority itself, which is best and truest when seen in close relation to the first. If I accept any part of the Bible as a final and ultimate equivalent for God, I put myself into an attitude of mind which all but insures a shallow and false interpretation of it. If truly divine, it must be an impress of an infinite and Eternal *Life*, and to limit myself to the propositions it contains is to make language the *measure*, instead of the mere sign of a living character. The Dogmatists, therefore, in trying to secure a safe human base of operations for their campaign in favour of Divine Truth—such a base as an infallible Church or book—fall into a worse error than their opponents, who quite truly deny that there is any such impregnable human base for the divine argument, but erroneously suppose that in doing so they have disproved the power of God to reveal Himself.

Both doubters and dogmatists take man, and not God—the finite, and not the Infinite—as the fixed centre of Truth, and it is obvious that such an assumption is one intellectual germ of Atheism. It seems sometimes strangely difficult to realise the significance of the truism that the Truth lies, and must lie, deeper than human certainty—that certainty rests upon Truth, not Truth upon certainty. *Our* grasp of the Truth can never be worth much; it is the grasp of the Truth upon us that men are willing to die for. And, therefore, the media by which Truth lays its hold upon our minds can never be exhaustively analyzed, because the analyst is himself smaller and feebler in every way than the power which holds him in its grasp. One living mind touches another at a thousand points, and no one can do more than indicate a few of them,—but this incapacity to understand does not weaken the power of the practical hold.

Hence it seems to me that both the sceptic and dogmatic schools of thought alike assume erroneously, that the true method of procedure is this,—'Granting man and nature, to prove God and the supernatural,'—a Sisyphus task which I am sure must for ever fail. The sooner we clearly apprehend that the higher proves itself to the lower, that the lower can only accept and welcome without measuring or numbering the resources by which that impression is made, the sooner we shall understand that we must neither expect to find human belief adequate to the eternal object of belief, nor human intellect adequate to exhausting the springs and sources of human belief.

The best analogy to follow in considering Revelation (though even that is but a feeble one), is the sort of command which a parent has over the avenues to a child's convictions. Encompassing him, as he does, almost on every side, he can reach his inmost faith by a multitude of approaches, of many of which the child is himself unconscious. Many of the impressions made may be inadequate,—some of them owing to the deficiency of the child's education or faculty may be refracted into positive falsehood,—while *all* the avenues to his mind are imperfect and liable to error. Yet we do not doubt for a moment that the parent *can* impress effectually, though imperfectly, his character and will through these avenues upon the mind of the child; and we are sure that the reality so conveyed is wider and deeper than the method of conveying it, while again the only rationale which the child could give of his own impressions would comprehend scarcely any true picture at all of the depth of those impressions. I infer, therefore, that in all revelations proceeding from a higher to a lower mind, there is an intrinsic necessity that the reality revealed must be wider and more comprehensive than the modes of revealing, while the modes of the revelation again are far wider and more comprehensive than the *evidence* which we can assign for accepting the revelation. There are three distinct levels in all impressions made from above on a lower nature :—First, the higher reality itself spreading out far beyond the channels of approach to the lower; next, these latter extending far beyond the range of the reasons which the learner can discriminate and assign for his conviction. God must be infinitely greater than the sources of our faith; these again must be indefinitely wider than the *evidence* which we give for our convictions.

I suppose that most people must be conscious of states of mind in which they are unable to believe what yet they know to be far deeper and truer than their believing power. 'It is too great for me—I cannot grasp it,' we say, ' and yet I know the deficiency is in me, not in the reality; and one reason that I believe it, is, because I am conscious that it is too great for my belief. I know that any divine truth must task and often seem to mock human belief; when I can best believe it, my mind is at its highest, but it escapes me again, not from any shadowiness in it, but from the contraction of my own spiritual and moral faculty.' This is the state of mind only adequately expressed by the words, "Lord, I believe; help Thou my unbelief." Such unbelief is, in a sense, even the evidence of truth, arising as it does, *not* from any *collision* between the Truth and the highest convictions of our minds, but merely from transcending them—from giving us the feeling of being lost in the attempt to embrace it. The belief in God Himself is of this nature. Often it is unreal, because it overpowers us. We apply to Him the diminutive scale of thoughts and affections by which we measure our finite world, and the contrast strikes us with a shadow of surprise and awe. We forget that though He can prove Himself to us, He does so only after His own discipline and purification of those inadequate thoughts and feelings by which we can never hope to prove Him to ourselves.

When, then, we say that all belief ought to be upon evidence, we only mean, or ought only to mean, that there should be *real* powers and influences, and reasons constraining our belief and worthy to constrain it; we do not or ought not to mean that all which legitimately affects our own convictions can be so translated into language as to have at second hand the same influence over others which it had, at first hand, over ourselves. This is less and less true in proportion as the object of belief is raised above us. Probably the widest and highest part of the influences which oblige men to trust in a personal God has never been expressed in human speech at all, though many not inadequate efforts have been made to indicate the directions whence these influences come. I have denied the possibility of any *proof* of an eternal reality from the human side, though not of course of that human certainty which results from the proof of it from the divine side—that is, which results from its divine manifestation to us. But though I should regard the possibility of giving any adequate human proof of any truth, as a sufficient and incontrovertible test that the truth proved was only of finite and human dimensions, there must be, of course, large portions of the real influence exerted over the mind by any Revelation which comes within the range of the intellect, and can be detained for analysis and examination. The direction of a few converging rays can be defined, though many of them, and perhaps the very ones which give out the most divine heat, may be invisible to the human understanding.

In the present essay I am anxious to indicate in this manner the direction of some of the influences which compel me to accept the Incarnation as the central truth of the Christian Revelation, after having rejected it first through the force of education, and subsequently from conviction during many years of anxious thought and study. If I can in any way succeed in doing for the Incarnation what has been so often done for the primary truth of Theism—in indicating, that is, some few really universal reasons why it should take a strong hold of the human conscience and intellect without aid from the *mere* external authority of either Church or Bible, I shall have done all I wish and more than I am sanguine enough to expect. It seems to me that no theologians have done more to undermine the true power of Revelation than those who have tried to force theology on men's minds by mere external authority, which has, I believe, no more capacity to influence the living faith of man, than a ray of light to affect the ear, or a sound to impress the retina.

A masterly writer, the Rev. James Martineau, has put very forcibly the great difficulty which occurs to every cultivated mind in discussing the truth of the Incarnation :—

"The truth is, this [Mr. Maurice's] school has never succeeded in settling accounts between the Eternal Divine facts, spiritually revealed by the ever-living witness, and the historical phenomena of the past, which, however connected with religion, are *cognisable* only through human testimony. In the joy of having found the former, even Mr. Maurice forgets the different tenure of the latter, involves them in the same feeling and treatment as if they, too, were entities apprehensible to-day independently of yesterday, and free from the contingencies of probable evidence. . . . The personal life of God in the world, of which his sense is so deep, seems to guarantee for him the particular Divine acts and manifestations enumerated in the Scriptures, and in the formularies of the Church; and his one standing appeal to us is, 'Believe in Him who is signified, and you will believe the signs;' yet it is plain that no prior apprehension of God would enable us to divine, before they came, the forms in which His agency would express itself; or after they have come and been reported, to separate the threads of reality from those of fiction in a narrative of mixed tissue. For knowledge of the Divine events, taken one by one, we are not less dependent on human attestation than for the biography of an emperor or an apostle, and it is vain to treat them as if they were deducibles from the primary spiritual truth, and were to stand or fall with it."[1]

Nothing can be better put. And it is needless to say that if we had no vestige of the Incarnation in history we should have no reason for believing it, though the want which it answers in the human heart would remain. But the question is not as to whether it is right to accept historical facts without historical evidence, but how far the belief in facts for which there *is* more or less historical evidence, is legitimately shaken

---

[1] *National Review*, No. XXVI. for October, 1861. Article, "Tracts for Priests and People," pp. 430, 431.

or strengthened by the tenacity with which they fasten on the conscience,—by their power of "revealing the thoughts of many hearts" in all races and all times. Some writers, like Strauss, for example, maintain that this power which some facts have of embodying human hopes and aspirations ought to render us *incredulous* of them as facts. Myths, he says, are human expectations, crystallized into the form of history; we ought, therefore, to believe much more easily what answers to *no* human hope than what does, for the hope may easily generate a fictitious echo of itself. Another school of writers maintains that historical beliefs should hang on historical evidence, and on nothing else; that the splendour of the Divine halo should be carefully shut out from the Gospel before we decide on its authenticity; that we should search into it as we search into the authenticity of Livy or Homer. To this school apparently the writer whom I have quoted belongs.

Now, it seems to me that in both schools there is a great want of distinctness of thought as to what historical evidence really means. We say that a witness who has no previous prepossessions at all on any subject is the best witness to a fact, because he judges simply by observation and by nothing else. We should trust more implicitly a supernatural story from a plain strongminded practical man, given to no nervous impressions than from a morbid nature like Cowper's, or a superstitious person full of ignorant fears and wonders. The best testimony we can get for very simple *physical facts* of any kind is, so to say, *accidental* testimony,—the testimony of men who have no theory, and no wish to have a theory. But what is a true and important criterion of the value of testimony in reference to very simple physical facts that come within the range of eye, ear, and touch, can never be legitimately generalised into a criterion of the general *evidence* of a complex, spiritual, moral, and physical event. Were we as a rule to mistrust the testimony of persons to events which could be proved to have been expected, feared, or hoped for by them beforehand, we should, in fact, often doubt events *because* they were probable. We judge of historical truth by two tests—by mere testimony, which is usually more safe if the event be (to the witness) entirely unexpected, but also by all evidence we may possess as to the causes previously at work, the knowledge of which necessarily tends to inspire expectation in all who have access to them, while those causes themselves tend to fulfil the expectations so inspired. And, of course, the very existence of an antecedent presumption will sometimes tend to weaken the mere scientific value of human testimony, while it incalculably strengthens our evidence for the fact testified. An astronomer who has calculated a new perturbation in the planetary motions may be a worse witness, in case of imperfect observation, as to the *fact*, than a casual observer, who is quite unaware that any such phenomenon is expected. But still the knowledge which causes us to expect (even doubtfully) such a phenomenon is rightly regarded as weighing far more in favour of the event than the partial invalidation of the personal testimony weighs in the other scale. The best witness of simple physical facts is the witness without expectation; but the whole evidence for expected facts is usually far stronger than the evidence for abrupt and insulated phenomena.

And this distinction has nowhere greater force than where the facts in question have their springs in personal character. Here we rightly prefer, and prefer almost indefinitely, the "evidence" of intimate friends to the "testimony" of strangers, and for the simple reason that so large an element in all human actions is other than physical—requires more than eye, ear, and touch, to perceive it—that no one who has not gained some familiarity with the character, can see its actions with any clear apprehension of their drift at all. Just as no one would trust an unscientific man's evidence on a chemical phenomenon, because he does not know *what* to observe, does not see where the pinch of the case lies; so no one compares for a moment, in most cases, the value of a friend's and a stranger's insight into a man's actions, unless where something is at stake which is likely to prejudice a friend's vision. In such cases previous knowledge of moral causes is far more important to the whole evidence than it is injurious to the impartiality of the testimony. Could the point to be observed in a chemical analysis be sharply and distinctly isolated, we would rather take the testimony of a man who had no idea what to expect than of a man who knew well what to expect; but it cannot; and therefore we say that the evidence of a chemist is worth ten times as much as the evidence of a non-chemist. And so also with regard to character: the very knowledge which helps us to criticise rightly, to some extent no doubt affects the independence of the testimony, since the expectation may infuse some colour of its own into the intellect; yet even so, that knowledge gives far more weight to the whole evidence than it takes from the weight of the physical testimony.

Now, to apply these considerations to God's revelation of Himself. No doubt the religious yearnings, the mysterious hopes, the premonitory prophecies which precede such a revelation, to some extent shake the mere sense-testimony of those who come within their influence. The "vision and the faculty divine" will, to some extent, perhaps, colour the testimony of witnesses. On the other hand, it seems to me simply unmeaning to say that the historical evidence in any large sense can be weighed without assigning the greatest importance to these prophetic visions and hopes. It is surely untrue, then, that for the divine facts of history we are "not *less* dependent on human attestation than for the biography of an emperor or an apostle." We are absolutely dependent on *some* human attestation for any historical fact; but I maintain that, beyond a certain limit, our belief in any such fact legitimately requires *less* external evidence in proportion as the previous knowledge or insight, leading us to anticipate it, is large or small. This is so, in some degree, even with regard to the biography of an emperor or apostle. If a newspaper tells us that a person of whom we have never heard has just attempted the French Emperor's life, we accept it as a mere newspaper rumour, and nothing more; but if it tells us that one whose fanatical political character and associations we intimately know, and whose vindictive vows we have recently heard, has done so, we attach far more importance to the intelligence. Its *evidence* is better, though it is certainly also true that the very causes which give us reason to believe it, may have induced somebody else to invent or colour the rumour. We see a not improbable origin for the false testimony, if it be false testimony; but, for all that, we hold much more firmly than we otherwise should, that the character in question has manifested itself in this way. We have seen the causes at work which might have led to this effect, and though they might also have led to a false anticipation of this effect, we rightly hold the evidence to be much stronger than if we knew nothing of the matter.

But if this be true even of the evidence for ordinary human biography, it is surely true that the historical facts of Revelation, which satisfy our highest religious yearnings, depend in an infinitely greater degree for their true evidence on completely corresponding to and extending that knowledge of God which He has put into man in the shape of such hopes and yearnings.

Of course, as I have already admitted, no one could believe in an historical revelation *without* a considerable mass of human testimony, because that testimony is as essential for the *how, where,* and *when,* of the Divine fulfilment of human hopes, as it is for the record of facts which faith had never presaged at all. But, given a certain substantial amount of such testimony, and I conceive that every man will, and must, be influenced in accepting or rejecting it by his own personal insight, or want of insight, into the Divine causes which might have produced such a revelation, and into the human wants which called for them. The principles by which we weigh the evidence of a historical revelation are *not* coincident with those by which we weigh the evidence for the biography of "an emperor or apostle," though, of course, they contain many common elements. My knowledge of what I may call the *à priori* probabilities, the moral presumptions of a human life, is entirely derived from the testimony of others. When I gain a strong and distinct impression of the individual character of the emperor or apostle, or any one brought into relation with them, I have, of course, a certain standard by which to judge doubtful evidence concerning their lives, but for such strong and distinct impressions themselves I am wholly dependent on the testimony of others. This is not so with regard to Divine causes. The certainty with which we apprehend God's righteousness and love is the highest certainty of which the human conscience is capable;

and hence, in judging of the truth of an historical revelation, much less in proportion depends on mere sifting of *testimony*, far more on the problem whether the facts accurately *fit* the Divine causes which we know to be in existence, and the human yearnings which we know to be of God's inspiration, than can ever depend on what is called "internal evidence" in ordinary history or biography. In the latter case, the standard of "internal evidence" is primarily derived from the external. In the case of Divine revelation, it is the first truth of our life, the deepest fountain of our being.

Well, then, to satisfy me of the truth of the Incarnation, there must be two distinct and coincident forces exerted on my mind. I must be historically satisfied that a Christ existed, claimed to be in some unique and eternal sense the Son of God and Lord of man; that He claimed the power to forgive sin, to search the heart, and to impose the yoke and the burden which set man free from all other yokes and burdens; I must be satisfied that others confirmed, then, and through the history of the world have ever since confirmed, this inward relation of Christ to their hearts;—of this much I must be sure as matter of history. And, secondly, before I can credit the inferences to which this would naturally lead me, or rather decide between those inferences and the incredulity to which so many philosophers' minds in all ages have been forced, I must be satisfied, as matter of the deepest inward conviction, that those hopes, and wants, and prophetic aspirations, which stirred the nations of antiquity before the dawn, and which have stirred still more deeply the nations of the modern world since the cross was set up on Mount Calvary, are not only adequately answered, but purified and strengthened by Christ's Incarnation, and not without it. As soon as men are convinced of both these series of facts—historically, that the claim of the eternal Sonship was made by Christ, and accepted as a new life by the mass of His followers in all ages,—spiritually, that the admission of that claim, and this alone, answers the cry of the ages and of our own consciences for Divine light and help, the two coalesce into an historical faith, which is something far more than assent to historical testimony—namely, assent to testimony concerning facts whose roots of causation we discern running deep into the very constitution of man and the character of God.

I will speak last of the historical testimony, for I know that in most men's minds in the present day, and know too with regard to my own, that it is not here that the true difficulty really lies. The real stress of the doubt felt is twofold. First, there is a strong impression which I long shared, that no fresh human power, no new insight into the divine world is given by faith in the Incarnation, which would not be equally given by an unfolding of the same kind of Christian morality and worship without the burden of that stupendous mystery which staggers the human intellect. Secondly, a positive metaphysical contradiction is supposed to be involved in the assertion that an infant, a child, a growing youth, a Jew, one limited in knowledge, subject to temptation, sensible of national prejudices, liable to sickness, overpowered by death, could in any sense be personally identified with the eternal and uncreated Son of God. Now, to me it seems that it would be and ought to be fatal, at least to all human faith in the Incarnation, if not to the fact itself, could it be shown as the first of these objections assumes, that the net moral and spiritual fruits of the Christian revelation can be reaped in full without accepting it. That it is *not* true seems attested by the clinging of the popular heart of Christendom throughout all the centuries to the confession that "for us men and for our salvation the Son of God came down from heaven, and was made man, and died upon the cross for us;" but falsehood so often mingles with truth in the popular mind, that it is not easy to accept as decisive the blind instinct even of ages, on such a point. No man ever is really convinced by the mere spectacle of strong faith in others; all that such a spectacle can do is to fascinate our minds till we can enter into its meaning for ourselves. I will try and show then, first, what I think is given by the Incarnation, which would not and could not be given by the fullest manifestation of Christian morality and piety,—were that possible without it.

1. We are told by it something of God's absolute and essential nature, something which does not merely de-

scribe what He is *to us*, but what He is in Himself. If Christ is the Eternal Son of God, God is indeed and in essence a Father; the social nature, the spring of love is of the very essence of the Eternal being; the communication of His life, the reciprocation of His affection dates from beyond time—belongs, in other words, to the very being of God. Now, some persons think that such a certainty even when attained has very little to do with human life. 'What does it matter,' they say, 'what the absolute nature of God is, if we know what He is *to us;* —how can it concern us to know what He was before our race existed, if we know what He is to all His creatures now?' These questions seem plausible, but I believe they point to a very deep error. I can answer for myself, that the Unitarian conviction that God is— *as* God and in His eternal essence—a single and, so to say, solitary personality, influenced my imagination and the whole colour of my faith most profoundly. Such a conviction, thoroughly realised, renders it impossible to identify any of the social attributes with His real *essence* —renders it difficult not to regard power as the true root of all other divine life. If we are to believe that *the Father* was from all time, we must believe that He was *as* a Father—that is, that love was actual in Him as well as potential, that the communication of life and thought and fulness of joy was of the inmost nature of God, and never began to be if God never began to be.

For my own part, I am sure that our belief, whatever it may be, about the " absolute " nature of God, influences far more than any one supposes our practical thoughts about the actual relation of God to us. Unitarians eagerly deny, I once eagerly denied, that God is to them a solitary omnipotence. Nor is He. But I am sure that the conception of a single eternal will as originating, and infinitely antecedent to, all acts of love or spiritual communion with any other, affects vitally the temper of their faith. The throne of heaven is to them a lonely one. The solitude of the eternities weighs upon their imaginations. *Social* are necessarily postponed to *individual* attributes ; for they date from a later origin— from creation,—while power and thought are eternal. Necessarily, therefore, God, though spoken of and worshipped as a Father to us, is conceived *primarily* as imagining and creating ; secondarily only, as loving and inspiring. But any Being whose thoughts and resolves are conceived as in any sense deeper and more personal than His affections, is necessarily regarded rather as benignant and compassionate, than as affording the type of that deepest kind of love which is co-ordinate with life ;—in short, rather as a beneficence whose love springs out of power and reason, than as One whose power and reason are grounded in love. I am sure that this notion of God as the Absolute Cause does tincture deeply even the highest form of Unitarian faith, and I cannot see how it could be otherwise. If our prayers are addressed to One whose eternity we habitually image as unshared, we necessarily for the time merge the Father in the Omniscient and Omnipotent genius of the universe. If, on the other hand, we pray to One who has revealed His own eternity through the Eternal Son—if in the spirit of the liturgies, Catholic and Protestant, we alternate our prayers to the eternal originating love, and to that filial love in which it has been eternally mirrored, turning from the "Father of heaven" to the "Son, Redeemer of the world," and back again to Him in whom that Son for ever rests—then we keep a God essentially *social* before our hearts and minds, and fill our imagination with no solitary grandeur.

It will be said that even if revelation does manifest to us any of the secrets of the divine eternities, they can influence us only so far as they have relation to us, and that to know what God is to man, is to know all that can affect our spiritual life. This is true, and yet it is, I believe, essential to know something of what God is, out of relation to man, in order to realise fully what He is in relation to man. Even in human relations we are never fully satisfied with our knowledge of any character, however intimately related with ours, until we know what it is and seems in other relations also. It is not that we distrust others, but that we distrust ourselves. "Subjectivity," as it is called, clouds the eyes; we want to know how far our own individual deficiencies, and sins, and impulses, colour our vision. And therefore we weigh others' experience as anxiously as our own. And just as we seek in this way to escape from the limitations of our own individuality in human affections, we yearn for some similar escape from the limitations of man's moral experience in divine affections. No masculine mind, at all events, will ever be really content with what is called "spiritual experience." Special knowledge is never fully trusted except it stands on a firm basis of general knowledge. For example, *national* convictions known to be such, though we may give way to them, never really take possession of a man as a faith, until he finds them in full accordance with, and adding something fresh to, human convictions. To know God as He is to us, we feel that we must know something of what He is in Himself and without relation to us. Then we feel upon a rock: otherwise we cannot tell what we ought or ought not to allow for the refracting medium of human error and sin. And I believe further, that the craving to know Him *out of relation* to us, is a sign of the maturity of the knowledge which arises from His relation to us. Just as it never occurs to a child to think of what its parents are to the outer world until the filial relation has reached a certain ripeness, when this further question seems to be the essential groundwork for a new and fuller filial knowledge,—so in religion, inspiration is first, revelation last; the former leading up to the latter.

It is objected, however, to this view, that such a yearning is a yearning for the impossible. "All human knowledge must be human, that is, subjective, relative—not exhaustive, absolute." No doubt; but there is a wide distinction between the mere subjectivity of our knowing power, to which we attach no profound sense of insecurity, and the subjectivity of the field of immediate personal emotions, to which we do. I do not mean by this to distinguish between the intellect and the rest of man's nature; for in all knowledge of *persons* the intellect alone is but the smallest part of the knowing power, and is fully as liable to error as any other. I mean to distinguish the *disinterested* knowing power from the interested—the reliance which we place in our own apprehensions when they are in no way agitated by egoistic considerations, from the hesitation with which we regard their assertions when they are. It is surely essentially healthy, and even a test of health, to measure the human by the divine, and not the divine by the human; just as a dislike and distrust of all the modern revivalist impressions is a token of health. And so, I think, to desire a solid foundation-rock outside humanity on which to build up human religion is a symptom of health. It is simply the disposition to trust more implicitly that which God says of Himself, when it does not *directly* and *primarily* affect our own personal life or self-love, but only reveals Him as He is, than when it affects us primarily and directly, and reveals Him only secondarily and indirectly. We can trust better our own moral experience when we have exercised it first on learning what God is, for we feel that we have a more open and calmer mind for apprehending His revelation of Himself than for learning the "regulative truths" concerning our own duty. Of course, "*doing* His will" comes before "knowing" of *any* doctrine; but knowing *Him* comes before knowing and understanding *ourselves*.

I believe, then, that the revelation of God through an Eternal Son would realise to us, if it can be adequately believed, that the relation of God to us is only the manifestation of His life in itself, as it was or would be without us—"before all worlds," as the theologians say ; that "before all worlds" He was essentially the Father, essentially Love, essentially something infinitely more than Knowledge or Power, essentially communicating and receiving a living affection, essentially all that the heart can desire. This is not, then, relative truth for us only, but the truth as it is in itself, the reality of Infinite Being. It is first proclaimed to us, indeed, to save us from sin, strengthen us in frailty, and lift us above ourselves ; but it could not do this as it does, did we not know that God was, and His Love was, and His Fatherly Life was, apart from man, and that it is a reality infinitely deeper and vaster than the existence of His human children.

And it seems to me that to know God to be in His own essential nature a Father, not merely a Father to us, is a very great step towards exalting the whole tone of our actual life. We are apt to take the word "Father" as metaphorical in its application to God—a metaphor derived from human parentage. But such a faith teaches us that the most sacred human relations, which we feel to be far deeper than any individual and solitary human attributes, are but faint shadows of realities eternally existing in the Divine mind. It is customary in many philosophical schools to regard the "absoluteness" of

God, the absence of all relation in Him, as a part of His Divine *privilege*. To me such a conception appears essentially atheistic, if really thought out, though, of course, practically consistent with the most genuine and fervent piety. Judaism never did think it out without hovering on the very margin of the discovery which Christ made to us. That discovery was, as it seems to me, in one aspect of it—that aspect in which it could be made only through an Eternal Son of God—this :—

'Never try to think of me,' it seems to say, 'as a mere Sovereign Will; never try to conceive my Infinitude as exclusive of all Divine Life, except my own: my infinitude is not exclusive but spiritual, and includes the fulness of all spiritual life, eternal love. Think of me as always communicating life, and love, and power—as always receiving love and obedience. Never pronounce the word 'God' without recognising that diversity of reciprocal life which *is* the highest life—the reconciliation of law and fidelity, of inspiration and submission, of life overflowing and returning, which cannot be without a perfect union of distinct personalities.'

2. The Incarnation, if believable, seems to me to throw a strong light on the seeming contradictions of human nature—contradictions which are only brought out into sharper relief by a fuller knowledge of the Creator. The more we acknowledge the greatness of God, the more are we perplexed by contending thoughts as to the nature of man. The knowledge we have gained either humiliates and crushes us, or produces an artificial ela-

tion. We either *crouch* with the highest of purely Jewish minds, or become urbanely self-content with the Pelagian-Unitarian thinkers. We either cry, "Woe is me! for I am undone, because I am a man of unclean lips and dwell amongst a people of unclean lips; for mine eyes have seen the king, the Lord of hosts!" or we congratulate ourselves that we are, by *inherent* right, children of God, "born good" as Lord Palmerston said, and have no profound need, therefore, of purification at all. The humiliation alone, and the exaltation alone, are alike false to the facts within us and destructive of the true springs of human hope. The "coal from the altar" which purified Isaiah's lips was a *special* deliverance from the abject humiliation of Oriental self-abasement — a kind of deliverance which is not universal enough for mankind; and, on the other hand, the persuasion that we ourselves are, in our own right, children of God, is a graver delusion in the other direction. What we want is some *universal* fountain of Divine Life within us which shall yet not blind us in any way to the truth that we ourselves are not by our own right children of God, but only become so through One who is. We need a reconciliation of the fact of the unhealthy egoism of our own individualities, with the equally certain fact of a divine Light struggling with that egoism, and claiming us as true children of God.

The Incarnation alone helps us adequately to understand ourselves; it reconciles the language of servile humiliation with the language of rightful children. Both are true. The unclean slave and the free child of Heaven are both within us. The Incarnation shows us the true child of God—the filial will which never lost its majesty, which never tasted the impurity of human sin—and so still further abases us; but then it shows Him as the incarnate revelation of that Eternal Son and Word, whose filial light and life can stream into and take possession of us, with power to make us like Himself. The Incarnation alone seems to me adequately to reconcile the contradictory facts of a double nature in man—the separate individuality which has no health of its own, and turns every principle to evil directly it begins to revolve on its own centre —and the Divine nature, which lends it a true place and true subordination in the kingdom of God. "We are not," said Athanasius, "*by nature* sons of God, but the Son in us makes us so; also God is not *by nature our* Father, but He is the Father of the Word, dwelling in us; for in Him and through Him we cry, 'Abba, Father.'" It is obvious that Athanasius uses the word "nature" here in a much narrower sense than Bishop Butler. In the largest sense it *is* our true "nature" to live in and through the Eternal Word. But what he meant—namely, that not by virtue of anything in our own strict *personality or individuality*, only by virtue of the divine life engrafted upon that personality or individuality, do we become sons of God—seems to me the very truth which St. John reveals:—" He came unto *his own*, and *his own* received him not: but as many as received him, to them gave he power to become sons of God." This teaching, and this alone, seems to vindicate the divine nature *in* us without leading us into the delusion that it is *of* us.

Two objections, however, will be made to this statement. It will be said that the same faith, in all its essence, may be held without the Incarnation; and secondly, that even if the eternal nature of the Son be granted as the source of human life and light, the difficulty is only pushed further back, and an intrinsic health and life ascribed to the subordinate person of the Son, which can only belong to the Father Himself. I have thought long and anxiously on both these objections, and will give what seems to me the truest answer to them. So long as we believe that we ourselves are, by the very essence of our own individuality, and not *through* the purifying and overshadowing nature of the eternal Son, children of God, we cannot but explain away and try to ignore the true struggle and weakness in us. We refer that weakness and that conflict to our "finite" nature, to our childish shortsightedness, to our "temptations"—to anything but the truth—which is, not that we are weak, not that we are childish, not that we are shortsighted and tempted, but that we have not in us, and can only gain through another, that *will* to be children of God which would overcome temptation and frailty. But, then, it is said, 'Admit this—why cannot we look to the Father directly to give us this will?' Thousands, nay, millions do thus look, and not in vain. But I do not think that, as a matter of fact, the faith in an eternal Father can either be adequately realized, as I have before said, without the faith in an eternal Son, or that, even if it could, it would fully answer the conscious wants of our hearts. We need the inspiration and present help of a perfect filial will. We cannot conceive the Father as sharing in that dependent attitude of spirit, which is our principal spiritual want. It is a Father's perfection to originate—a Son's to receive. We crave sympathy and aid in this *receptive* life. We need the will to be good *as sons*, and to this the vivid faith in the help of a true Son is, I think, essential. Such a revelation alone makes humility divine, rather than human; eternal, instead of temporary and finite; such a revelation alone refers the origin of self-sacrifice to heaven rather than earth. And to make humility and self-sacrifice of essentially human birth is false to our own moral experience. We feel, we *know*, that those highest human virtues, humility and self-sacrifice, are not original and indigenous in man, but are grafted on him from above. This faith, that from the life of the Son of God is derived all the health and true perfection of humanity, is the one teaching which robs Stoicism, Asceticism, Unitarian and Roman Catholic good works, and the rest, of their unhealthy element of pride, by teaching us that, in some real sense, every pure feeling in man, everything really noble, even self-sacrifice itself, comes from above; that God's virtue is the root of all man's virtue; that even the humility of the child of God is lent us by Him who lived eternally in the Father's will before He took upon Himself our human life.

It may be thought that this is, in some sense, a transcendental and unreal philosophy. On the other hand, I believe it to be *the* popular root of the faith in the Incarnation in almost all ages. Certainly it was the root of that faith in St. Paul, the greatest of all Christian thinkers and teachers. To him, as much as to St. John, the faith that Christ was the vine, and men the branches —that it was from His divine life that the health and unity of the social system proceeded—pervaded every letter that he wrote. The great epistle to the Romans turns solely on this point. "Not I, but Christ that liveth in me," was the solution of all his difficulties concerning human good works. His want had been the assurance of a power close to his heart, not his own, by which the law could be fulfilled. He found this assurance when Christ was revealed "*in* him," and it solved for him the great problem of social renovation. Christ, the head, sent a new pulse of life through all the members, which gave a due subordination to each, and yet held together the social body in a single coherent whole. The law had been a hard task-master to St. Paul—even the divine life of the Father and Creator had not been sufficient for him—till this divine fountain of sympathy, brotherhood, humility, and self-sacrifice, had been also revealed. This was the power and mystery of the Cross. Now, no longer, need every good act of man's be tainted by a sort of evil self-gratulation on thus fulfilling his duties as a child of God. The Son was revealed as the fountain of humility and the source of all true sympathy, as aiding our prayers, fascinating our cold neutral wills with the fervour of His filial will, rendering it possible for us to love and hope and pray with full knowledge of the true source of human strength in Him whose love and hope and faith is eternal, and eternally in contact with our own hearts.

But, then, I have heard it said, this faith, if we hold it, only pushes the difficulty further back. If the eternal Son of God could be intrinsically good, though originating a new type of goodness—the filial and dependent—which He could not share even with the Father, why could not men in their finite sphere originate, *at first hand*, all the virtues of filial beings simply through their direct communion with the Father? I am sure I cannot answer this question; but is it not a question of fact? Why we are what we are, no one knows. But *is* there in us—in our individual selves or personalities—any essential *will* to good, any essentially filial free will? Surely we know that it is not so. That we have no essential will to evil, I believe. But the truest self-knowledge teaches us that our highest individual power consists in distinguishing between the Spirit of God and the spirit of self-will; and our only goodness, *not* in willing what is good for ourselves and out of our own love of good, but in surrendering the reins to One whose true love of good, and will to good, we can discern. If this be true, what have we to do with its mystery? That we *might* all have been, in free spiritual will, perfect children of God, like Christ, is conceivable certainly, but *false*. We know that our highest nature is to be taken up into another's nature, instead of clinging to our own centre. The law of life for the branches is not the law of life for the trunk. Is not this enough for us? We see that the law of Christ's nature was a higher one— that in Him filial goodness is original—while we have only the power of gaining it by a voluntary submission to His life. The metaphysical difficulty, if there be one, may, perhaps, only be pushed further back; but then, as a matter of fact, we find it is *solved by being relegated*. He was a true Son of God, and we are not. We can only become so by admitting *Him* into our hearts; He needed nothing; eternal dependence on the Father was the law of His free will.

3. And this brings me to the supposed metaphysical contradiction in the fact of Incarnation, which I used to think fatal. That difficulty was, that an infinite being *could* not become finite, or take up a human form, except as a mere simulated appearance. To me, it would be far more painful to believe in the unreality of Christ's finite nature and human condition, than to give up Christianity altogether; in fact, it would involve giving up Christ to believe it for a moment. But this metaphysical contradiction, which once seemed so formidable, does not now exist for me at all. That the Son of God, even though eternal, co-eternal with the Father,

may pass through any changes through which any derived being may pass, seems undeniable. When we note how little the powers which we ourselves possess, and which seem to belong to us, are identified with our personality—how by a stroke of paralysis, for example, a man of genius is stripped of all his richest qualities of mind and reduced to a poor solitary *ego*—or if that be not so, how he lives in two worlds, in one of which he is a feeble, helpless, isolated will, and in the other (if there be another in which he is still his old self) a man of genius still—when we note this, it seems to me to be simply the most presumptuous of all presumptuous assumptions to deny that the Son of God might have really become what he seemed to be, a finite being, a Jew of Jewish thoughts and prepossessions, and liable to all the intellectual errors which distinguished the world in which He lived. If there is an indestructible moral individuality which constitutes *self*, which is the same when wielding the largest powers, and when it sits alone at the dark centre—which, for anything I know, may even live under a double set of conditions at the same time—I can see no metaphysical contradiction in an Incarnation.

Indeed, the phenomena of *growth* are surely not less wonderful than those of limitation. If individual powers can be bestowed, and in some sense closely united with our individuality, they can be withdrawn. If infinite power and knowledge can be given by the Father to the Son, they can be limited as He wills. I am sure that Jesus of Nazareth was a Jew, a human being, ignorant of many things, only at times penetrated by the light of His infinite nature—One who could understand all human temptations, who looked forward to pain and death with human shrinking, and who saw the shortcomings of His disciples' love with human anguish. What eternal reality, then, was it that was revealed in that life? The *will* of a perfect Son, still resting in that of the Father, and ordering the human passions and desires with the sole purpose of doing that Father's will. The essential difference, the only essential difference between the life of Jesus of Nazareth and of any human being, seems to me to be that His free will was always fastened, so to speak, on that of God's, so that, though He felt temptation, the predominant *passion* of His will (if it is legitimate to apply such a word as passion to a fountain of perfect freedom) prevented the slightest trembling in the balance : while the free will of all other men is intrinsically indifferent, and needs a divine countervailing force to aid it in escaping from the solicitations of human temptation. And Christ, in revealing this perfectly filial will, revealed it as the power in the protecting shadow of which, and by the sympathy with which, we might also escape the sin which He understood, but never experienced. It was not as an *example*, but as the very source of the divine light which was to stream into us, that His life was revealed. What the Incarnate Word *was* in Him, *that* it would have the power to make us, if we would but yield ourselves up absolutely to its guidance. In point of limitations, temptations, frailties, His life was no better than ours. The will alone was better, intrinsically better; and that will would engraft itself on ours, and guide and sway us, if we would but surrender the reins.

I have now, in a certain very inadequate way—consciously inadequate to the strength of my own conviction—explained why the Incarnation, *if it be a fact*, would to my mind be a new power, a new fountain of life and hope to man; and I have said all that seems to me necessary to remove the only plausible *à priori* impossibility that ever got a strong grasp of my mind. But now, on what testimony can a rational mind justify its belief in so stupendous a fact, of which, even if true, the evidence would seem to be so far removed from the reach of human criticism?

In the first place, it seems to me impossible for any one who accepts the historical records of Christ's life as in any degree genuine to doubt that Christ asserted for Himself a spiritual and eternal Sonship, which was the true and universal ground of all men's filial relations to God. I held the existence of this claim to be indisputable long before I held that claim to be justified, and I believe that all the more critical schools of Unitarians, both in Germany and this country, grant it—at least, so far as they admit the fourth Gospel to contain an authentic account of Christ's own words. Of course, it is quite a tenable position to admit the fact and deny the inference that what a mind so high and simple held concerning its own relation to God need be accepted by other men. But at present I only wish to discuss the fact of Christ's own expressed belief. And as St. John's Gospel—though to my own conviction the completest exposition of the truth of the Incarnation—is doubted by many sincere critics who accept the first three as genuine, I could scarcely rest my faith on it, did it not seem to me that the other three, though certainly not compiled by, nor originating with, men who had thought out and realized the meaning of the revelation, are full of the same truth—full of it, that is, just in that shape in which it would be recorded by witnesses who had not yet found their way to its true significance.

What, for instance, can be better identified with the personal preaching of Christ than the whole series of parables speaking of the prophets as imperfect messengers from God to man, whose teaching had failed to reveal Him adequately, so that at last He sent His "own Son" to claim for Him His kingdom? Is it not clear that in all these a distinction *in kind* between the prophet and the Christ is meant to be imprinted on the heart? He, the last of the series, is not a servant of God, but "the heir." Again, it is recorded by all the synoptical gospels that Christ asks Peter whom men suppose Him to be. Peter replies that some say He is John the Baptist, some Elias, some one of the prophets. "But whom say ye that I am?" Peter saith unto Him, "Thou art the Christ"—"the Son of the living God," adds St. Matthew.

And the same Evangelist records the reply of Jesus :— "Blessed art thou, Simon, son of Jonas, for flesh and blood hath not revealed it unto thee, but my Father which is in heaven." Can any assertion be stronger, that between God and Christ there was this mysterious, special, and hidden relation which eye could not see, which spirit could not discern, unless God Himself had breathed it into the conscience of the disciple? To say that the spirit of such a passage does not wholly refute the notion that Christ's own conception of Himself was the modern Unitarian model-man conception, seems to me a violence to all true criticism. But it is not on one or two passages that I could rest such a belief. What is the spirit of all the three first narratives? It is this: —they describe and attempt to delineate a man who spoke, with an authority of His own, of the secrets of God's spirit. At times He forgives sins, and treats the healing of bodily diseases as a mere pledge of that deeper power to restore health to the spirit. At times He speaks of His own lowliness; but though always with the humility of a Son towards God, it is in the attitude of a King towards men. " He that loveth father or mother more than me is not worthy of me, and he that loveth son or daughter more than me is not worthy of me ;" what an assertion for any man, however good, to make!—an assertion only the more inconsistent and incredible, the better he might be: an assertion, in short, which could only be made by one conscious that His spirit was in direct *organic* communion with the spirits of those to whom He spoke—such communion that love to Him and love to God were inseparable emotions. The language St. John puts into Christ's mouth, "I in them and thou in me," seems only a clearer enunciation of the whole spirit of the first three Gospels, which implies as direct a spiritual communion between Christ and men as existed between the Father and the Son. For example, take the words, "He that receiveth you receiveth me, and he that receiveth me receiveth Him that sent me." This is not the language of a servant of God, but of one who shares His eternal attributes. The mere prophet speaks simply in the name of Him whose message he delivers, and does not regard his own personality as any necessary link in the chain.

The truth is, that the pervading and deepest characteristic of Christ's language concerning Himself is the humility, *not* of conscious unworthiness (like St. Paul's), but of conscious submission, of filial perfection. And to me, the most touching and satisfying words that have ever been uttered by human lips, are those which no mere man could ever have uttered without jarring every chord in the human conscience:—

"Woe unto thee, Chorazin! woe unto thee, Bethsaida! for if the mighty works which were done in you had been done in Tyre and Sidon, they would have repented long ago in sackcloth and ashes. But I say unto you, it shall be more tolerable for Tyre and Sidon at the day of judgment than for you. And thou, Capernaum, which art exalted unto heaven, shalt be brought down to hell:

for if the mighty works which were done in thee had been done in Sodom, it would have remained until this day. But I say unto you, that it shall be more tolerable for the land of Sodom in the day of judgment than for thee. At that time Jesus answered and said, I thank thee, O Father, Lord of heaven and earth, because thou hast hid these things from the wise and prudent, and hast revealed them unto babes: even so, Father, for so it seemed good in thy sight. All things are delivered unto me of my Father; and no man knoweth the Son but the Father; neither any man the Father save the Son, and he to whomsoever the Son will reveal him. Come unto me, all ye that labour and are heavy laden, and I will give you rest. Take my yoke upon you, and learn of me, for I am meek and lowly in heart, and ye shall find rest unto your souls: for my yoke is easy and my burden is light."

Can there be, even in the Gospel of St. John, a more unqualified assertion that it is *the* Son of God who spiritually reveals to all men their Father, and so enables all to become true sons of God; or that Christ Himself knew Himself to be that divine Son and universal light of man?

Again—

"But he answered and said, An evil and adulterous generation seeketh after a sign, and there shall no sign be given to it, save that of the prophet Jonah.[2] The

---

[2] I leave out the verse in which the very far-fetched parallel between Jonah's supposed adventure in the fish's belly and our Lord's

men of Nineveh shall rise in judgment with this generation, and shall condemn it; because they repented at the preaching of Jonah, and behold a greater than Jonah is here. The queen of the south shall rise up in judgment with this generation and shall condemn it, for she came from the uttermost parts of the earth to hear the wisdom of Solomon; and behold, a greater than Solomon is here."

In short, I cannot open a page of the Gospels without finding in Christ a complete absence of that self-reproach which we identify with humility, but which only belongs to it among imperfect and sinful men, and yet the fullest presence of that filial humility which recognised dependence on the Father as the true law and spirit of life, which lived in the will of another, and yet concurred freely in that will. Now, this combination seems to me, and is, I believe, unique in history. Wherever we find deep humility amongst men it is accompanied by self-distrust and self-accusations, as in the case of St. Paul. Wherever we find tranquil self-reliance it is *un*accompanied by the dependent and filial spirit; it is found, if at all, in some Goethe, standing with

---

three days' burial in the earth is interpolated, not only because St. Luke omits it and gives the natural significance to the passage, but because it destroys the whole force of our Lord's meaning, and is evidently a blunder of some Jewish scholiast. The whole drift of the passage is, that the spiritual sign is enough, and that the craving for a physical sign is bad. Jonah was a sign to the Ninevites, because he touched them with a sense of their evil; and so, too, our Lord claimed to be a sign to that generation.

serene brow above the clouds of human sorrow and weakness:—

> "He took the suffering human race,
> He read each wound, each weakness clear:
> He struck his finger on the place
> And said 'Thou ailest here and here.'
> He looked on Europe's dying hour
> Of fitful dreams and feverish power,
> And said, 'The end is everywhere.
> Art still has truth, take refuge there.'
> And he was happy—if to know
> Causes of things, and *far below
> His feet* to see the lurid flow
> Of trouble, and insane distress
> And headlong fate, be happiness."

Such is the attitude of the most complete human self-adequacy; but it is not the attitude of Christ, who proclaims to us everywhere, "I am come in my Father's name, and ye receive me not; if another shall come in his own name, him ye will receive."

And it seems to me that this unique combination of child-like lowliness with perfect kingliness and serenity of conscience extorts a witness to it from human nature which is equally unique. We say to our hearts, 'This is not an independent will, but a filial will; and yet this is not an imperfect sinful man, but one who shares the eternal life of the Father whom He reveals.' The ultimate distinction between Christ's human nature and our own lay not, it seems to me, in any exemption from human ignorance, sensitiveness, temptation, but in the ultimate divinity of His free will, which moulded itself according to the Father's will without a moment's trembling in the balance. Of the perfect concord, perfect submissiveness, perfect dependence of this will, He Himself was aware, and this gave Him His tone of authority towards man. But God's purpose was often concealed from Him on earth; He could discern only the general outline of His destiny, and this only with the fitful uncertainty of that prophetic prescience which estimates perfectly the evil and the good, and yet can hardly bring itself to believe in any even temporary triumph of evil. "If it be possible, let this cup pass from me: nevertheless, not as I will, but as thou wilt," is surely the highest expression of a perfect filial will full of humility, but wholly untouched by humiliation.

But it will be said, that, granting that Christ was convinced of this ultimate divinity of His own nature; admitting that His disciples believed partially and fitfully at first, more profoundly and spiritually afterwards, in the same truth—how can we accept such a stupendous assertion, on the evidence of beings whom we admit, not only not to be infallible, but to be touched with all the natural limitations of their social condition, their nation, and their era? Must we not necessarily connect such confidence in their testimony with some doctrine of infallibility such as has turned the religion of whole countries into superstition, and built up the inflated theory of an infallible Church, or an infallible Bible? How can you take one of their beliefs, and reject another—accept the one which admits of no historical verification, and reject that which has been historically tested and disproved—hold to their Christology, and smile at their crude notions of "meeting the Lord in the air"—defer to their faith in the secrets of eternity, and push impatiently aside their demonology? Is there no substantial reason for leaving such a faith as that in the Incarnation, to be held by men who combine with it a superstitious treatment of apostolic authority, or the letter of Scripture?

I hold not; and I think, moreover, that the faith in the Incarnation, in its largest sense, is absolutely inconsistent with this superstitious treatment of the human authority of apostles, or the literal text of the Bible. To me it seems certain, that St. Paul and St. John alone, among the apostles whose writings are recorded, had gained anything like a conscious grasp of this truth. The authors of the first three gospels, though they mention facts which point to it, as the rays from behind a cloud point to the hidden position of the sun, certainly had never grasped the magnitude of the truth that they were helping to reveal. Even St. Paul apprehended it, I think, only in relation to the *conscious* life of faith. He held, doubtless, that the Son of God had been the centre of Jewish unity and nationality, throughout the history of the Jewish nation; that the fathers of the nation who passed through the Red Sea "did all eat the same spiritual meat, and did all drink the same spiritual drink; for they drank of that spiritual rock which followed them, and that rock was Christ." He held, too, that Christ was equally the centre and root of the social unity of the Christian Church; that His life was in all its members, and the real bond of its organisation; but I can see no trace that he had yet learned to extend the same truth to the whole world of heathen humanity, that he had grasped the fulness of St. John's teaching, that " He is the light which lighteth *every man that cometh into the world.*"

To me the Incarnation seems to be revealed in exactly a similar way, and through similar channels of various degrees of authenticity, as the existence of God itself. We all hold that God manifested Himself through a variety of avenues to the mind of man —that at length He set apart one nation to witness more especially to His personal unity and righteousness —that through its means, without neglecting the manifold approaches to the conscience of the heathen world, the great truth gradually struggled into the field of human vision, and convinced the world of its reality, without ever shutting itself up in the form of a logical demonstration. The existence of God lay at the root of so many natural facts, that it gained access to the mind just as the personality of other men or the laws of nature gain access to the mind. In the same way, and in that way only, I hold that the Incarnation has proved itself;—Christ's own belief in the divinity and eternity of His own personality occupying exactly the same position in relation to this truth, that the belief of God's "peculiar people" in the government and providence of God occupied in relation to Theism. But the Jews' conviction that their destiny was guided by God, and Christ's expressed conviction in the divine eternity of His own life, were great powers to *aid* belief in other men; but without echoes in our own experience would and could not be decisive. And the gradual dawning of this faith on the imperfect and often contracted minds of Christ's followers produced, no doubt, as many false lights and colours, suffused their experience with as much special error, as the belief in the special relation of God to their nation produced in the minds of the Israelites.

Every great and infinite truth dawning upon minds but half-prepared to receive it must create a certain degree of excitement, which will collect a fringe of broken colours round the central glory. That this was actually the case with the disciples of Christ, as well as with the Jews, I do not doubt. Their millennial expectations seem to me a clear instance of it, and I believe there are others. But so far from supposing that this invalidates the great reality itself, I think it would be as wise to say, that the fanaticism into which the Jewish people frequently fell, in identifying themselves as "*the* people of God," disproves the fact that they were separated by God for a special purpose.

But history touches this truth, not merely in relation to Christ's own life, or that of His immediate followers; it records a long series of connected facts which preceded, and a long series of connected facts which succeeded, this. Does the one seem to anticipate and to culminate fairly in the mere sending of a new and great prophet? Does the other seem to derive its vital influence over the ages from the mere enunciations of a great departed prophet? Or does the harmonious development of the world's history seem to require at this point, some great focus of the world's life, some actual union of God and man—an Incarnation? There is no doubt that, at this point, the history of an Oriental people, whose great work it was to learn and to teach the personal government of a righteous God, blends with the history of the Gentile nations, with the fountains of Greek art and philosophy, with the system of Roman equity, with the whole civilization of the West; and all that it thus takes up into itself becomes coloured by a revolutionized form of the old Oriental faith. But may not the great crisis be accounted for by this very fact —the confluence of different streams of national life —without assuming any divine act greater than the sending of a new and more Catholic-minded prophet? I think not; for I think the Jewish history culminated *before* the influence of Greece or Rome rushed in; and that the Christian began, in germ and essence, *before* the confluence alluded to, though it was materially modified thereby. To me it seems that both the Jewish history is truncated and the Christian history maimed, if you disbelieve in a real Incarnation at the point where the two coalesce. The one would be a gradual ascent without a summit, a chain of purposes without a consummation

—the other a wide and permanent stream with a shallow and temporary source, a new life for man without a new source of inspiration. I will try and explain my meaning further.

The Jewish faith in a supreme supernatural Will, by whose fiat every event of Nature and every duty of man was determined, had, clearly, I think, an overpowering and overwhelming effect on the national character, as this Will grew into distincter outline. Righteous it was, but its righteousness was of a kind impossible and almost terrible to man; the Law was brilliant light, but it cast a heavy shadow; the prophets said, almost in despair, "Why should ye be stricken any more? Ye will revolt more and more. The whole head is sick, and the whole heart faint." It was felt that a link was wanted between the absolute, supreme, original Will, in whom all the universe rests, and the actual child-like life of human duty. The people of Israel, as I have said before, *crouched* beneath the brightness of God's presence. Their prophets felt more and more that it was not merely as a righteous king that God could reveal Himself so as best to purify and win back the nation; there must be, they began to learn, *between* the Father and human nature, some being lowly as the latter, perfect as the former, whose kingliness would not consist in mere righteous power, but in righteous humility, who rules man as man learns to rule himself, by perfect obedience and homage to Another. Hence the series of prophecies which are said to be fulfilled in Christ, which in the truest sense *are* so fulfilled, but which in the prophet's mind were often applied to more obvious and visible rulers. There was a yearning for a spiritual king whose title to rule should be lowliness and sympathy, who should be greatest of all, because "servant of all." The prophets discerned such a rule over the human spirit as real, though the ruler Himself was still behind the veil. Besides the Father, they began to speak of One who should be as "a shadow of a great rock in a weary land," of whom it might be said, "In all their afflictions he was afflicted, and the angel of his presence saved them; in his love and in his pity he redeemed them; and he bare them and carried them all the days of old;" of One who should suffer with us, and so rule us; who should be "wounded for our transgressions, bruised for our iniquities," and by whose "stripes we should be healed." Through all the later prophets this vision of a divine king, not original and absolute, not king in His own right, but by right of His humility, obedience, love for One above Himself, is as a softening thread which subdues the awfulness of the old faith, and strives to bridge the chasm between the human world and the immutable Jehovah.

The Babylonian conception of a hierarchy of angels tended, no doubt, to deepen this vein of thought, and to bridge the chasm of that solitary Omnipotence in which the old Jewish creed had enthroned God. But it was a moral more than an intellectual insight which revolted from this stern type of monotheism. The Jewish imagination was overwhelmed by the weight of unrelieved absolute power. It asked for a Messiah, not so much to restore the nation's destiny, as to fill up this fearful chasm between the created and finite life of man and the awful will of God. There was a growing hope that some king would appear who would not only vindicate the truth of the ancient promises, but supply the missing link between the creature, who cannot rule, and the Creator, who cannot obey. Such a yearning, such a shrinking from solitary Omnipotence, seems to me to run through the prophecies of Isaiah, and the meditations of Job, with a vividness that no adequate critic can ignore. And how the yearning for a Messiah, and for a *union of divine and human attributes* in that Messiah, grew between the return from captivity and the birth of Christ, we find, I think, extraordinary proofs in the growth of the Alexandrine Judaism, represented by Philo, and the strong leaning of the higher minds among the Jews, such as St. Paul's, towards the spirit of its teaching. It is clear, I think, that no new prophet, however great, could have satisfied this yearning, could have supplied the natural summit to this Jewish history, or the natural consummation of the chain of divine purposes which that history had embodied.

Again, looking from the chain of events which prepared the way for the Christian revelation to the chain of events which followed it, it seems still more difficult to believe that the latter could have derived their explanation from the oracles of a great prophet. Contrast the history of the Christian Church with that of Mahometanism. That Mahomet was a great and genuine prophet with a divine mission, I heartily believe. His prophecy has engraved itself on the hearts of millions who have never felt the fascination of the Christian faith. But history shows in many ways that it has its root only in the past; there is no growth in the faith, no power of adapting itself to the new ages. Mahomet *as he was* rules Mahometans *as they are*. His word was petrified and crystallised in Mecca, and can assimilate no new truth. It is an inorganic faith—a faith not only founded on, but imprisoned in, a rock. But the history of the Christian Church is a history of constant growth in spite of sacerdotal resistance, and I believe that the upward force of that growth has ever been the communion with a living Christ. Mere Theism, no doubt, has in it some expansive force, as the history of the Jews shows; but the immutability of the eternal attributes on which it rests throws too awful a shadow over human life, and requires a filial mediator in order to adapt them to the changing colours of human affections. A growing and social religion must, I feel sure, blend indissolubly the human with the divine. It was because Judaism was struggling upwards to this, that it did *not* become stereotyped and crystallised like Mahometanism.

And every great era in the Christian Church has been marked by a new insight into the bond between the divine and human attributes of Christ; the Father has been more or less vividly worshipped just in proportion as the life of the Son *in* humanity has been realised. To read the history of the Christian Church without the belief that Christ has been in vital and organic relation with it, seems to me to read it under the impression that a profound illusion can, for centuries, exercise more power for good than the truth. The Gospel, if it merely did for Christ, as Unitarians hold, what the Koran and personal traditions did for Mahomet, would have been an iron system of oracles, instead of a picture giving distinctness to, and interpreted by, a living inspiration; and the sooner it had been laid aside, except as a mere auxiliary to the living voice of God, the better. Surely all the expansive power of Christianity, all that adapts it to the purpose of the ages, has been directly due to the faith in a "light that lighteth every man which cometh into the world," and in the incarnation of that light in the human life of Jesus of Nazareth. Without this belief in the inward light, the reverence paid to the external life is a mere idolatry; without the belief in this external incarnation, the inward light is too apt to nourish human conceit and pantheistic dreams. And I cannot understand the history of the Christian Church at all if all the fervent trust which has been stirred by faith in the actual inspirations of a nature at once eternal and human, has been lavished on a dream.

It may be said that the importance assigned in this essay to the correspondence between a revelation and an inward want, is fatal to all doctrines of historical evidence

—that if our belief in facts is in any degree to vary with our *wish* to believe in them, history ceases to be a science, and becomes more or less mythic. But I think the objection is very easily answered to all who do believe in God. *That* reality, it is clear, is not exactly matter of historical evidence, though history and personal experience generate our faith in it. And once accepted, the evidence as to any of His outward actions must consist of two portions—its correspondence with the faith He puts into our hearts, and the external testimony. I could hold no fact of historical revelation without external testimony. Without Christ's assertion of His relation to the Father, without the evidence of St. Paul, and all the disciples, then and since, to His relation with their own spirits, in short, without the light which this faith throws on the history, both of the Jews and the Christian Church, I could not venture to build anything on the inward want for an incarnation. But with these external facts of history before me, I feel that I have far more right to build, and to build confidently, on that want which God puts into the heart, than I should have to think any evidence I receive of a friend's actions confirmed by correspondence with what I had known of his character.

Indeed, much of the argument which is directed against the possibility of evidence for the Incarnation, appears to me to go a good deal deeper and to be applicable directly to disprove the possibility of evidence for the existence of God. For instance, the same masterly writer whom I before quoted, the Rev. James Martineau, says in another essay, "Such a *fact* as the Incarnation, namely, that a seeming man, born, suffering, dying, was really Infinite God, incapable of birth, suffering, death, could never be assured to us but by those who are admitted behind the scene of the finite world. Mere witnesses, few or many, are useless here; they can tell us only what they have seen and heard; and this is a thing neither visible nor audible, and traceable by no characteristic and exclusive signs. Unless, therefore, those who affirm it can make good and claim to know what, humanly, is unknowable, the doctrine must be left to its place among the historical developments of religious faith," *i. e.*, as I suppose Mr. Martineau means, among the developments of religious fancy. Now substitute the following, and I do not see how whatever cogency this reasoning may have is diminished:—'Such a fact as the personal existence of an infinite God, incapable of change and passion, yet infinite in love, and divine provision for every temptation and suffering of finite creatures, could never be assured to us but by those who are admitted behind the scene of the finite world. Mere witnesses, few or many, are useless here; they can tell us only what they have seen and heard; and this is a thing neither visible nor audible, and traceable by no characteristic and exclusive signs. Unless, therefore, those who affirm it can make good a claim to know what, humanly, is unknowable, the doctrine must be left to its place among the historical developments of the reverential sentiment.' Yet Mr. Martineau would probably make very short work with this argument. Of course, no one supposes that the mere spectators of Christ's life, *simply as such,* can give any testimony as to His divine nature. Our Lord Himself expressly denied the possibility of such external testimony. When Peter made his confession, "Thou art the Christ, the son of the living God," He replied, "Flesh and blood hath not revealed it unto thee, but my father which is in heaven." St. Paul speaks, in precisely the same terms, of God having revealed His Son *in* Him, nor can I understand how any revelation at all of divine personality is possible, if it is not equally possible for the Father and the Son. That all revelation implies "admission behind the scene of the finite world," is, I should think, more of a truism than a truth. There is, certainly, no more intrinsic difficulty in God's communicating to the spirits of men, "This is my beloved son, hear ye him," than in His communicating, "I am that I am." And to my mind the former communication is the natural complement of the latter. Historical evidence seems to me to have nearly the same relation to the development of Theism as to the development of Christianity; and as the fact that Judaism shows a wonderful development in its teaching as to the character of God, is no subversion, but rather a confirmation of its divine claims, so the fact that Christianity shows a wonderful development in its teaching as to the nature of Christ, seems to me no subversion, but rather a confirmation of its divine claims.

And now, to come to an end, let me ask myself, and answer the question as truly as I can, whether this great, this stupendous fact of the Incarnation is honestly *believable* by any ordinary man of modern times, who has not been educated into it, but educated to distrust it, who has no leaning to the "orthodox" creed as such, but has very generally preferred to associate with heretics, who is quite alive to the force of the scientific and literary scepticisms of his day, who has no antiquarian tastes, no predilection for the venerable past, who does not regard this truth as part of a great system dogmatic or ecclesiastical, but merely for itself—who is, in a word, simply anxious to take hold, if he so may, of any divine hand stretched out to help him through the excitements and the languor, the joy, the sorrow, the storm and sunshine, of this unintelligible life? From my heart I answer Yes :—believable and more than believable in any mood in which we can rise above ourselves to that supernatural Spirit which orders the "unruly wills and affections of sinful men"—*more* than believable, I say, because it so vivifies and supplements that fundamental faith in God as to realise what were otherwise abstract, and, without dissolving the mystery, to clothe eternal love with breathing life. God Himself is not believable while we wander helplessly in the labyrinth of mere natural phenomena, or lose ourselves in the mystery of "the infinitudes," or surrender ourselves captive to the newest phase of "modern thought," or disguise our true natures with the affectations of antique mannerisms, or attempt to create Him out of our own conscience, or to find a place for Him in our dogmatic creeds.

But whenever and however we so escape from ourselves as to acknowledge a living and eternal Lord, then it seems to me to be not harder, but easier, to confess Him as something more than this; as One who has revealed to us the very essence of His nature through the Son who was with Him before the world was. It is not harder, but easier, to trust in a Will unveiled, than in one still veiled; to confess the Father of that eternal Son who pours the light of filial love into every human conscience, and who has shown us that not power nor knowledge, but free goodness alone, is of the inmost essence of the divine nature. I confess that human reason is wholly unable to comprehend eternity, but it seems to me far easier to *apprehend* it, to take hold on it, to believe in it, *with* this revealing Incarnation than without it. To *fancy* that we trust in God may be easier while He remains simply what He was to Faust, the "All-embracer, the All-sustainer;" but to trust in Him really, to believe He can help us to reduce the vulgar chaos of our English life to any order resting on an eternal basis, is far easier if we believe that the very same mind is shining into our own consciences which entered into the poorest of lots among nearly the most degraded generation of the most narrow-minded race that the world has ever known, and made it the birthplace of a new earth. To trust in God adequately we ask not merely to recognise His power, but to know Him as He is—His character, His *actions* as distinct from our actions. The answer comes to us in the shape of a revelation that the Father is no solitary and self-enveloped being, that there is One who shared with Him eternity, who is always at the sources of our human life, who entered into our very lot in one of its least attractive forms, and of whom it is said, "This is my beloved son; hear ye him." Surely it is easier to trust in One so revealed than in any glory from which the veil has never been withdrawn. To me, at all events, it is so. This faith alone satisfies me that I do not aspire after anything "higher and holier than the truth," but that the truth which lays hold upon my mind is infinitely higher and holier than anything I can elaborate for myself. Without the Incarnation, Christianity seems to me a vague idealism. In it alone I find the Word, "who is quick and powerful as any two-edged sword."

VIII.

M. RENAN'S 'CHRIST.'

M. RENAN'S 'Vie de Jésus'[1] is no common book. To me, indeed, it seems an attempt to conjure up, by the aid of great learning and greater imagination, a mighty phantom in the place of the Son of God and the Son of Man;—to paint the majestic lines of His character who "spake as never man spake," as converging on an imaginary focus, and as presenting, therefore, a distorted and exaggerated image of humanity, instead of the simple beauty of divine life. Still, it is a book that is honest, learned, and vigorous: studded here and there with touches of true genius, and, above all, is a sincere endeavour to solve the problem which scepticism usually repudiates, wilfully depriving itself thereby of all popular claim. If the world is to be robbed of the great and

---

[1] 'Vie de Jésus.' Par Ernest Renan, Membre de l'Institut. Paris, Michel Levy; London, Williams and Norgate, 1863.

solemn objects of its trust, those who undermine its worship are, I think, bound to substitute, so far as they can, what they do believe themselves, in place of the popular images which they break before our eyes. Hitherto they have not done so. They have been content with Strauss and Baur to dissipate by analysis forms and scenes which they have not attempted, even where it was possible for them, to remodel and restore.

M. Renan does not fall into this error. His purpose differs from that of former sceptical critics mainly in this, that he attempts to *reconstruct* the life of Christ, though without any supernatural elements, instead of to analyse those elements away,—that he strives to restore by the bold strokes of no contemptible art the life-like features of a portrait in which all the most characteristic traditional expressions have been condemned as spurious. What Strauss and Baur have rejected, M. Renan for the most part rejects also; but, nevertheless, he does not despair of giving back purpose, power, and majesty, to the figure thus disrobed of all the drapery in which centuries of faith had enveloped it. I think it has, in fact, proved the destiny of this book to awaken the educated intellect of Europe far more effectually to the greatest problem of human history, than any of its more theoretical predecessors. It is exactly because there is little or no novelty in its premisses, nothing that has not long been familiar to every student of the recent criticism, that it has strung the intellectual nerve of the Christian Church to face honestly and answer adequately the greatest question that can task human thought. For it is the first time that any man of high power, putting aside what he believes to be supernatural and therefore false, has sought to explain honestly to himself,—without, except in one memorable instance, needlessly narrow and ungenerous criticism,—the part which our Lord has played in the history of the world. M. Renan fails, of course, utterly, as every effort of imaginative genius, however great, must fail, in trying to exclude from his vision the radical fact with which he has to deal,—to think vividly, and yet think away the very essence he is handling; but he fails honestly and sincerely, never intentionally suppressing anything, and allowing us to see clearly at every step that the rationalistic hypothesis which he professes to take as the groundwork of his picture, is one whose essence it is to dissipate almost all the true colours that he strives to lay on. He grapples with his subject with a great and often subtle force that cannot but rouse all the genuine vigour of Christian conviction to interrogate its own thought in the same spirit. There is but one blot on the manner in which, granted his premisses, his work has been done.

The first sketch of his book was traced amidst the scenes of the Gospel history, and it was concluded under the very shadow of death. Its dedication, though to English ears it may want the reserve in which, perhaps, we too much delight to shroud private grief, is too striking a guarantee of the earnest purpose of the book to be passed over by those who wish, as I do, to reproduce honestly the sort of impression it is calculated to make, before they attempt to point out how its genius and insight seem to be in conflict with the ground-principle which underlies and runs through it. In 1860 and 1861 the French scientific mission for the exploration of Phœnicia, headed by M. Renan, led him to reside for some time on the borders of Galilee, and to travel repeatedly through almost every scene of our Lord's life. During the summer he retired with his sister to Ghazir, in the Lebanon, for rest, and while his impressions were yet fresh in his mind wrote out rapidly his preliminary sketch of the 'Life of Jesus.' It was to this stay that we owe the following dedication :—

"TO THE PURE SPIRIT OF MY SISTER HENRIETTE, WHO DIED AT BYBLUS, 24TH SEPTEMBER, 1861.

"Do you remember, from your rest in the bosom of God, those long days at Ghazir, where, alone with you, I wrote these pages, inspired by the scenes we had just traversed? Silent at my side, you read every leaf, and copied it out as soon as written, while the sea, the villages, the ravine, the mountains, unrolled themselves at our feet. When the overwhelming light of the sun had given place to the innumerable army of stars, your fine and delicate questions, your discreet doubts, brought me back to the sublime object of our common thoughts. One day you said that you should love this book—first, because it had been written with you, and also because it pleased you. If sometimes you feared for it the narrow judgments of the frivolous man, you were always persuaded that spirits truly religious would in the end be pleased with it. In the midst of these sweet meditations Death struck us both with his wing; the sleep of fever seized us both in the same hour; I awoke alone! You sleep now in the land of Adonis, near the holy Byblus and the sacred waters where the women of the ancient mysteries came to mingle their tears. Reveal to me, my good genius, to me whom you loved, those truths which over-master Death, which wholly prevent us from fearing, and make us almost love it."

These are lines which no man could trace without a deep conviction that his thoughts had been double-sifted through both a sincere intellect and a sincere spirit: and so, in truth, painfully as M. Renan's pages often impress me, I believe it to be. Indeed, even before his sister's death, his familiarity with the scenes of Christ's life seems to have powerfully affected his imagination:—
"All this history," he says, "which at a distance seemed to float in the clouds of an unreal world, now took a body and solidity which astonished me. The striking agreement of the text and the places, the marvellous harmony of the evangelical ideal with the country which served as a frame to the picture, were for me like a revelation. I had before my eyes a fifth gospel, injured but still decipherable, and from that time forward, through the narratives of Matthew and Mark, in place of an abstract being whom one might think had never existed, I saw an admirable human figure live and move." Let me try to reproduce M. Renan's "admirable human figure," before I attempt very briefly to criticise his work.

Jesus of Nazareth, then, he sketches as originally a simple, contemplative, innocent, rustic saint, with a villager's childlike ideas of the kingdoms of the world and the glories of a Court. These ideas he expresses in his parables about kings, says M. Renan, with the most delightful *naïveté* and want of *connaissance des choses*,— but with a religious fire of love burning in his heart, a profound apprehension of God as his Father, and that ardour to bring others to the same love of Him, which gives force, dignity, and breadth to the least experienced wisdom. His whole nature revolted against the hard and false sanctimony of Pharisaism. With regard to the Law, he had eagerly accepted the teaching, then widely disseminated among the Jews, of the school of Hillel, who, his predecessor by fifty years, had "by his humbly borne poverty, by the gentleness of his character, by the opposition which he offered to the hypocrites and priests, earned the right to be regarded as the true master of Jesus, if one may speak of a master at all in relation to an originality so great." But it would not be for even the widest interpreters of the Law, says M. Renan, that Christ can have felt any great fascination. The Psalms, Isaiah, and the more recent Messianic literature, beginning with the Book of Daniel, and continued in the Apocryphal Book of Henoch, had for many reasons a greater imaginative charm for the genius of the young prophet. It is from the Book of Daniel that he drew the Messianic title of "Son of Man," which, with a fine appreciation of his own exquisitely human genius, he reserved especially for himself. Moreover, the attempt in these books to sketch the future course of history was the origin of Christ's own great millennial dreams, and the source of much of his imaginative power over his countrymen.

It was the sublimity of these visions which raised the popular poetry of the Jews so far above that of the classical nations. "Greece," says M. Renan, "traced charming pictures of human life in sculpture and poetry, but always without evanescent backgrounds or distant horizons. Here there are wanting the marble, the practised workman, the exquisite and refined language. But Galilee raised for the popular imagination a more sublime ideal, since behind its idyls you see swaying in the balance the destiny of humanity, and the light which shines upon its pictures is the sun of the kingdom of God." Into such a heritage of thoughts and pictures Jesus, says M. Renan, early entered, feeding his heart first upon his own spiritual intercourse with his Father, then upon the gentle and anti-ceremonial wisdom of Hillel, lastly on the pure poetry of the Psalms, the wonderful visions of the Prophets, and those growing stores of Apocalyptic literature which, in boldly venturing to identify the destiny of the Jews with the destiny of the whole human race, had given the first impulse to what we now call the philosophy of history, and so rivetted the high speculative imagination of Jesus. It is now no more possible, says M. Renan, to throw ourselves back into Christ's position, "than for the earth to understand the phenomena of the primitive creation, now that the fire which then penetrated it has died out." Jesus had no notion, indeed, says M. Renan, of physical law, and to him the miracle which arrests sickness and death was nothing but "the free volition of God," and, therefore, nothing extraordinary. "But in his great spirit such a belief produced effects quite opposite to those which it produced on the vulgar. With the vulgar, faith in the particular action of the Deity brought with it a silly credulity and the trickery of charlatans. With him it led to a profound idea of the familiar relations between God and man, and an exaggerated belief in the power of man,—beautiful errors which were the secret of his power; for if they were one day to lower him in the eyes of the physician and the chemist, they gave him a power over his time of which no man ever disposed either before or since."

Add to all this the freedom of his life in Galilee before his boldness brought down upon him the death he almost courted,—a freedom which no modern society, hedged in by conventional rules and positive laws, can understand,—for the medical laws of France alone, says our author, would have at once put a stop to that irregular and empiric practice of healing the multitude which was one great source of his power with them,—and M. Renan gains some faint vision of the favourable conditions under which his great character grew to such unexampled sublimity. In the free life under the open sky of Galilee he risked everything, no doubt, but great risks are only a stimulus to a truly creative mind; it is the petty fetters of an omnipresent social police, cutting and clipping life to a given pattern, which dwarf the growth and stunt the greatness of modern humanity. "That mountain summit of Nazareth, where no man of modern days can sit without a troubled feeling, perhaps frivolous, about his destiny—there Jesus sat twenty years without a doubt. Delivered from self-seeking, the source of our troubles, which makes us seek bitterly for some interest in virtue beyond the tomb, he thought only on his work, on his nation, on the human race. Those mountains, that sea, that azure heaven, those high table-lands on the horizon, were for him not the melancholy vision of a soul which interrogates Nature about its lot, but the certain symbol, the transparent shadow, of an invisible world and a new heaven." Thus love of his spiritual Father, Hebrew poetry, the living spirit of the Law, the visions of a Messianic age that should include the whole race of man, his ignorance of science and belief in the plenary force of divine volition, the political freedom of his time which scarcely interfered with individual action except to slay at once, the beauty of Nature about him, and —part result of all these, part cause,—his wonderful power of inspiring love in the simple men and women around,—all tended, says our author, to raise to the highest intensity a character of marvellous breadth and force.

One touch is so true and so original in M. Renan, that believers in our Lord may thank him heartily for it, and I have, therefore, reserved it to the last. There was never in the world, says M. Renan, a character so little capable of entering into shades of thought and feeling (*nuances*) as the Semitic. The hard contrasts and bitter ruptures which mark all the Jewish history are full of testimonies to this defect. The lines of dividing light and shadow are more harsh and strong than the shadow lines of moonlight. But "Jesus, who was exempt from almost all the defects of his race, and whose dominant characteristic was an infinite delicacy," was an exception to the rule. Hence, in great measure, perhaps, his wonderful power over women, whom, says M. Renan, he,—wrapped in divine ideas, and, half careless of human ties, except as ministering to the development of human thoughts,—treated with the tenderness of "a vague poetry." Finally, and for much the same reason, our author thinks that, while tolerating the State or civil power, he always speaks of it with an essential "irony," and regarded it in his heart as at best an external alleviation, and utterly inadequate remedy, for the ills of human society.

Such is a sketch, in many respects remarkable for insight and beauty, of the character of Him from whom M. Renan wishes to withdraw all faith that may not be given to man. It is not easy to feel equal respect for the spirit of his narrative of our Lord's life. Working with the unmanageable hypothesis that everything supernatural is false, there are two constant and perpetually recurring obstacles to anything like a high appreciation. In the first place, Christ's whole life is inextricably intertwined with a belief in His own kingdom and His absolute relation with God, through which, indeed, others might come to the Father, but not without His intermediate agency to bestow the true spirit of the Son; next, it is not only full, but fuller and fuller as the end draws near, of the assertion of His power—if men will only consent—to break every yoke from that of sin and suffering to that of death itself.

M. Renan sees this, and is forced to adopt the hypothesis of a partial degeneration of the character of Jesus, as the *exigeant* claims of his own asserted Messiahship forced him to vindicate them to the world. Had he died after the Sermon on the Mount, or the declaration of that "only absolute religion" by the well of Samaria, "God is a spirit, and they that worship him must worship him in spirit and in truth," then "there would not have been in his life any page to grieve us;—but greater in the eyes of God, he would have been ignored by man. He would have been lost in the crowd of great unknown spirits, the greatest of all." Fortunately for us, says M. Renan, it was not so. Jesus did not come "stainless out of the struggle of life," or he would have been unable to influence life. "*Au fond* the Ideal is always a Utopia." "Every idea loses something of its purity from the moment it aspires to realise itself." It was the instinct of genius for acting upon the world that led Jesus into the Messianic groove of thought. It was that, says M. Renan, that soiled his purity, though without it he could never have founded a lasting Church. If he had any original defect it was a want of that which we moderns call absolute sincerity with ourselves—a virtue almost unknown to the ancient world, scarcely possible to its half-developed consciousness, and its wholly undeveloped science. Modern veracity, M. Renan thinks, is half a product of exact science, which has given to faithfulness in details a new importance. If, therefore, M. Renan denies this to Jesus in its highest degree, he deprecates the notion that he is denying to him what the same denial would mean in modern times, and in the west of Europe. "Sincerity with oneself," says M. Renan, "has not much meaning with Orientals, little habituated as they are to the delicate distinctions of the critical spirit. Good faith and imposture are words which, to our rigid conscience, are as irreconcileable as logical opposites. In the East there are, in passing from the one to the other, a thousand shades of evasion and indirectness. All great things spring from the people, but one cannot guide the people except by concessions to their ideas. . . . The philosopher who, knowing this, isolates himself, and entrenches himself in his nobility, is worthy of high praise. But he who takes humanity with its illusions, and seeks to act upon it and with it, could not be blamed. Cæsar knew very well that he was not the son of Venus. France would not be what she is if men had not believed for a thousand years in the holy vial of Rheims. It is easy for us, impotent as we are, to call this Falsehood, and, glorying in our timid honesty, to treat with disdain the heroes who have accepted, under other conditions, the struggle of life. When we have done with our scruples what they did with their falsehoods, we shall have won the right to be hard on them."

Accordingly, M. Renan, trying to conceive the truth of the life of Jesus from a rationalising point of view, sees even in his first years, " innocent artifices," such as the attempting to persuade Nathanael into the belief that he had a certain supernatural knowledge of his thoughts under the fig-tree; and believes that the Messianic claim which he set up in perfect good faith, and held earnestly to the last, led him deeper towards the close of his career into that Oriental *finesse* for a good end, which M. Renan deems so little blameable. He believes that throughout, Jesus, believing himself in his own miracles of healing, was still uncomfortable as to the extent and amplitude of his powers, that in consequence of this feeling, as well as the deeper fascination of his spiritual and Messianic ideas, he felt and frequently betrayed that impatience of the appetite for miracle which occasionally escaped him, and that, in short, he rather underwent (*subissait*) the miracles which the people and his disciples demanded of him, than worked them, or, still less, courted the opportunity of working them. But this demand upon him grew as his claims to the Messiahship spread. And hence M. Renan seeks to explain the great miracle of the resurrection of Lazarus in a fashion wholly unworthy of his own purely naturalistic conception of Christ—in a fashion which is, indeed, the great literary blot on his book. He inclines to believe that a fictitious resurrection was got up as a "pious fraud" at Bethany by the family of Lazarus, and that their Master, after weeping genuinely for the supposed death of his friend, on Lazarus's return from the tomb permitted the reputation of his miraculous recall to life to be attributed to him without denial. The friends of Jesus would never have hesitated, he thinks, to force thus the hand of their Master. "Faith knows no law but the interest of that which it believes to be true. If *this* proof were not solid, how many were! Intimately persuaded that Jesus was a worker of wonders, Lazarus and his two sisters might have helped one of his miracles into execution, as so many pious men, convinced of the truth of their religion, have sought to triumph over the obstinacy of men, by expedients of which they well knew the feebleness. . . . As for Jesus, he was no more than St. Bernard and St. Francis of Assisium, able to master the greediness of the crowd and of his own disciples for the marvellous. Death, besides, was about in a few days to give him back his divine liberty, and to rescue him from the fatal necessities of a part which became each day more *exigeant*, more difficult to sustain."

Thus has the "innocent artifice," which began by playing a moral legerdemain with Nathanael's conscience, developed into a toleration of a "pious fraud" far grosser than even Pharisaic consciences were wont to tolerate! The woe which Christ had so lately denounced on "the scribes and Pharisees, hypocrites, like unto whited sepulchres, which appear beautiful outwardly, but within are full of dead men's bones and of all uncleanness," would surely, according to this great literary no less than spiritual blunder, have recoiled on the head of M. Renan's 'Jesus.' Such a conspirator as this cannot be identified even with M. Renan's great but rapidly degenerating hero. It is the only thread of thought in the book which I feel inclined to call not only erroneous, but impious.

Moreover, the necessity of his false Messianic position led our Lord, in M. Renan's view, not only into duplicity but fanaticism. I will conclude the merely expository part of my review with a very remarkable passage, in which he strives to delineate the growing fever which burnt up the soul of his imaginary hero as the necessity of his position grew more and more urgent :—

"We easily understand that for Jesus, at the period at which we have now arrived, all that was not the kingdom of God had absolutely disappeared. He was, if one may say so, entirely beyond the limits of nature (*totalement hors de la nature*)—family, friendship, country, had no longer any meaning for him. Without doubt he had from this time made the sacrifice of his life. Sometimes one is tempted to think that seeing in his own death a means of founding his kingdom, he deliberately conceives the purpose of making his foes kill him.[1] At other times, though such a thought was not till much later elevated into a dogma, death presents itself to him as a sacrifice destined to appease his Father and to save men.[2] A strange taste for persecution and tortures penetrated him (Luke vi. 22, and following). His own blood appeared to him like the water of a second baptism with which he had yet to be baptized, and he seemed seized with a strange haste to anticipate this baptism, which alone could quench his thirst. The grandeur of his views on the future was at moments surprising. He did not conceal from himself the fearful storm which he was to raise in the world. 'You believe, perhaps,' he said, with boldness and beauty, 'that I came to bring peace on earth; I did not come to bring peace but to throw down a sword. In one house of five persons three shall be against two, and two against three. I came to bring division between the son and the father, between the daughter and the mother, between the daughter-in-law and the mother-in-law. In future, a man's foes

---

[1] Matthew xvi. 21-23; xvii. 12 and 22, 23.   [2] Mark x. 45.

shall be those of his own household.' 'I came to bring fire on earth, and so much the better if it be already burning.' 'They will deliver you from the synagogues, and the hour will come when, in killing you, they will think to render God service. If the world hates you, know that it hated me before you. Remember the word I have said unto you, the servant is not greater than his Lord. If they have persecuted me, they will persecute you also.' Carried away by this frightful access of enthusiasm, compelled by the necessities of a preaching more and more exalted, Jesus was no longer free. He belonged to his part, and in a sense to humanity. Sometimes one would say that his reason was disturbed. He had something like agonies and interior agitations.[3] The great vision of the kingdom of God glancing without cessation before his eyes, turned him giddy (*lui donnait le vertige*). His disciples at moments believed him insane.[4] His enemies declared him possessed.[5] His temperament, full of passion, carried him every instant beyond the bounds of human nature. His work being one not of reason, and playing (*se jouant*) with all the classifications of the human spirit, what it demanded most imperiously was 'faith.' This word was that which was oftenest repeated in the little church. It is the word of all popular movements. It is evident that none of these movements would succeed if it were necessary that their leader should gain all his disciples, one after the other, by good proofs logically deduced. Reflection leads only to doubt, and if the authors of the French Revolution, for example, had had to be preliminarily convinced by adequately long meditation, they would have all arrived at old age without doing anything. Jesus, in the same way, looked less to inspiring regular conviction than to carrying away his hearers. Urgent, imperative, he suffered no opposition. One must be converted; he is waiting. His natural sweetness seems to have deserted him; he was sometimes rough and *bizarre*.[6] His disciples at times did not understand him, and felt before him a sort of sentiment of fear.[7] Sometimes his displeasure against all opposition carried him

---

[3] John xii. 27.
[4] Mark iii. 21, and following.
[5] John vii. 20; viii. 48; x. 20.
[6] Matthew xvii. 16; Mark iii. 5; ix. 19; Luke viii. 45; ix. 41.
[7] Mark iv. 40; v. 15; ix. 31; x. 32.

away into acts inexplicable and even absurd.[8] It was not that his virtue was declining, but his struggle in the name of the ideal against reality became insupportable. He bruised himself, and recoiled from contact with the earth. Obstacles irritated him. His notion of the Son of God became troubled and exaggerated. The fatal law which condemns the idea to decay from the moment that it seeks to convert men took effect in his case. Men, in touching him, lowered him to their level. The tone which he had taken could not be sustained beyond a few months; it was time for death to come and unloose the knot of a situation of the extremest tension, relieve him from the impossibilities of a path without issue, and, by delivering him from a trial too prolonged, introduce him, for the future sinless, into his heavenly peace."

Such is, I think, a fair, at all events an anxiously candid account of a book, which I believe to contain the most genuine and devout attempt to explain our Lord's life, if I may reasonably use such an expression, *from below*, that I have ever met with. Wholly and painfully at issue with its principle, I sincerely believe the book has done almost unmixed good. It is too earnest in tone to attract mere sceptical levity. And for thinkers of any other kind, whether holding to the Incarnation or not, it has put for the first time the full issue, in a practical form, before their—I will not say imaginations, but rather before *themselves*. If M. Renan's striking picture has not called up within them a figure far more striking, and yet also far more real, if their hearts have not so far burned within them even at the traits which M. Renan occasionally brings out so finely as to shrivel up to dust much of his appended literary theory, if even through

---

[8] Mark xi. 12, 14, 20, &c.

this sincere but warped interpretation, "the thoughts of many hearts" have not been so far revealed as to awaken other and deeper thoughts, which M. Renan either ignores or rejects, I must have read this book under the shadow of some great illusion. I have never read a professedly sceptical book that tended more powerfully to strengthen the faith which it struggles to supplant. In trying to dispel the darkness cast by mere negative criticism, and to throw the light of the new theory more fully on the image of Christ, M. Renan seems to me to have constantly and involuntarily used expressions which snatch us away altogether out of the ostensible plane of his own thought. You shift your point of view uneasily to catch his meaning, and re-examine the citations by which he supports it, and suddenly his words take a new effect on the mind, and instead of justifying a forced criticism from below, they unseal your sight to a fresh illumination from above.

The one great difficulty, it will have been seen, which M. Renan evidently feels most keenly, is the reconciliation of something large, sunny, and sometimes almost playful, in the character of Jesus, with the vehemence, the force of passion, the overbearing self-sacrifice of tone which he discerns in other passages of Christ's life, and which seem to his keen eye to put Christ almost altogether "out of the plane of Nature," and present Him as living for the Ideal, every human tie sundered or despised, in bitter conflict with reality. The bright vision of the kingdom of God seems, at times, says M.

Renan, to turn the brain of Jesus giddy, and burn too fiercely and exhaustingly into the tender sympathies of His humanity; at other times the "vague poetry" of His tenderness for women, the delicate sense of moral *nuances* amid the bleak forms and desolate grandeur of the Semitic thought, the sweet elasticity of His filial faith, that could bear all things except hypocrisy, the patient tolerance of His bearing towards the civil power, the sunny freedom of His love for nature, strike M. Renan with equal surprise, as the characteristics rather of a wise poet than a burning prophet.

The two do seem inconsistent, and the scientific artifice by which M. Renan has reconciled them is scarcely worthy a moment's consideration. As we have seen, he gets over the difficulty by pushing back the gentle characteristics into the earlier period of the life of Jesus, and postponing the more passionate to the later. On examining his references, however, one may see that there is not the remotest biographical ground for this device. Many of the more commanding and scathing words attributed to Him belong, if there be any reliable dates at all in His career, to the earliest period of our Lord's life. M. Renan, with what I believe to be a thoroughly true critical insight, holds to the external narrative of St. John's gospel, though unfriendly, and, indeed, thoroughly unjust, to its report of Christ's discourses. But, judged by this gospel, the severest and most decidedly Elijah-like act of Christ's life, His cleansing of the Temple, was immediately consequent on His first intercourse with John the Baptist. And looking not only to that, but to all the other gospels, I cannot doubt that the severest of His conflicts with the Pharisees is by no means to be placed in the last period of His ministry. Probably, there is no period in His life which is so fully penetrated with the divine sunlight of His tenderness as the period before and during the last parting. If tradition has any chronological value at all, that period, when the box of ointment was shed upon Him, when He wept over the doomed city, when He warned Peter of his coming fall, washed the feet of the disciples, told the daughters of Jerusalem to weep not for Him though the cross was even then being set up before His eyes, but to weep for themselves and for their children, and finally prayed for forgiveness on His enemies, was not a period of zeal withering all human ties, and putting Him beyond the plane of Nature, but of marvellous and surpassing love, such as could not easily be matched in our accounts of the Galilean period. M. Renan's attempt to trace a history of gradual absorption into an idea, of a dizzied brain, and enthusiasm almost drying up the fountains of human charity, has not even the shadow of a foundation. If there be a period still traceable in our imperfect records of a more prophetic force of denunciation than any other, it is an *earlier* period, before the end closed in, and there still seemed to glimmer some hope that the Pharasaic phalanx might be pierced. Yet that there are these two striking contrasts in Christ's character,—the luxuriant beauty and the forked lightning,—M. Renan has truly discerned; may not Christ's own constantly repeated account of their origin be the true one, "Whatsoever I speak therefore, even as the Father saith unto me, so I speak"? The divine charity and the divine wrath are only rays broken in two by the imperfections of man. In the Son of God, whose mind moves in perfect harmony with His Father's, they may exist together, though they shine separately for us.

The same voice which runs through the Old Testament, a voice awful with tender reproach, reminding the Jewish people that God had chosen them, not they Him, that He had purged their vision that they might discern Him, that He had sanctified them by patient discipline, "line upon line and precept upon precept,"—this same voice runs also through the Gospels. " Thou Israel art my servant, whom I have chosen, whom I have taken from the ends of the earth, and said unto thee, thou art my servant, I have chosen thee, and not cast thee away. Fear thou not for I am with thee; be not dismayed, for I am thy God." "Ah, sinful nation, a people laden with iniquity; they have forsaken the Lord, they have provoked the holy one of Israel to anger, they have gone away backward." Such is the constant refrain of the Old Testament; and the voice of the Gospels is its human counterpart : "Ye have not chosen me, but I have chosen you." "Be of good cheer, it is I, be not afraid." "Oh faithless and perverse generation, how long shall I be with you, how long shall I suffer you?" The tenderness may be greater in the New Testament—for the deep sense of human brotherhood is there, which but barely tinges now and then the greatest and maturest of the prophetic visions of the Old—but the Christ of the Gospels is, even when gentlest and most fraternal, a softened and reflected image of the Hebrew Jehovah:—the fierce sun of the desert mirrored in the Galilean lake. "The Lord found Israel," says the song of Moses, "in a desert land, and in the waste howling wilderness; he led him about, he instructed him; he kept him as the apple of his eye. As an eagle stirreth up her nest, fluttereth over her young, spreadeth abroad her wings, taketh them, beareth them on her wings, so the Lord alone did lead him." "Oh Jerusalem, Jerusalem," says our Lord, "that killest the prophets and stonest them which are sent unto thee, how often would I have gathered thy children together, as a hen gathereth her chickens under her wings, and ye would not!"

M. Renan has delineated with almost equal power that aspect of Christ in which He "cometh from Edom, with dyed garments from Bozrah, glorious in apparel, travelling in the greatness of his strength," and is said to have "trodden the winepress alone," and that in which it is said of Him that "in all their affliction he was afflicted, and the angel of his presence saved them;" and that "in his love and in his pity he redeemed them, and he bare them and carried them all the days of old,"—only M. Renan has severed the blended rays, and so disguised from us "the glory of God shining in the face of Jesus Christ." Yet I have learned afresh from his negative criticisms that the character which looms so awfully through Jewish history is presented to us again in the Gospels, though with the new attitude of an upward and filial as well as the downward and protecting gaze. For the rest, all the lineaments of awe and pity, royalty and love, everlasting patience and fire-sifting judgment, are the same. And M. Renan, while he proves once more the indisputable imperfections of the human records, leaves me with a far more burning image in my heart of that eternal character of which all Jewish history is full to overflowing, than I could have had, had he not thus ably striven to divide by an infinite chasm the "life of Jesus" from the life of God.

Indeed, to those who can believe entirely in the reality of the Incarnation, and at the times when they can utterly believe it,—to those who can have faith in the entrance of the eternal Son for a season into a finite nature and mortal consciousness,—who can see that this is something far as the poles asunder from that *affectation* of a human part by Omniscience, which pseudo-Orthodox theology so often confounds with it,—for these all M. Renan's difficulties fade away, while all the gleams of new light his book has given, remain. The *naïf* and inexperienced Galilean peasant, speaking of Courts with a villager's vague impressions, and looking at the world without any sign of insight into the scientific discoveries of ages yet to come, foreseeing with rapture the divine kingdom and divine judgments, but only through the semi-transparent light of those "times and seasons which the Father hath kept in his own power,"—showing forth adequately His divine personality and origin only in the fulness and perfection of His communion with His Father's will, but unfolding that will to man through the limited forms and imperfect conceptions of His age and nation,—working miracles, as He spoke, not at His own will, but at the will of Him who sent Him, in short, continuing under the conditions of shortsighted humanity the spiritual life He had lived in the plenitude of His heavenly intercourse with God, and so linking together eternity with time, the divine purposes *behind* the laws of nature, with their steady and seemingly inexorable course,—this figure, surely, is far more true, as well as far more noble, than M. Renan's composite Jesus.

Nay, more, this mystery seems to me in no way harder, in many ways far easier to lay hold of, than M. Renan's Absolute Spirit, who inspires man with ideas which necessarily degenerate in practice, who can breathe into man true thoughts, but cannot teach him to act true actions. If one could concede that a belief in *revealing* miracles is justifiable only by such external evidence as would be required for mere marvels,—if one could grant, too, that Christ's avowed spiritual certainty of the unique and immanent character of His relation to the Father was necessarily a fanatical belief, then M. Renan's doubts and his imputations of innocent artifice and Oriental unscrupulousness would be all justified; while his gleams of insight would remain monuments of generous credulity.

I could grant neither premiss; but have to thank this spiritual sceptic for new glimpses into the power of a faith which he regards with pity; and for a deeper apprehension of that purity which he considers safe from pollution only while it remains unmanifested,—while it is cloistered in the solitude of a fruitless ideal world.

IX.

M. RENAN'S 'ST. PAUL.'

"JE persiste donc"—says M. Renan, in concluding his estimate of the apostle of the Gentiles,—"je persiste donc à trouver que dans la création du Christianisme la part de St. Paul doit être faite bien inférieure "à celle de Jésus,"—a "persistence" which surely, on any view whatever of Christianity, hardly requires greater courage than that of the astronomer who should say, 'I persist, then, that in the constitution of our system, the part of the planet Jupiter ought to be accounted very inferior to that of the sun.' But what a little surprises me, and has, I think, surprised a good many of M. Renan's readers, is to find themselves compelled to "persist" that in the brilliant French critic's history of the sources of Christianity, the volume on St. Paul is very inferior to the volume on Christ. I had anticipated that the man who could come so near to painting a divine intensity of light, even while strenuously interpolating those dark lines in its spectrum which are admitted to be characteristic of human weakness and sin, would have given a portrait of St. Paul such as almost every one would have admired and recognised as absolutely faithful, however much they might have differed as to the truth or fallaciousness of St. Paul's beliefs and hopes.

But it would seem that M. Renan's interest in the problem of Christianity fades rather rapidly as he recedes from the central figure of the faith. He strained every nerve to explain to us how he accounted, on rationalistic principles, for the one great light which has so gone out to the ends of the earth that hardly anything in human history is hid from the heat thereof; but when he comes to account for those who were not that light, but only bore witness of that light, his interest declines visibly, and the great superior planet with its satellites painted in the present treatise, are lit up by his imagination not only far more faintly in themselves, but far more faintly even in proportion to their relative magnitude and brightness in Christian history, than was the central sun itself. I do not think he has even approached the power of his first essay. I doubt if St. Paul will be at all more visible to any of his readers when they close the volume than he was when they opened it. There is scarcely an attempt to realize St. Paul's state of mind in relation to Christianity *from within.* The dualism of effect between M. Renan's sketch and his occasional extracts from the letters of St. Paul is quite painful. Even St. Paul's character itself seems to me not unfrequently fundamentally misunderstood—as when "jealousy" is described as its basis, in reference, of course, to St. Paul's intense anxiety to be recognised as an apostle of equal authority with the twelve. The ruggedness of his hero fills M. Renan with a sort of disgust. He harps on the impassable chasm between St. Paul's crabbed theories of justification and the gracious parables of the gospel. He relates, too, almost with contempt, St. Paul's celebrated effort—a very clumsy effort he evidently regards it—to Christianize Athens, intimating very explicitly that if St. Paul had the advantage in some respects, the Athenian sceptics who heard him had much the advantage in others hardly less important.

On the whole, what I have gained from this volume is, almost exclusively, picturesque detail, some acute textual commentary, and a much distincter conception of the *numerical* poverty of the Churches which rewarded the apostle's personal exertions over that vast field of labour. St. Paul himself seems to me hardly so intelligible a character on laying down the essay as he seemed when I first took it up; for while M. Renan has a genuine tenderness for St. Peter, and a picturesque sentiment for Mary Magdalene, his conception of the " ugly little Jew," whose spirit was stirred within him when he mistook, as M. Renan thinks, the exquisite art of Athens for the idolatry so abhorrent to his Hebrew forefathers, is, on the whole, unfriendly, wavering, and often fanciful. Even where M. Renan's insight is truest, he does not reconcile his own descriptive touches, but leaves them in their apparently bald contrast without a word.

He calls St. Paul, with some justice, at once the true ancestor of Protestantism and the most perfect "director of consciences" who ever belonged to the Christian Church, but he does nothing towards indicating the characteristic which fitted him alike for these seemingly opposite functions. He ascribes to St. Paul the ambition, the jealous love of influence over men, and the capacity to exert it, of a great practical organizer who cannot help contracting a certain amount of stain from the world he impresses,—who has, indeed, so true an insight into what is politic and expedient, that he often sacrifices to it the finer scruples of virtue; and now and then M. Renan even uses words of St. Paul which might almost apply to a diplomatist like Talleyrand. And yet he charges St. Paul (far more plausibly) with a "frenzied" attachment to particular dogmatic theses, a passion for transcendental paradox, and "contempt for reason," which are certainly no characteristics of the diplomatic intellect; and here, again, he makes no effort to blend these ópposite characteristics in his delineation. He freely and gratuitously imputes to St. Paul little personal unveracities in the cause of religion, such as the assertion that he went up "by revelation" to Jerusalem, and that he had received "of the Lord" the words of consecration in the Communion Service, when the apostle must have known, hints M. Renan, that no revelation had been given him in either case; yet he equally gratuitously attributes to the apostle a superstitious belief in his own (fancied) power to pass sentence of death on the incestuous member of the Church at Corinth, *i.e.*, to pledge God to execute the sentence which he had, according to our author, passed. Again, he expresses his distaste for St. Paul's ostentation of indifference to women, and of his indisposition to marriage; yet he hints his grave suspicion that the apostle may have been married to Lydia of Philippi (on the strength of the expression, "true yokefellow," σύζυγε γνήσιε, addressed we know not to whom in the epistle to the Philippians), though St. Paul did not, it is admitted, take a wife with him on his journeys, and speaks of himself, clearly enough once, as unmarried. In a word, M. Renan's estimate of St. Paul seems to me almost purposely fanciful, and, in respect to the very highest side of the apostle's mind, unfinished in outline, and confused in colour. Most of all do I feel the want of any attempt to harmonize the apostle's theology, as shown in his letters, with the great French sceptic's view of his character—that of a fiery missionary and propagandist, whose great impulse is to build up a great institution, to *succeed*. The detached essays in Mr. Jowett's 'Thessalonians, Galatians, and Romans,' seem to me to have an immeasurably higher value in this respect than this book of M. Renan's, where what he calls the "transcendental," and what I should call the mystic and theological side of St. Paul's nature, is simply regretted and pooh-poohed. Is it quite impossible to form some image of St. Paul more distinct in itself, and more in harmony both with his correspondence and his missionary achievements, than is here given us?

It seems to me a matter of some significance that St. Paul's first appearance in the history of Christianity s a foretaste of his whole character and work, in that sense at least in which contraries, or even contradictories, in human character are so often foretastes of each other. He appears, first, not simply as inquisitor and persecutor, nor even as an inquisitor and persecutor of Christians, but as specially directing his inquisitorial persecution against the Greek or Gentile extension of the Christian Church as represented by Stephen. The special charge against Stephen—the charge, doubtless, which kindled St. Paul's highest indignation against him —was the "blasphemy against the law and the temple" involved in saying that Jesus of Nazareth should "destroy this place, and change the customs which Moses hath delivered us." This suggests to me, in its connexion with the whole tenor of St. Paul's subsequent writings, that the great problem which had haunted him since his youth had been the true relation of the national Hebrew faith and expectations to that great world, thoroughly saturated with Greek ideas and Roman institutions, in which at Tarsus, and everywhere except Jerusalem, he must have found himself. St. Paul's was not an intellect to be startled at a paradox, however strong. On the contrary, as M. Renan himself somewhat contemptuously indicates, though he seems to me to miss the enormous importance of the thought in reference to St. Paul's writings, to St. Paul faith was of the essence of paradox. But even while he clung with characteristic vehemence to the paradox involved in the prediction that the narrow Jewish ceremonial, with all its paraphernalia of legal technicality, both in matters of ritual and matters of morality, was one day to be accepted and conformed to by the whole world, by the keen Greeks, whose ironic incredulity he felt to his very soul, and by the stolid Romans, whose utter indifference to all these local superstitions galled him perhaps even more powerfully,—the magnitude of the paradox itself must have grown ever more imposing. Doubtless he early perceived that his own religious chiefs—the high priest, for instance, from whom he received letters of recommendation to the orthodox Jews in Damascus —really looked upon him coldly as a hot-headed, "dangerous" young man, for whom, indeed, it was essential to find inquisitorial work, since he asked for it, but for whom they were glad to find that work at a safe distance, like Damascus, instead of permitting him to get the hierarchy at Jerusalem into trouble with the Roman government. St. Paul, while he realised most intensely the enormous practical paradox involved in any fulfilment of prophetic anticipations such as the orthodox Jews looked for, must have very quickly caught the impression that his own hierarchy did not truly realise what they taught; no doubt, indeed, they were as much disposed to get rid of excitable young persons who wanted to carry out logically the principle of their own teachings, as our Church in the last century was disposed to get rid of Wesley and Whitfield. Probably the ruling Pharisees—his own master Gamaliel, for instance,—thought him feverish and unsafe, and would in secret have preferred going on quietly in the old way, even though the hopes they professed to cherish should seem growing ever more distant and fanciful.

It was in this state of mind, doubtless, while brooding, just as he still did after he became a Christian, over his favourite Hebrew truth that the foolishness of the world and the base things of the world, and the things which are despised, are chosen by God to bring to naught the mighty and strong and wise things of the world, that the great revolution in St. Paul's heart began. Realising even more intensely than usual how foolish and base in the eyes of the world was the very fanaticism by which he himself was actuated,—a fanaticism marvelled at as gross superstition by all the clever men of his acquaintance in Greek circles, disapproved as restless and anarchical by the Romans, distrusted as over-zealous by the prudent Pharisees of Jerusalem,—his mind may have begun to ask itself: 'Is not this doctrine of a crucified Messiah precisely one of that class of offences and stumbling-blocks which, because they involve the greatest abnegations of human pride and dignity, are chosen by God to confound the things which are mighty and strong in human wisdom?' If he himself were pursuing a line which even prudent Jews thought folly—a line of over-zeal, of believing too much, of interpreting the law too literally in using force to extirpate a heresy humiliating to Jewish pride,—what were those doing who were the willing victims of this persecution, and that, too, on behalf of such a paradox as the assertion that the Messiah *had* been put to death and ignominiously crucified before returning to earth to reign? The uplifted face of the dying Stephen, with his prayer, "Lay not this sin to their charge," would recur to him as a type of those "weak things of the world" which are destined to confound the mighty; and yet at the same time his acute intellect would discern at once that there was something in this new heresy which, as it had actually won over Greeks like Stephen, might promise a reign far more universal than any faith of which the Hebrew temple was the only centre, and the Hebrew ritual the sole condition, could hope for.

It was, I imagine, in this doubting, unsettled attitude of mind, oppressed on the one hand with the feeling that his own party, the Pharisees, were proud, stiff, and formal, and quite indisposed to favour any line of action based on a childlike trust in God's promises against the evidence of all the overwhelming plausibilities and probabilities of life, and oppressed, on the other hand, with the equally disheartening conviction that, even if Pharisaism renewed its youth, and became fiery, zealous, earnest, it would yet be simply hopeless to try to subjugate to it the searching Greek intellect and the imperialist Roman contempt for provincialism,—that St.

Paul, half catching at a new and very powerful means for *widening* his faith, half welcoming a new element of divine humiliation in it to Jewish exclusiveness, was suddenly converted on the way to Damascus by the vision of our Lord. Certain it is that in *every* version of that vision, both that in the Galatians and all the three versions in the Acts, the prominent feature is the same, and is *not* the feature we should *à priori* expect to mark the conversion of a strict Pharisee,—namely, that he is the chosen instrument to preach "*to the Gentiles.*"

It seems to me therefore quite clear that St. Paul's mind must have been profoundly preoccupied long before his conversion with the paradox involved in supposing that his own strict Judaism could ever take forcible hold on the great Gentile world, and that, in compelling himself to cling close to his faith, despite the paradox, he naturally began testing his own confidence in it by agitating fiercely against any heresy which seemed to relax the chains of Judaism and concede something to the heathen. In the heat of this crusade it must have flashed upon him more than once that there might be a still diviner paradox implied in the humiliation of the proud, stiff, Jewish orthodoxy, than even in the subjugation of the keen, free Greek intellect or the haughty Roman imperialism ; so that when his conversion came, he was instinctively groping after a double conviction : (1) that the hard Jewish legalism was not divine, was *not* one of those weak things of the world destined to confound the things which were mighty, but rather one of the typically proud things of the world destined to be confounded, and (2) that whatever was destined to supersede it must have far larger affinities for the Gentile world than the strict Judaism could ever have had.

Admit this profoundly Hebrew basis and starting-point for St. Paul's theology—that man and his systems are nothing, that God and His grace are everything; that either a man or a Church that begins to rely on intrinsic merits is losing divine help; that the Cross is the type of what is divinest, because it is the type at once of what is weakest and the most conscious of weakness, and of what can shine therefore only by borrowing glory of God,—and I seem to gain an insight into the secret of St. Paul's eloquence and persuasiveness such as M. Renan, in his contemptuous and hasty notice of the apostle's unfortunate liking for the "transcendental absurd," has necessarily been debarred from. Who that has studied St. Paul at all has not noticed that bold, soaring, and—I might almost say by an audacious anachronism, if it did not give so false a conception of its intellectual motive—*Hegelian* dialectic, with which he rises from the forms of our finite and earthly thought to the infinite and the spiritual life embodied in them? "Who then is Paul and who is Apollos, but ministers by whom ye believed, even as the Lord gave to every man? I have planted, Apollos watered, but God gave the increase. So that neither he that planted is anything, neither he that watereth, but God that giveth the increase. . . . Therefore let no man glory in men. *For all things are yours;* whether Paul, or Apollos, or Cephas, or the world, or life, or death, or things present, or things to come; all are yours, and ye are Christ's, and Christ is God's." What ease and swiftness, and power of wing in this indignant upward flight from the petty conflicts of the Corinthian Church; an upward flight which does not cease till the poor subjects of contention, though he himself was one of them, seem lost like grains of sand beneath the bending sky!

M. Renan makes an exception to his general distaste for St. Paul's religious writings in favour of the famous chapter on charity. But though St. Paul's rapid and, as it were, spiral upward flight is never seen to higher perfection than in this cumulative description of the attributes of divine love, which at every stroke seems to rise into a more triumphant and beatific vision, yet what I may fairly call its *method* is common to all the higher passages of St. Paul's reasonings and exhortations, which habitually aim at dissolving away the "beggarly elements" in morality and religion, and making us see that it is only participation in the divine nature which gives any meaning at all to human virtue. If it be not the "transcendental-absurd" to say "Charity never faileth: whether there be prophecies, they shall fail; whether there be tongues, they shall cease; whether there be knowledge, it shall vanish away; for we know in part, and we prophesy in part, but when that which is perfect is come, that which is in part shall be done away;" if *that* be not absurd, even though it be transcendental, how is it more so to reason that "God, who commanded the light to shine out of darkness, hath shined in our hearts to give the light of the knowledge of the glory of God in the face of Jesus Christ; but we have this treasure in earthen vessels, that the excellency of the power may be of God, and not of us: we are troubled on every side, yet not disturbed; perplexed, but not in despair; persecuted, but not forsaken; cast down, but not destroyed; always bearing about in the body the dying of our Lord Jesus Christ, that the life also of Jesus might be made manifest in our body"? In both passages alike, as in all illustrative of St. Paul's peculiar and characteristic persuasiveness, the very essence of that principle which M. Renan calls "the transcendental-absurd" is at the heart of the apostle's thought, simply because it was at the very root of his own life—I mean the conviction that it is the only true glory of man to renounce glory for man and seek the glory of heaven; to dissolve or widen his own selfish and limited love in the ever-flowing charity of God; to be thankful for the poverty of the earthen vessels which force him to turn to that divine fountain of grace, from their capacity for containing which, and from that alone, they derive their worth. If M. Renan had had even the slightest sympathy with the very moving principle of St. Paul's life, he could not have designated as the "transcendental-absurd" that which really was the life of both conscieuce and intellect alike, and which made St. Paul what he was.

For observe that St. Paul's door of escape out of the Jewish narrowness and exclusiveness was precisely by this outlet,—his distrust of all human self-sufficiency as such, his "transcendental" merging of all human powers and genius in Christ. His objection to the circumcision was *not* a refined dislike for a barbarous custom and tradition, but that it gave the Jew something to reckon upon, and to trust to apart from God—something by which to exalt himself above the Gentiles. Again, his craving for some closer bond with the Gentile world, for some affinity with the keen philosophical intellect of the Greek, and the stately jurisprudence of Rome, is shown in a hundred passages: in that careful study, for instance, of the Greek religious nature which made him appreciate so fully the side of Theism *approaching nearest to Pantheism*, and speak to the Athenians of the *inwardness* of that God who gives to all, "life, and breath, and all things . . . . that they should seek the Lord, if haply they might feel after him and find him, though he be not far from any one of us, for in him we live, and move, and have our being, as certain also of your own poets have said, 'for we are also his offspring;'" and not less certainly in that earnest respect for Roman legislation which made him inculcate on the Roman Church the divine sanction of all secular government, and speak to them of rulers as "ministers of God," "not bearing the sword in vain." I see the same feeling in the evidently profound yearning of St. Paul to see Rome,— a yearning which he avowed in the only letter we have of his addressed to a Church he had not seen—the Epistle to the Romans; and his latent desire to get nearer to the heart of Roman influence is sufficiently attested in his many evidences of deference to Roman rulers, in his guarded submission even to Felix, one of the very worst of those rulers; in his still greater courtesy and deference to the "most noble Festus;" in his appeal to Cæsar; and in the many indications of pride in his Roman citizenship recorded by his biographer in the Acts. But though the proofs of St. Paul's craving for a closer sympathy with the two great Gentile powers, the intellect of Greece and the governing genius of Rome, are stamped everywhere on his history and writings, he felt no more disposition to value the national genius of Rome or Greece for its own sake than he did to value for its own sake the national genius of Israel, as embodied in the law of Moses. He *feared* Gentile powers and traditions less, because they had never, as far as he knew, been set up as human merits justifying man before God. But he knew no mode of attaining that closer sympathy with the Greek and Roman, for which he had evidently been craving long before he assisted at the martyrdom of Stephen and set out for Damascus bent on pushing the rigours of Judaism to their utmost limit, except by levelling *all* human grounds of pride, and denying all gifts alike the slightest intrinsic value, unless so far as they drew their owners closer to Him who gave them. St. Paul was always reiterating to himself that in the divine sight "there is neither Greek nor Jew, circumcision nor uncircumcision, barbarian, Scythian, bond nor free, but Christ is all and in all." He broke down "the wall of partition" between the Jew and the Gentile by his assertion that "*no* flesh could glory in Christ's presence," and it was only through that confession that he learned to appreciate the gifts which *other* flesh than the chosen people had received at the hands of God. His universalism was gained by stripping all peoples alike naked, as it were, of any special glory of their own, till he learned to look on every national gift as a mere temporary loan from above, the object of which was to merge the possessors in the joy of human weakness and conscious indebtedness to God.

St. Paul's faith was the precise antithesis of our modern humanism. He delighted to present humanity as a naked, shivering, worthless beggar, scarcely an entity at all until it recognised freely its weakness and nakedness, after which that very weakness and nakedness became its strength and glory, as attesting whence it borrowed all that might seem to be of any worth in what it had. Christ Himself had taught the same before; but He taught it from above, without that incessant sense of the supernatural division between man and God—the flesh and the spirit—which St. Paul was ever striving to express. St. Paul shrinks, with true Hebrew trembling, from the light, even as he welcomes it and plunges in it; he feels the human kernel rattle, as it were, even in the protecting shell of divine grace and love.

I do not think that without thoroughly realising this,

which is the very essence alike of St. Paul's theology, of his morality, and of his individual self-consciousness, it is possible to appreciate fairly what we call his *character*, *i.e.* his social manner, his peculiar temper, his political dexterity, his power as a "director of consciences," his pride in maintaining himself, his yearning after appreciation, his exquisite and heartfelt joy in the full recognition of his services by the Churches he had served. St. Paul's very essence was a pervading sense of personal humiliation, dissolving into gratitude to God for a vision of marvellous glory. It seems to me that the key to his character is his confession to the Corinthians:—"Lest I should be exalted above measure through the abundance of the revelations, there was given to me a thorn in the flesh, the messenger of Satan to buffet me, lest I should be exalted above measure. For this thing I besought the Lord thrice, that it might depart from me; and he said unto me, My grace is sufficient for thee; for my strength is made perfect in weakness: most gladly, therefore, will I rather glory in my infirmities, that the power of Christ may rest upon me . . . *for when I am weak, then am I strong.*" This is another instance of what M. Renan would call "the transcendental-absurd" in St. Paul; but if so, it is impossible to understand St. Paul himself in the least without understanding "the transcendental-absurd" too. Shrinking infirmity and self-contempt, hidden in a sort of aureole of revelations abundant beyond measure—that was St. Paul. And he believed, too, that there was a real law of direct proportion between the darkness at the core and the brightness of the spiritual envelope,—that when he was cowering most beneath his sense of despicable infirmities, then the power of Christ rested most conspicuously upon him, —that when he was least dissatisfied with himself, then the radiance of heaven began to pale and dwindle round him. Combine a nature and experience such as this with a temper of unusual fire, and a very keen eye for the relative political advantages of the various grounds open to him in any contest, and we shall see in St. Paul not so much the "eminent man of action" whom M. Renan delineates—for eminent men of action are almost always profoundly self-confident, without any trace of shrinking and infirmity of soul—as a man of passion with a very few great gifts for action, gifts almost exclusively limited to a profound and delicate genius for winning the sympathy of individuals by alternate self-abnegation and the most eloquent exposition of his own desires and hopes.

St. Paul loves to appear as a suitor to even the most humble of his followers,—loves to supplicate, as the most powerful mode of command. Pride he has, but the pride that loves to abase itself in order to secure itself. He throws himself, as it were, at the feet of his disciples in order to win them back; he points to his sufferings, enumerates his labours and his griefs, but all in order to melt away their pride of resistance, in order to give the most obdurate a sufficient excuse and self-justification for expressing their sorrow, in order to make them feel that they are *giving*, even more than giving up, when they relent. He treats every one who acknowledges his influence as doing him the greatest of favours. "I am *debtor*," he says, "both to the Greek and to the barbarian," meaning that he had gained both Greeks and barbarians to Christ. Eminent as a man of action he was, but only because he was so very much greater as a man of passion. It was in the generous parade, as it were, of his weakness and sufferings, in his boundless willingness to entreat where he might have commanded, in the passion with which he was ready to descant to every one on the overflow of the divine grace which had rescued him from what he was, that he found his power of action. It was not *organising* power, as far as I can see, nor strength of will, nor impressiveness of manner, nor any manipulation of the secrets and private jealousies of the various communities he visited, which made him a great man of action, but simply the generous passion with which he lavished himself, revelations, visions, shame, sufferings, hopes, pride, everything, for the purpose of claiming or reclaiming any one who seemed within his reach.

Of course a nature like this, so apt to despise technical moral rules so long as it kept God in sight, so lavish and unhesitating in its use of personal entreaty and in the sacrifice of every personal reserve for the same end, could not but have its weak side. No doubt St. Paul sometimes condemned himself for going too far in the way of *tactics*. I think his appeal to the inflamed partisan passions of the mob of Sadducees and Pharisees at Jerusalem, "I am a Pharisee and the son of a Pharisee, and for the hope of the resurrection of the dead I am called in question this day," caused him some compunction afterwards; at least, he declares afterwards to Felix that there had been no cause of offence given by him to the Jews, "except it be for this one voice, that I cried, standing among them, Touching the resurrection of the dead I am called in question by you this day." Clearly that was what we should now call a *dodge*, and St. Paul knew it, and was ashamed of it. But it was of the very essence of his type of faith not to be overscrupulous in details so long as he made himself of no account and made God all in all; and this led him, perhaps more than once, into seizing hold of weapons close at hand for making an impression, which he could afterwards see were *not* divine instruments at all. The same scorn for a legal morality, and tendency to make the letter nothing and the spirit everything, no doubt diminished now and then the restraint he might otherwise have put upon his temper. "God shall smite thee, thou whited wall; for sittest thou to judge me after the law, and commandest me to be smitten contrary to the law?" is the kind of outbreak which, though it was immediately withdrawn and apologised for, an equally great man of more reticent and regulated moral temperament would hardly have indulged in at all. If the epistle to Timothy is spurious, there is the skill of a true literary forger in the sentence, "Alexander the coppersmith did me much evil; the Lord reward him according to his works." Again, the apostle quarrelled vehemently with Barnabas; and there is something positively grim in the Eastern ferocity of the wish expressed in the epistle to the Galatians (v. 12) against the false brethren who troubled the Church by insisting on the strict Jewish circumcision, ὄφελον καὶ ἀποκόψονται οἱ ἀναστατοῦντες ὑμᾶς. But then the same all but reckless prodigality of nature which made St. Paul now and then use a stratagem, and now and then launch a thunderbolt, in the fervour of his pleading, is the spring of all his finest touches, as when he wishes himself even "accursed from Christ" if it could save his Jewish brethren; when he pathetically desires that Agrippa and all who heard him might be made like to him "except these bonds;" when he declares that "*neither death nor life*" (speaking of life as far more formidable than death) shall be able to separate him "from the love of God which is in Christ Jesus our Lord;" or when he confesses frankly to the Corinthians the shrinkings, the changes of purpose, the painful irresolution he felt about his third visit to them, lest they should have been excited against him by his former letter. St. Paul could hardly have been thus lavish of himself, thus eager to expose even his most private feelings to the light, had he habitually reviewed his impulses before giving any of them free play. It is truly wonderful, I think, that in the course of controversies so fierce, conducted by a mind of such heat and such marvellously quick sympathies, we have not far more of violence and manœuvre than we have. Had St. Paul been chiefly "a man of action," as M. Renan thinks, but of the same ardent temperament as he actually betrays, it could not but have been that he would have waged a far more personal and terrible war. Had he not been what he was,—a man of ardent *inward* life, who, living "in weakness, and fear, and much trembling," yet had the gift of using his ardours and his fears alike, as means of persuasion to others,— his warmth of temperament could not but have taken far oftener the form of practical interference and personal denunciation, and his ready-witted insight the form of diplomatic strategy.

Again, M. Renan will not have it that St. Paul was a man of either the highest virtue or even of a loveable nature. St. Paul himself would probably have agreed with his critic. But for my own part I doubt whether there can ever be human virtue higher, or human disinterestedness of this impersonal kind more loveable, than St. Paul's. No doubt he was, what M. Renan calls him, "an ugly little Jew," painfully conscious when amongst Greeks and Romans of his own insignificance, and one who felt the ties of faith much stronger even than the ties of friendship. But if it be virtuous habitually to overcome "weakness, and fear, and much trembling," and not to count life dear, so that he might but "finish his course with joy" and work out the trust committed to him, then was St. Paul the most virtuous of men, surmounting the greatest obstacles to reach the highest end.

And if it be loveable to think and feel so ardently for others as is implied in such words as the following, for instance, addressed to a distant Church:—"Out of much affliction and anguish of heart, I wrote unto you with many tears; not that ye should be grieved, but that ye might know the love which I have more abundantly unto you,"—then St. Paul was assuredly in this sense the most loveable of men.

M. Renan, however, thinks him insincere, charges him with inventing private "revelations" for the sake of insuring submission on the part of his converts. I cannot conceive a charge more grossly improbable. That St. Paul tried to distinguish most scrupulously between his own judgment and the inspiration of God, and believed, though admitting to himself at times a doubt whether his judgment were his own or inspired (see 1 Cor. vii. 40), that he could do so, we have the most ample evidence. The doubt expressed in the passage I refer to, shows that St. Paul may or rather must have been at times mistaken. Doubtless, in announcing to the Thessalonians the approaching day of judgment and end of the world—assumed to be likely to happen during his own lifetime—he was profoundly mistaken in interpreting, as divinely inspired, thoughts more or less due to his own limited conceptions. But I cannot conceive clearer evidence of any man's scrupulous sincerity in such matters than we have of St. Paul's. Indeed, in making this charge, M. Renan seems to me to go out of his way to accuse St. Paul of a sort of sin of which he has given us the most ample evidence that he was absolutely incapable. That he could manœuvre in the heat of a moment of excitement (and afterwards repent it) I have admitted. But without vehement impulses, the highest kind of human *virtue* is, as I suppose, impossible. It seems to me difficult to conceive any nature less easy to harmonise and control than St. Paul's. At times shrinking, trembling, almost cowering, dwelling with nervous irritability on one topic,—such as the discord and demoralization at Corinth; wavering between tenderness and severity; full even of a consciousness of personal infirmity which seems almost to have amounted now and then to self-disgust (as if at a sort of meanness of soul in himself), yet conscious of a heat of imagination and an ardour of faith such as none of those who marvelled at and half-despised him could understand,—it seems truly marvellous that he should have been generally so calm and foreseeing in compromise, so courageous without defiance in self-defence, so tender and gentle even to womanliness in dealing with those whose feelings he was compelled to wound, and so magnanimous towards his colleagues and rivals in missionary work. How M. Renan can speak of jealousy as the foundation of St. Paul's nature in the face of his generous acknowledgment of the work of Apollos in his own peculiar field, I confess I do not understand. He was jealous as a mother is jealous over his infant Churches, jealous with what the Bible calls a godly jealousy, lest they should be persuaded that legal and ritual observances were the appointed means of extinguishing sin in the heart; and for the same reason he was jealous of his apostleship, since the spiritual equality of the Gentiles depended on the equality of his apostleship to that of the Twelve; but of the sort of jealousy which must have been felt *towards* him by the Twelve, if M. Renan is right (which I exceedingly doubt), in referring to St. Paul the denunciations recorded in the Apocalypse of those "which say they are apostles, and are not," I think there is absolutely no trace at all. St. Paul is always eager to acknowledge himself the least of the apostles, "that am not meet to be called an apostle, because I persecuted the Church of God." At all times he is eager to abase himself in any way to win his cause, which was not his own, but his Master's.

Indeed I can never think of "the ugly little Jew," with his tender remembrance of all the old women and slaves in his various little Churches, his "outward fightings and inward fears," his visions and his humiliations, his signs and mighty deeds and his fears and tremblings, his anxious distinction between that which his Lord had told him and that which he had thought himself; that fine tact which *might* have been strategic; that fiery temper which *was* sometimes fierce; the flesh which struggled against the spirit, and the spirit which dissolved away the flesh and painted man as, at his best, hardly approaching anything so purely good as a vacuum for God to fill; his rapidly mounting eloquence that rushes with the whole universe into the presence of God, and his sudden cries of shame and sin,—without feeling that in him we reach the highest conceivable degree of that human virtue which is *not* moral beauty, and that loveableness of spirit which is not sweetness or harmony. I have never felt that I could heartily apply to our Lord those words of Isaiah usually referred to Him, concerning His having no beauty that we should desire Him, for surely He is "the first and only fair." But I can apply them with my whole soul to St. Paul:— "He hath no form nor comeliness, and when we see him there is no beauty that we should desire him; he is despised, and rejected of men, a man of sorrows and acquainted with grief; he was despised and we esteemed him not." Yet is not his the sort of despicability which is soon better honoured and better loved than anything else that ever entered into our world, except indeed the light which it reflects, and the love which it reveals?

X.

THE HARD CHURCH.[1]

THERE is a school of theological speculation, as well Nonconformist as Conformist, which may fairly be classed as the 'Hard Church.' It is a degraded variety of the solid, sagacious, strong-minded form of Christianity. This latter, in its undegraded phase, is sincere, eager, pious, good sense, a little stony, but not without a very valuable function in testing the strength and metal of more sentimental and shadowy schools of thought; indeed, it may be called the Church of Common Sense. In its spoiled form it is a hard arrogant infliction, uniting the tone of a schoolmaster to a spirit of intellectual scorn, essentially a *Hard* Church. I should be very

---

[1] 'Perversion; or the Causes and Consequences of Infidelity. A Tale for the Times.' Smith, Elder, and Co.

'Selections from the Correspondence of R. E. H. Greyson, Esq., Edited by the Author of the 'Eclipse of Faith.' 2 vols. Longmans.

sorry to think that this last type could be found *pure* in many theologians. It has infected with more or less virulence the writings of several. The school, itself, however, in its best phase, is rather an intellectual than a moral phenomenon. It has contained many able and careful thinkers very far removed from any kind of intolerance, and who would look down on the flogging theology with gentle wonder and warm disapprobation. Paley may be said to have founded the school, not only by bequeathing to it a good fixed capital of masterly argument, but, what is more important, by giving the most pronounced example of its *mode* of thought. He, first of all men, as the Cambridge tutor, in the fondness of his admiration, happily expressed it, "had the credit of putting Christianity into a form which could be written out at examinations." To have a compact statement of the whole gist of Christianity is the principal "note" of the Common-Sense Church. Its followers have often, indeed, more or less repudiated Paley—whose temporising ethics are certainly quite separable from his theological system. The late Archbishop Whately, one of the ablest and most agreeable writers of the Common-Sense Church, supplied it with a logic; Dr. Mansel has elaborated for it the higher metaphysical philosophy; Mr. Rogers, the most slashing and merciless of its captains, has thrown up defences round the conception of authority, and insulated the region of inspiration; and Mr. Binney caught its exact spirit when he once addressed to young persons, after Paley's manner, a suggestion "how to make the best of *both* worlds."

But, after all, Paley's "case" is but little changed. Its hinging point is the habit of resting the main stress of belief on the argument from design, and the miraculous credentials of revelation. And in this all the school agree, from the Aristotelian thinkers who concede free will and at least the elements of a natural conscience, to the necessarians and utilitarians, who base morals wholly on the positive authority of Revelation. Broad in inclusion, only because it demands but *few* articles of belief, not because it is wide in theory, the Church of Common-Sense, which always tends towards the Hard Church, is the resort of the strong-minded theologians, and forms a court standing midway between the narrow crypts of Low Evangelical doctrine beneath, and the venerable decay of the High Church towers above. Its heroes are men of somewhat menacing understanding—not Broad-Church men, if Mr. Maurice, Dean Stanley, Mr. Lynch, and Mr. Baldwin Brown are of the Broad Church—latitudinarian, but not Catholic in the tone of their theology—sharp and confident in their logic—given to browbeat their adversaries on the spot rather than to going *with* them their mile, or at least up to the utmost point of common conviction—dry and ungenial towards intellectual doubt—shrewd partisans—eager assailants of "extremes"—and champions of that neutral precipitate of Christian theology, orthodoxy in its cooling stage.

The Hard Church sees in theology neither a deep philosophy, like Coleridge; nor a response to the heart, like Neander; nor a divine reconciliation of the many contradictory yearnings of human nature, like Mr. Maurice. Its idea of a theological system is a decisive chain of circumstantial evidence, with a result confirmatory of all sagacious views of life. Its aim and effort is to draw up so masterly a statement of these, that you would think yourself a fool to put a business-agency into the hands of a man so insincere or so dense-minded as to withhold his assent. Its great anxiety is to appeal to no strictly individual experience, but to make it "equally conclusive to all beings of equal rationality." There is something essentially unsympathising in its overweening sense. It steadily endeavours to conceive men as so many units of crystallized intelligence, representing different interests, but each fixed in its own type, and all like enough to each other to render a wholesale method of treatment the most remunerative. The Hard Church glories in hard sense. And what *is* hard sense but that which has learned to dismiss rapidly from the mind, as immaterial or practically misleading, all those fluctuating elements of human life which do not seem to be deeply imbedded in the average notions of average men? Is it not, in short, the power of generally regulating the judgment according to the force of *numerical* impressions? The Hard Church, therefore, necessarily relies on what may be called the *inorganic* laws of human thought and action, and ignores the more delicate laws of growth and change discoverable in social and individual character. The fixed skeleton-truths of social life which never change in form or composition, but remain always alike, at least at the same stage of human history,—such as the first principles of economy, of utility, the elements of political justice, and the general rules of evidence,—these are always recurring again and again *in the same form* in men's experience, and, like inorganic bodies, therefore, their properties become more and more familiar with every-day experience. These, therefore, hard sense involuntarily appropriates; and it loves well to discover and re-discover their influence in every part of life.

But it will not be so with what one may call the *organic* truths of human character; those which change their shape and disappear and reappear, undergoing various transformations at different stages of their influence on men. These, really appearing at different times under different aspects, cannot leave the same impress even on the keenest general observation, and must count as different truths, the real link not being detectable without a special and individual insight which would spoil the judgment for its rough general work. Social truths, or truths of character in their different stages of the stalk, the leaf, the bud, the flower, must really count as different things, not as various aspects of the same thing, to a mind that *ensures* itself, as it were, against the many probable errors of *primâ facie* impression by the very great number of cases in which it is obliged to act upon them, and in a large majority of which it will hit sufficiently near the mark. Thus, to the hard understanding, *organic* truths, *i. e.* truths of continuous life which have a history and a development of their own, are split up into a number of loose inorganic truths with their links missing. A great number of disconnected *fixed* notions take the place of insight into the gradual and complex growth of slowly maturing life.

Hence the great men of the Hard Church are apt to spend their whole strength in demonstrating the futility of all religious positions which represent genuinely organic and individual convictions; and are apt to scold quite as much at the eccentricities of any positive faith which is not accommodated to their common-sense rules, as at the eccentricities of scepticism and unbelief. They seem to have concentrated all their strength on the task of sweeping away the "cobwebs of philosophers," and exhibiting how many counterfeit theologies are in contact with our actual life, instead of finding out the points where true theology connects itself with those counterfeits. I do not depreciate in the least the services of those who expose shams; but I do believe that he does pure harm who delights in "studies" of shams, without bringing them into living relations with the real wants which they pretend to appease. Mr. Carlyle—in spite of his mournfully hopeless no-reply to such wants—has done whatever good he once effected (and it was not small) for the thinkers of England, not by a cold skill in painting shams everywhere, even where they were not to be seen, but by showing them in sad contrast to the famishing spirits to which they were offered as nourishment. The Hard Church, though they do reserve a private theological solution for the problems of life, are more cruel and more useless teachers to those whom they think it their duty to assail. They seem to think that it is not the endurance but the *infliction* of hardness which makes a true soldier of Christ. They go about like theological detectives, without any care or compassion for the sins (imaginary or real) of the defaulters they arrest. They "expose" shallowness and weakness, or hypocrisy, in the spirit which seems to say, not only 'Here are men deceiving themselves with an imposture,' but 'Here are men who have no deeper wants, no deeper life that is left unsatisfied by this imposture; here are men who have completely imposed on themselves.' They paint, not only the sham *clothing* of men's minds, but sham minds altogether—and give you the impression that God has retained no witness of Himself in the spirits of much more than half His children. They even give no sadness to the tone of their delineations. It is coarse triumph over the wretchedness of supposed or real evil. This is not the style of exposure that makes men look into their own hearts. It is the style that makes men hurl back the charges at their accuser. A section so mischievous as the Hard Church, Christendom does not contain. It is wise and useful to tear away the veil from all imposture, intellectual or spiritual. But it is neither wise nor useful, for it is untrue, to tear away such a veil and show no human nature beneath it, restless under its unreality, and bitterly seeking to dissemble ease.

There is no end which a Christian writer can have in view, so noble as a crusade against the moral Atheism of the day, and the resistance to the death of that self-centred philosophy and worship of blind Nature which is fostered by the modern idolatries of beauty, and force, and law. But how are we to fight this battle? By admitting that God has lost all influence in the world, except over the holders of true doctrine? By refusing to believe in the signs of the goodness which we see, because it is associated with that which we dislike? Why, it is the intellectual analogue of the massacre of St. Bartholomew. The orthodox Church exterminated the heretics from hopelessness of their conversion. It gave up in despair the task of availing itself of the true doctrine in their hearts to introduce a truer. And this is exactly the intellectual policy of the Hard Church. Instead of rejoicing to indicate the good there is, and bringing out clearly its conflict with that which they regard as evil, they intellectually *ignore* the more hopeful elements that are bound up with scepticism, that they may indulge themselves in more unrestrained ferocity against it.

Can any faith be *real* which is not eager and grateful to recognise that God has done much, because it cannot recognise that God has done all? I have no words to express my intense horror of that Hard Church spirit that rather grumbles because scepticism is not sceptical *enough*, and drives away those amongst the sceptics who cling fervently to the belief in the sinfulness of sin, and the duty of prayer, with a taunt that it would be more *consistent* to embrace a better developed type of infidelity. If there is one sign more hopeful for this century than the last, it is the more Christian type of sceptical thought; and unless the application of the Hard Church scourge, reduce to a bitter silence the spirit of the higher minds amongst the doubters, I believe it will issue in a general return towards Christianity of all unselfish and veracious-minded sceptics. Can it be a Christian divine who preaches thus?—

"I acknowledge, indeed, that if I were to yield myself to the guidance of the speculative understanding, I could not stop short of that system of Atheism which it is now the fashion to call Pantheism; for I quite agree with you in finding no resting-point in the shallow Deism of Theodore Parker or Francis Newman; indeed, I cannot imagine how any one who has read Butler should ever have halted at such a half-way house. But I can feel deeply the attractiveness of Spinoza's creed, or rather of that ancient system of oriental speculation of which Spinoza has been the greatest modern exponent; but to which he added nothing essential that had not been said by Chinese and Indian Pantheists three thousand years before him. So far as the mere intellect is concerned, I could embrace that grand idealistic philosophy which identifies the perceived with the perceiver, matter with spirit, and man with God — which represents all physical and all moral phenomena as unalterably determined by antecedent fate—all things but parts of one tremendous whole—all wheels in one vast machine, impelled by irresistible and incomprehensible laws. I could believe (with Fichte) that 'every thing is what it is of absolute necessity, and cannot be other than it is;' or (with Miss Martineau) that 'I am as completely the result of my nature, and impelled to do what

I do, as the needle to point to the north, or the puppet to move according as the string is pulled.' And I could proceed (with Emerson) to identify good with evil, and could quote Goethe to prove the idleness of wishing to jump off one's shadow.

But when the understanding has entangled me in this web of necessitarian Atheism, conscience rises in rebellion, and cries out indignantly that good is different from evil, that sin is sinful, and that guilt demands atonement. And the longing of my heart convinces me that I cannot do without a heavenly Father to love me, a heavenly deliverer to save me from myself."

The "shallow Deism of Francis Newman" is precisely that Deism which "cries out indignantly that good is different from evil, that sin is sinful," and that prayer is the atmosphere of the moral life. And is this, then, really *shallower* than a Pantheism which identifies good with evil; which ignores those moral assumptions on which *alone* Christianity is conceivable; which has the credit of dissolving away the faith in a personal Father, and so denying not only the kingdom but the possibility of the kingdom of Christ? Atheism then is less "shallow" than Theism; fatalism is deeper than the recognition of divine law and moral freedom; and the more profound is your trust in God and the voice of conscience,—the more *realities* you confess,—the more ashamed of you and angry with you is the Hard Church that you cannot be more *thorough* in ignoring truth. It is an evil sign for the Christian Church when Theology wishes you to choose between orthodoxy and *nothing*, and regards it as a proof of a shallow mind that God and God's law should be recognised *at all*, unless they are recognised in their fullest truth. Do these confuting gentlemen ever realise to themselves how vast a step any real and deep Theism that holds fast by prayer, is towards Christianity? Do they ever distinctly remember that God thought this *enough* for the spiritual life of His own people during some thousands of years? Does it never occur to them how striking is the contrast between their scornful alternative, "Pray believe *either* more or less," and the spirit of one who, in reply to a hearty confession of the first two commandments, instead of "exposing" the weakness of such "shallow Deism," replied, "Thou art *not far* from the kingdom of God"?

The dread felt and expressed by the reactionary school of liberal theology towards any thing that falls short of their approved minimum of Christian dogma, arises, I believe, in a totally false and unworthy suspicion of a tendency in too wide a charity to sap the strenuousness of personal conviction. 'Unless we attribute,' so they seem to argue, 'a certain *necessary* wickedness and moral discredit to heresy, we shall not be able to keep our own faith and other people's from oozing away in the genial atmosphere of the world. Let us draw our line in common charity as low as we can; but let us keep no terms with any thing that falls below it. For if we ever cease to regard doubt as a disgrace and a danger to others, there is no reason why we should not fall into it ourselves.'

It may be wise to guard against that mere geniality of thought which proceeds only from a universal liking for men of all sorts, not from a deep trust in God; but this is *not* the basis of a genuine catholicity of faith, which is far more widely removed from latitudinarian carelessness as to what men may think, than any dogmatic bigotry can ever hope to be. The trust that Truth is the living Word of God communicated to men as a *character* can alone be communicated—to different minds by different teaching, and by differently winding courses,—to some slowly but intensely, in points of vivid light with large intervals of unintelligent darkness,—to others with rapid evolutions of the general outline and meaning of His providence and discipline, yet perhaps with a less deep and constant sympathy of moral life,—to all who eagerly seek what is right with a gradual clearness and eventual certainty,—this is the trust on which alone true catholicity of feeling can be based, and with which indifference is wholly incompatible. Those who fancy their opinions *private* property are likely to be angry at the shock of finding them unconfirmed by others, and so to fall into bigotry,—or, on the other hand, to be so perplexed at many differences as to fall into apathetic indifference. But those who know that what they see, they see only because God has shown it to them,—that it is a partial and gradual manifestation of Him, and one which was granted only on difficult terms, that has given them faith,—will hesitate to think that, in His dealings with others, He must have made the same truth clear precisely in the same way and at the same time; and yet they will know that it can never pass away.

Indeed, this delusion, that our human belief is commensurate with the spiritual influences of God,—nay, is a sure pledge, and the only pledge, of those influences,—constitutes not merely the essence of bigotry and pride, but almost all the other far from capricious peculiarities which distinguish the inquisitorial theology of the Hard Church. This it is which makes its theologians so eager to find, in marks of *bare power*, some grounds for God's authority quite distinct from His *character;* because, having an idolatrous regard for faith, as a sort of charm, they want to find some iron foundation for it sufficiently unspiritual to remain unshaken when God Himself is hidden from the heart. They think they have discovered that foundation. They believe it unassailable; they think that wherever God acts at all, they should recognise Him by this mark; they look out for that mark: if they do not see it, they scold and say, 'God is not with you; on the contrary, corrupt human nature is with you; what you struggle to express is wholly opposite in nature to what I have attained; my belief is even more certain to me than any conviction I could possibly have that God has any part in your belief or no belief; you are either a liar or an idiot.' This is no exaggeration of the—uncharitableness, I will not say—but rather unlimited insolence, of temper which characterises this Hard Church religion. It is an insolence almost impossible to *mere* nature, an insolence essentially due to the artificial combination between natural arrogance and an evil idolatry of belief. It is an exaggeration of the native dogmatism of human nature, caused by fancying for oneself a private monopoly in God. It cannot but spring up, if one holds with equally absolute certainty that He is *not* present with another, and that He *is* endorsing one's own opinions. Take the following illustration of this Hard Church spirit from Professor Rogers's method of dealing with Atheism,—not, remember, an individual case of Atheism which he could trace to personal immorality, but that which has been so common in the working classes for a generation past at least :—

"My dear Sir,—I cannot offer a single word of apology to your 'secular' guest for what I said. You know he distinctly affirmed, in consistency with some of the 'secularist' authorities of our time, that he believed it was desirable to get rid of the conception of a presiding Deity under any possible modifications !—and that the absence of any such notion was more favourable to human virtue and morality than its presence. This opinion is asserted, as in some other atheistical works (all obscure enough, to be sure), so in a little one which proposes it as the "task of to-day" to annihilate the—Deity ! No doubt it will be the task of to-morrow also, and, I should think, the day after that. You will recollect, that when your 'secularist' acquaintance affirmed the above strange dogmas, I gave him a fair opportunity of retracting, by saying that if he merely meant that *such* a God as millions had worshipped,—a Belial, a Moloch,—an obscene and cruel Deity,—even a Venus or a Bacchus,—might possibly be as bad as none (or worse), many might agree with him ; but if he meant *such* a Deity as implied perfection of wisdom, justice, power, and goodness, none but a liar or a madman would. He positively re-affirmed, however, his opinion that, under *any* modification, the idea of a God was pernicious ; that Atheism was better than Theism ; and particularly appealed to those great 'authorities' M. Comte, Mr. —— and Miss ——. It was then I said, if you recollect (what I still say, and am prepared to maintain), that I hold myself absolved from arguing with any one who can affirm that the idea of a perfectly holy, invisible, ever present infallible Governor (sincerely entertained), is *more* unfavourable to virtue than the notion that there is no God at all ; or that, so far as it has any conceivable bearing on human conduct, it can be other than auxiliary to every imaginable motive to morality ; that I was convinced, so long as the human intellect was constituted as it is, that the man who asserted such a paradox must be regarded by ninety-nine men out of every hundred as a liar, and that the hundredth would only shield him from *that* by supposing him *mad*. I still hold to every syllable of that declaration. It is impossible, constituted as we are, that we can believe any man other than a hypocrite or an idiot, who tells us that, if you *add* a motive or two motives *coincident* with ten others to these last, the whole will be diminished in force : that the supposition of an unseen judge over the *thoughts* as well as *actions*, and who will infallibly reward or punish them in accordance with what your 'secularist' acquaintance himself *believes* to be true principles of human conduct, will be an impediment to right doing ! Would it not be just as easy to believe that two and two make five ? . . . . I am quite ready to argue with any candid atheist, if such there be (of which I have my doubts), as to whether there is a God or not ; I am sure he will not descend to this sort of knavish or idiotic paradox. If sincere, he will say, 'Well, if there be *no* such God as you have described, so much the worse for the world. I admit *that;* one must confess that it is *desirable* there should be such a one ; but that does not prove that there *is* one.' This is what I should call intelligent and candid ; and the argument might go on. As to what he says of my want of charity—but let the man say what he pleases. If he be a liar, who would, and if an idiot who could, reason with him ? And that he is either one or the other, is beyond doubt with me. . . . ."[2]

Now did it ever occur to Mr. Rogers, that if almost all great minds have passed through a stage of the

---

[2] 'Selections from the Correspondence of R. E. H. Greyson, Esq.,' edited by the author of the 'Eclipse of Faith.' 2 vols. Longmans, 1857.

darkest scepticism, there must be not only a discipline in such scepticism, but such a discipline, that to some, at some periods of their career, it might well seem to be true that religion is wholly hurtful? If, instead of proclaiming from the heights of his supposed Christianity that this Atheist was either a "liar or an idiot," Mr. Rogers had taken the pains to elicit the state of mind which could alone render such a paradox honest and real, might he not have gained something of valuable conviction, even for his own Christianity?

At least I have met with those who, being neither liars nor idiots, have enunciated the same astounding paradox; and who, I believe, were at that very time under the discipline of a divine education. I could even conceive it most natural that the passage from a narrow and confidently selfish system of belief to that large and tasking form of Christianity, whose only infinite certainty is the unveiled holiness and love of God, should lie through such a period of vehement scepticism as this. For is it not, in fact, good that some men should know what it is to the heart to believe itself *alone?* is it not even desirable that *if* man could find his highest purity and virtue in self-reliance, he should do so? is it not a most divine discipline that he should be robbed, not only of the "motives" to virtue which religion gives, but of the living help which trust gives, if he can indeed fancy himself a self-dependent being? Is he not even better when he is trying for himself how firmly he can walk alone through the dark mystery of life, than when leaning only on the false supports of a selfish and degraded theology? And may not the destined experiences of that "dim and perilous way" teach him something truer far of the spiritually dependent nature of man,—of what he has falsely mistaken for God,—of what God really is,—than Mr. Rogers himself could ever learn while he kicks against the pricks of Atheism, and instead of striving to see whether that too may not sometimes be a divine as well as a satanic discipline, brutally offers an opponent his choice between the epithets of a "liar" or an "idiot"?

To me the Hard Church seem to evince a most melancholy ignorance of the true meaning and history of doubt, when they meet it as they do. Were they devil's advocates, they could do no better. To jeer and taunt a doubter with the shallowness of his thoughts, even if they be shallow, can have but one of two effects —to scare him into apparent concession without solving his real perplexity; or to fortify him in his resistance, not from any deeper appreciation of his own position, but from irritation at yours. The insolent method proceeds, as I have said, from complete distrust that God's realities are any wider or more various than the self-confident understanding of man. Now the method which is really pursued with our minds, if dogmatists would only take the trouble to note it, is totally opposite. Often, no doubt, temporary scepticisms do arise in moral weakness far more than in moral strength. But in all cases we are made to feel and sound the whole depth of our doubts before there is any progress to their removal. We are not dragged away from them, or mocked out of them, by the spiritual providence of God. We are taught *all* they mean before we are taught the true solution. Superficial doubt becomes real and searching before it passes away. Real and searching doubt itself often brings on, or else is guided into, a practical crisis in the outward life before it is laid to rest. At the very time when the coarse theologian is telling the sceptic that his brains "must be a mere lump of cotton-wool,"[3] or that his difficulty is of no account whatever "in the estimation of any body who does not deserve to be shut up in Bedlam"[4] the spiritual experience of life may often be expressly adapted to exhaust and then solve the problem by which He whom the theologian professes to confess and defend, has tasked and disciplined the sceptic's mind; and it is well if the arrogance of man do not counteract, or at least weaken, the efficacy of the inward experience prepared by God.

It is this wretched assumption, that the petty moulds of our own faith define and limit the spiritual activity of the divine object of faith, which makes us so eager to check and punish, instead of adopting and pursuing, the line of thought by which for the first time the doubter's mind has been brought into any real contact with the spiritual world. If we really believed that God had any intercourse at all with the sceptic's mind as well as with our

---

[3] Vide supra, vol. ii. p. 328.   [4] Ibid. p. 329.

own, we might often look on genuine doubt as the first stirrings of genuine trust; and, instead of practising the throttling art of such controversialists as Mr. Rogers, might learn from Socrates that the first great step is to make a man hold his doubts clearly and seriously, to bring them into really articulate life, to let him see their full depth, and be fairly haunted by their practical urgency; and then perhaps, but not till then, might we be able to help him to realise where the answer to those doubts had been revealed. The scolding theology of modern orthodoxy is mainly engaged in striving against the very Spirit for whose honour it is so bitter—in resisting the spiritual unfolding of difficulties which it is, in truth, its duty to assist. The reason why half the faith of Christendom is so hollow and valueless, is to be found in the mistrust of theologians lest no sounding-line, however divine, should be able to fathom the depths of honest doubt. At least they act as if the kingdom of God depended on their penning-in intellects of every kind and depth between some miserable and wearisome logical alternatives, by which they fancy their own convictions have been guided. That is, they believe in a God as large and no larger than their own capacity for faith; and hence they are never led to see whether or not, perhaps, that small capacity might be enlarged.

The Hard Church believes in a Hard Master. It evidently holds that the reception of Christianity is not caused by a divine Spirit working *with and in* human nature,—subduing it into its most perfect harmony,—

answering its own deepest wants,—bracing with new strength its own highest powers; but working *against* it,—irritating its pride, browbeating its natural faiths, disappointing its hopes with the bitterest irony of Providence, and silencing by the mere stentorian force of loud omnipotence its indigenous doubt. This is what the author I have just quoted, who, I admit, caricatures in some respects even the Hard Church, says of the Bible:—

"You cannot say that 'The Book has not given you every *advantage;*' for never was there one which more irritates the pride and prejudices of mankind, which presents greater obstacles to its reception, morally and intellectually;—so that it is amongst the most unaccountable things to *me*, not that it should be rejected by some, but that it should be accepted by any. 'It is, I grant,' said an old Deist, 'a very strange thing that Christianity should be embraced; for *I* do not perceive in myself any inclination to receive the New Testament.' *There* spake, not Deism only, but HUMAN NATURE."

The same doctrine is repeated by the same author in other places. Christianity, he tells us, goes "desperately against the grain of human nature;" and his own writings seem in this respect to be a humble attempt to imitate this feature in his conception of Christianity. "The theories," he tells us in another place, "of Christianity and Deism are *antipodal;*" and hence clearly his attempt to identify himself exclusively with that form of Christianity which recognises least truth, and least desire for truth, in every system which it regards as extra-Christian. He seems to think that Christianity was given, not "that the thoughts of many hearts might be revealed," but that they might be suppressed and suffocated; and assumes in all his controversy that it must be by choice and of set purpose, not from any inward constraint, if any man find difficulties in the Christian evidences,—a purpose which must be put down by "strong" measures. He considers Christianity in the light, more of a disagreeable medicine than a Gospel, administered by the benevolent compulsion of God to reluctant humanity.

But the day when such a conception could have been generally accepted, if it ever were, is now long past. To the Jew, no doubt, the revelation of the purposes of God was conceived of as, in a measure, *absolute*,—as independent of his own fears or cravings,—as a Voice from the great darkness of Omnipotence, to be listened to and obeyed. But even the Jew had the strongest feeling that this voice did not merely overrule but refreshed the true nature within him, *answered* rather than silenced his questionings when he was overpowered by the mysteries of the national destinies, and made him feel that nothing true within him was crushed, but every thing elevated, by the life of obedience to that divine teaching. And assuredly St. Paul expressed the general yearning of both Jew and Gentile when he said, that the "creation groaned and travailed" for the birth of Christianity; that its new knowledge and its new power were not useful and wholesome remedies forced on reluctant minds, but a divine fountain, springing up after long expectation to assuage the burning thirst of nations and of centuries. Had St. Paul thought that in the words, "I perceive in myself no inclination to receive the New Testament," human nature itself was speaking, he would scarcely have spoken with so much confidence, to an audience of Greek philosophers, of all nations as "seeking the Lord, if haply they might feel after him and find him," or have proved that confidence by his eagerness to proclaim, alike to the rude idolaters of Lycaonia, the trained intellects of Athenian schools, the Jewish people and king, Roman prefects, the Roman emperor, and the Spanish barbarians, truths which human nature, as such, had neither longing nor inclination to accept.

And if this were so *then*, assuredly every century of the subsequent eighteen has made it more and more, not only true, but obvious, that the deepest evidence of all divine truth is in the intimations and cravings of the ordinary human heart. As human history unfolds, it becomes more and more obvious that wants which seem completely finite and earthly often break their limits by the force of an inward and irrepressible inspiration, and give their witness for a spiritual world,—that the most patient and plodding industry will burst into the most passionate excitement if denied the sense of a spiritual freedom it would never practically desire to *use*,—that the disinterested social and political ties for which men suffer and die absorb a larger and larger proportion of the most ordinary daily duties,—that that even the lowest and commonest of human appetites acquire by their association with politics and science countless associations and ties with deathless Art, with the ceaseless success and endeavour of the human intellect, with the greatness of spiritual virtues and spiritual sins, with the belief in infinite suffering, the agony of despair, and the joy of trust.

It is literally true that, as human history goes on, spiritual disorders and wants descend deeper and deeper into the core of physical life; responsibilities are distributed over society at large which were concentrated on one or two points,—and are not only distributed, but more generally understood and felt; the social and political bearings of individual selfishness or unselfishness are more and more more deeply realized; spheres of life that were formerly conceived as totally unconnected with the spiritual world, are now seen to be poisoned by spiritual rather than physical diseases; poetry and art penetrate more and more homely retreats, drawing out everywhere the latent forces of voluntary evil and good, and the full expressiveness of human beauty and deformity; even our very laughter comes from deeper springs than that of the ancient world, and has in it a fuller consciousness of all that human nature seeks to be, and all that it is. In short, the craving for a divine religion that arises in *strictly* human inclinations—in the unsatisfied tossings of human desire and want and emotion—in the fever of restless thought, driven on to ask for infinite satisfaction, and finding only finite—in the gnawing sense of unreality and insincerity that accompanies all temporary pleasures and all temporary aims,—was never so deeply felt as in the present day. If ever there were a time when it was simply false to say that human nature, as such, has "no inclination" to receive Christianity, it is now.

And certainly there never was a time when it was so hopeless to force any revelation on it, from without, that is not first dimly shaped forth within; for there never was a time in which, taking it in its largest sense, human nature had so much faith in *itself*. Even Atheism clings vainly and passionately to this faith; and glorifies and worships the *Etre Suprême* of humanity,—the *Einheit des Menschengeschlechts*—after it has discarded God. And this is no sign of mere degradation, but the last remnant of a true devotion. It is because even Atheism sees that a spirit draws men into one national or universal unity, of a diviner and *more* human kind than any which divides and sets them at variance, that it desires to worship humanity at large, and recoils from the notion that each should separately worship himself. I am perfectly sure that no religion, and no so-called phase of Christianity, has the slightest chance of universal reception in the present day, which strives to bear down and silence the spiritual testimony of human nature, taken in its strictest sense, to the religious wants and pains and hopes which are already fermenting there, and which only need to be quickened into clear responsible knowledge by divine affirmation given through the external history of man. Unless a universal divine spirit be recognised as living *in* man, there will be no chance of recognising any as living *above* man; no revelation would be credible from a divine king that did not reveal also the long-brooding thoughts of a divine humanity.

The Hard Church care not at all to start from common ground, and bring men on to a higher level; their only care is to make men feel as uncomfortable and wretched as possible on the ground they occupy. Had Christianity been really revealed in the way in which the Hard Church endeavour to reveal it, it would have begun by enforcing on all men, except the Jews, that they believed nothing at all, and had no capacity for judging even of what they wanted to believe,—in fact, by asking contemptuously for the surrender of all the groundless faith they had; and would then have presented them, as offensively as possible, with a series of confessedly pugnacious truths, demonstrated by thunder-claps of power and by an appeal to their coming preternatural success. Was it thus, or by the fascination and development of all the faith that the world still retained, that Christ and His apostles riveted the ears of Jew and Greek and Roman? Had they argued with the unbelieving nations in the *spirit* in which the school I am dealing with argues with Deists and Atheists, and yet with the marvellous force they actually displayed, they would have produced a mighty recoil into passionate and rebellious Atheism instead of the renovation of the whole western world.

The unspiritual religion of the Hard Church has commonly another characteristic, which is, in truth, only a deeper form of that want of faith, and consequent want of large spiritual charity, of which I have been speaking. A belief which narrows the spiritual agency of God to the narrow channels it has already sounded and marked out for itself, has, as I have said, no patience to estimate anxiously the deeper grounds of other men's difficulties, or to go with them their full mile of common road before breaking off into the diverging path of private opinion. But this narrowness of spiritual trust often generates a still more marvellous characteristic of theological discussion. Does it not betray the utter unreality of much religious conviction, that even in discussing the grounds of all reality,—the very nature and influences of God,—nothing is more common than to catch eagerly at the mere accidental weaknesses of an opponent's *statement*, as distinguished from his *meaning*, so as to achieve a logical victory over his form of expression without touching the body of his thought?

That sane men should profess to believe in the universal Spirit of God, and yet in controversy concerning that Spirit should ever be glad to stop short of encountering an opponent's *fullest* thought, is perhaps the most extraordinary example in existence of the power which men possess to distort the spiritual world into the image of their own littleness. Of course there is no full consciousness of the self-deception; a logical fencer strikes too eagerly at the weak point to consider whether the victory he gains is one of words or of thoughts. But this is just the very sign that his creed is in fact only a beaten track of thought in his own mind, not a trust which goes *out* of himself into a real reliance upon God. If the object be to measure intellectual strength with an adversary, of course the detection of a deficiency in *expression* is of some moment. But if the object be, by comparing mutually a real mental experience, to obtain a clearer insight into what God's ways with us are, a theologian would be eager to strengthen by every means in his power the force of his opponent's case, that he might as fully as possible reach that mental reality in which alone the divine Spirit could have had any participation. It is a sure sign that a man's religion is rather a codified mass of opinions concerning God than a personal relation, or even a *desire* for a personal relation, to Him, if he be not eager to remove as completely as possible the film of confusion which words interpose between the religious life of men and any thoughtful comparison of the convictions to which that life gives rise.

If controversialists had any deep trust that God were really with them *all*, they must be much more anxious than they are to get over imperfections of expression in order to grasp the reality behind. Look at the skill and patience with which in human affairs any one who believes that there is something of *real fact* to elicit, and is eager to elicit it, will question and cross-question, and probe the very depths of another's memory. And ordinary religious controversy shows its real unspirituality in this, that the disputant has not, in truth, the slightest conviction that there is any background of *fact* to elicit; he does not really believe God has any living relation at all to the mind of others, and therefore he makes no effort to see what that relation is. He simply wishes to confute a troublesome opinion ; he conceives it to be all matter of distant *inference*, not of moral *experience ;* he avails himself eagerly of weak exposition, because, while he has no belief that thorough and fair exposition would add in the least to the data or premises in dispute, he has a very just and rational belief that it would give him a great deal more trouble ; and hence the rareness of bold and eager thought in theological controversy. You see it in science, because each party really assumes that the other also is in contact with the *facts*, though perhaps judging of them hastily. You see it in psychological and moral disputes, because again the same capacity for personal observation and study is conceded, and the object is really to arrive at what the other has got a certain hold of, and reconcile it with what we ourselves have a certain hold of, and not to compare the arbitrary meanderings of the vaguest possible inferences from the vaguest possible data. But you do not see it in theology, because so few fairly admit that there is any living spring of independent conviction in every distinct mind ; so that the boldness and eagerness which are in place in any real collision with facts, are utterly out of place when you only see a new combination of troublesome words without any new combination of realities. It is the absence of true faith in a universally Revealing Mind that destroys altogether the only possible field of theological discussion, since only phantom combatants can fight in phantom lists.

That must be unspiritual religion which cares to criticise and triumph over logical forms of error, instead of trying to appreciate the facts which those logical forms more or less inarticulately express. This seems to me, however, to be the pervading fault of the class of writers I am considering. They are not, I think, consciously unfair, but excessively *unreal;* grappling with the hasty statements instead of the mental tendencies of their opponents; impatient to confute and to trample upon an adversary, utterly careless as to the comprehension of his fullest meaning. The blows fall thick on the weakest points of weak assailants; and triumphantly quell objections which may very likely be real, but certainly are not adequate, exponents of deep popular perplexities on the subject of religion. Nothing, for example, can be much more disgusting than the following portion of a letter to a younger friend on the philosophy of prayer. Directly a real spiritual difficulty is started, the writer sets up just such a hue and cry as if he were a slave-catcher sighting a runaway negro, instead of a theologian grappling with the most mysterious of all subjects; and in place of desiring to see into the depths of the perplexity, he seems to dance round it with half ferocious exultation, discharging blunt missiles at it from time to time :—

"I have heard (need I say with dismay?) from your relative, and my dear friend, Mr. W—, that you have become such a 'philosopher' as to have discovered the inutility of all 'prayer,' and that you have resolved to give it up!

"Pardon me for saying, that it would have been better if you had given up your 'philosophy' *such* philosophy, I mean; for it is a 'philosophy falsely so called.' True philosophy demands no such sacrifice ; and I hope, from the regard you have for me, you will at least read with patient attention what I have to say to you.

"Philosophy ! why, my dear youth, one *fact*, which, I am told, you acknowledge to be still a *puzzle* to you, is enough to show that a genuine philosophy,—the philosophy of Bacon,—the philosophy you profess to revere so much,—distinctly condemns your conclusion as utterly *un*philosophical. You confess, it seems, that seeing the clear inutility of prayer, from the impossibility of supposing God to contravene the 'order of antecedents and consequents,' or to infringe His own laws (of all which babble by and by), it is to you a great 'puzzle' that the overwhelming majority of the race in all ages,—of philosophers and peasants—of geniuses and blockheads,—of the refined and the vulgar,—the bulk even of those who plead for the doctrine of 'moral necessity' itself,—have contended for the propriety, the efficacy, the necessity of prayer ! that man, in trouble, seems naturally to resort to it ! that, for the most part, it is only in prosperity that those who deny its value can afford to do so ; that when they come to a scene of distress, or a deathbed, even they, in the greater number of cases, break out,—if they believe, as you do, in a presiding deity at all,—into cries for help, and supplications for mercy ; just as naturally as they weep when sorrowful, or rejoice when happy !

"You call these facts a *puzzle;* they seem a curious example of human 'inconsistency,'—of the tardiness of man to embrace a genuine philosophy ! Ha ! ha ! ha !

" I fancy there is another explanation that smacks a little more of a *genuine* philosophy. Surely if the great bulk of mankind, all their lives long, whimsically admit in theory the propriety and efficacy of prayer, even while they daily neglect it in practice,—if multitudes, who would *like* very well to have a burdensome and unwelcome duty which they neglect proved to be no duty at all, are still invincibly convinced that it is such,—must not a genuine inductive philosophy confess that such a concurrence of wise and vulgar, of philosophy and instinct, and all too against seeming interest and strong passions,—is an indication that the *constitution of human nature itself* favours the hypothesis of the efficacy and propriety of prayer ?—and if so, ought not that to be taken into account in your philosophy ? *I* contend that it is decisive of the controversy, if you are really to philosophise on the matter at all. Meantime it seems, you account it merely a great *puzzle,* amidst that *clear demonstration* you have, of the inutility and absurdity of prayer!

"If you say, 'I have confessed it is a puzzle; what does it prove?' I answer, 'Prove? my fine fellow; why it proves *this,*—that *the* fact which ought to determine your philosophy on this question is against you. Yes;—*the* fact which a Bacon would take principally into account, utterly refutes you. Stick fairly to your *induction,* and I will give you leave to infer as long as you will. The facts you call a 'puzzle' prove that the normal constitution of human nature pleads distinctly both for the propriety and efficacy of prayer. Such facts say as plainly of man he was made to do this or that,—it is his *nature* to do this or that,—as the fire to burn or the sun to shine."

And when at length this author vouchsafes a reply to his opponent's difficulty, it is this:—

"Let us suppose—and I am confident I may defy you to disprove it—(I indeed believe it is the absolute truth), that amongst other 'pre-arrangements' of Divine wisdom, and to the maintenance of which, therefore, all that 'immutability' on which you found so much is pledged,—it has been decreed that prayer shall be one of the indispensable conditions of the stable enjoyment of God's favour; let us suppose He has decreed, and for ever, that only *he* shall be truly happy, get what he hopes, and receive what he needs, who seeks 'His face;'—let us suppose, I say, all this (and I am very certain you cannot show its improbability or absurdity), what then? Why just this, that if this *be* a condition of the Divine conduct towards us, if it *be* one of the 'wise pre-arrangements,' one of the 'unvarying laws,' your philosophy, my young friend, is still very true, but unluckily confutes your conclusion: I have introduced, you see, but another of your pleasant antecedents, and your little syllogism holds no longer."

After this explanation, which he offers as, in his conviction, the absolute truth, the writer goes on to explain, that this "antecedent condition" of divine favour—prayer

—may therefore be regarded as in the nature of a "peppercorn-rent" to God for all his blessing :—

> "I have not thought it of moment to reply to the logical refinement sometimes urged, that even if it be granted that prayer is an indispensable *pre-condition* of the Divine favour, its inefficacy as a *proper cause* may still be maintained ; for I am convinced that you would not urge it seriously. As to the *event*, it is all one, and I do not think it worth while to discuss such subtleties.
>
> "If a man were to offer you an estate on the payment of a peppercorn-rent (and our 'prayers' are worth not so much to the Deity), it is certain that the man's bounty, and not the peppercorn, would be the *cause* of your good fortune ; but as without the peppercorn you would be without the estate, I imagine you would have little inclination to chop logic with him about its being 'causal' or otherwise."

I have seldom read a theological argument showing so utter a want of moral appreciation of the thought, so painful and contemptuous a disposition to mere logical fencing. To me, at least, the difficulty is left just where it was ; but by the closing illustration is presented in the harshest possible form. It is the oppression of the thought that man's eager life, his love, his anguish, his piercing cries, *are* mere "pre-arranged conditions," "peppercorn-rents" to the great proprietor of the universe— hinges in an inexorable system of pre-established machinery—inevitabilities in one vast frame of inevitability,— which robs us wholly of the desire to pray. If communion with God be not the free interchange of a living trust for a living love, if it be not a voluntary appeal looking for a voluntary reply, if the imploring agony be a mere flash of vital force pre-ordained to precede a fixed proportion of the divine blessing, if, in short, individual prayers do not individually affect the divine Spirit except as determinate signals in a mighty plan upon the appearance of which an act of love becomes due,—then, I say, the true difficulty remains, that with such a conviction intensely stamped upon the mind, it would be totally impossible to pray. Prayer can never be the fulfilment of a "pre arranged condition," the "payment of a peppercorn rent," without utterly ceasing to be prayer. It is, and can only be, possible on the assumption that it is a real influence with God; that whether granted or denied, it is *efficient* as an expression of our spiritual want and resolution; that the breath of power which answers it is a living response, and, like all living responses, the free utterance of the moment, not the pre-ordained consequent waiting for a pre-ordained antecedent; that there is a sphere beyond all necessary law, in which both the divine and human life are not constrained by immutable arrangements, but *free*. This, I say, is the only intellectual assumption on which prayer can be a natural act; and though any intellectual assumption at all is far from needful to most persons in a sphere of being so mysterious, it is the only one which meets the moral perplexity which the opening reason of man will frequently start. Whether Professor Rogers's reply be true or false, it leaves the heart of the spiritual problem quite untouched, while attaining a barren victory over its logical form.

I will quote one other instance of the same kind, from the writings of the same author, which present instances of the same method on almost every religious subject he touches: it is on the subject of the Atonement. The creed of the writer requires that Christ's *suffering* should be regarded as, for some reason or other, a real *substitute* for human suffering, and an indispensable condition to God's forgiveness. He argues on it thus:—

"We can only reason a little way; but as far as we *can* reason, I do not flinch from saying that every *fact* we know is against the theory of your simple unconditional forgiveness.

"We can but reason in reference to a subject so vast, and in all its bearings so infinitely transcendental to our comprehension, by *analogy*. Now it is certain, that in any moral government with which we are acquainted, or of which we can form any conception, —in any government whose subjects are ruled by *motives* only, and where *will* is unconstrained,—the principle of the prompt unconditional pardon of crime on profession of repentance and purpose of amendment would be most disastrous; as we invariably see it is in a family, in a school, in a political community. Now, have we any reason to believe that in a government most emphatically *moral*,— a government of which all the moral governments with which we are acquainted are but imperfect imitations, and which are, indeed, founded on a very partial application of the laws which a perfect moral government implies,—similar easy good-natured lenity would be attended with less ruinous effects? If we have none, then, since we cannot think that God's government will or can *cease* to be moral, or that He ever will physically constrain His creatures to be happy or holy,—indeed the very notion involves a contradiction in terms,—would not the proposed course of universally pardoning guilt on profession of penitence prove in all probability most calamitous? Let us then, suppose (no difficult thing) that God foresaw this;—that such a procedure would be of pernicious consequences, not to this world only, but, for aught we know, to many; that it would diminish His authority, relax the ties of allegiance, invite His subjects to revolt, make them think disloyalty a trivial matter? If so,—and I defy you to prove that it may not be so, — then would there not be benignity as well as justice, mercy as well as equity, in refusing the exercise of a weak compassion which would destroy more than it would save? Let us suppose further, that knowing all this, God knew also that His yearning compassion for lost and guilty man might be safely gratified by such an expedient as the Atonement; that so far from weakening the bonds of allegiance, such an acceptance of a voluntary propitiation would strengthen them; that it would flash on all worlds an indelible conviction no less of His justice than of His mercy—of His justice, that He could not pardon without so tremendous a sacrifice; of His mercy, that He would not, to gratify it, refrain even from this; that it would crush for ever that subtle sophism so naturally springing in the heart of man, and which gives to temptation its chief power—that God is too merciful to punish;—I say, if all this be so,—and I fancy you will find it difficult to prove that it *may* not be so,—does not the Atonement assume a new aspect? Is it any longer chargeable with absurdity or caprice? May it not be justly pronounced a device worthy of Divine wisdom and benignity? Is it not calculated to secure that which is its proposed end?—at once to make justice doubly venerable and mercy doubly dear?—justice more venerable, that it could not be lightly assuaged; mercy more dear, that it would be gratified though at such a cost?"

I take it that the real difficulty sincerely felt by most Christians who have doubted or rejected the doctrine of Christ's vicarious sufferings is here completely evaded; for the analogy drawn from human affairs has two main features: one, that it grounds the necessity for inflicting suffering before granting pardon on the uncertain nature of human *professions* of penitence; the other, that it grounds the same necessity on the danger that any omission to vindicate the majesty of law on those who have *themselves really* transgressed it, will bring the law itself into less respect. Now neither of these points of analogy has the slightest application to the case in point: for, with regard to the first, no one ever ventured to say that Christ's sufferings could redeem any uncertain or superficial penitence from its full spiritual burden of misery. There is no difficulty with God in judging that which no human Court of justice dare attempt to determine; and if some absolute infliction of pain somewhere be needful in human Courts only to provide for the countless cases where professed penitence is insincere or incomplete, it would not be needful before a divine tribunal at all, since half-penitents must suffer until they are thoroughly changed in heart, and true penitents need suffer no more. And, on the second and deeper point, that pardon could only be conditional on some display of the just severity of the law, lest the law itself should lose its awfulness,—the reply is clear that the law is not vindicated, but broken anew, by the substitution of one who has not violated it for those who had. If it is sin against the law to pardon the guilty, it is no less sin against the law to inflict suffering on the innocent; and to add that infliction to the remission of a penalty that is duly incurred, is to double the transgression of the majesty of offended law, not to cancel it.

The simple truth is, that though it is one of the deepest laws of human society that we should bear each other's burdens—that when "one member suffers all the members suffer with it"—that there is no such thing as the isolation of a sin, or even of the misery that proceeds in widening circles, though with slackening force, from every centre of sin,—though it is the law of human fellowship that the good must suffer with the guilty (and the more willingly the higher they are in goodness), as *the price of that fellowship*,—yet this is not a law of vicarious *punishment*, a law by which the penalty *proper to sin* is borne by one who has not committed that sin, but rather a law which intensifies a hundredfold instead of removing, the sense of social responsibility, and consequently the burden of social guilt. And so the sufferings of Christ have, I believe, never legitimately lightened a single fear of a guilty mind by suggesting any subtraction from the penalty in store; but rather, by revealing the true law of the social unity of humanity, have increased those fears a hundredfold. It is only by rendering true penitence *possible*, by emancipating us from the despair of human weakness through the revelation of a divine power in whose might we may trample on sin and death, not by cancelling any balance of suffering due to us *after* true penitence, that the death of Christ can set us free.

Nothing ever can, or ever ought, to dissuade the human heart from believing, that if once it can be utterly and profoundly penitent, a free pardon from God is *certain*, and always was certain, and needed no "forensic arrangement" of any sort to make it more certain. But how to attain that true penitence without the revelation of a triumphant power close to and even participating in our sense of human helplessness, was the great problem; —the answer to which has been parodied in the hideous and pagan theory that infinite justice must inflict some punishment *somewhere* for every violation of law, but whether on the offender or on a voluntary proxy is comparatively unimportant. The Hard Church habitually glances at the most superficial aspect of the difficulty, and never attempts to realise the essential meaning of objectors. Dr. Mansel, who is the great philosopher of the Hard Church, has, as I have shown in a previous essay, treated the same subject in very much the same style.

I have now done with the Hard Church. The temper which fixes the eye rather on private demonstrations of God and of His revelation than on God Himself and the substance of His revelation ;—which is so occupied with its fancied monopoly of the privilege of defending God's ways, that it forgets the object of faith in the expertness of its endeavours to fortify the approaches ;—and which never practically realises that all private avenues to belief are, if God be a living and universal Father, capable of indefinite enlargement by studying the infinite variety of His spiritual dealings with *others*,—is I know, a temper to which we are all liable, but which fills me with genuine dread. Indeed, when I read these books of small confident logic on subjects so high as to task our nature to the full, I sometimes ask, 'Is not scepticism the next stage in the education of such confidence as this? Is it not likely that such thinkers must pass through some discipline in the blinding night,—some groping, some "feeling after" God, to teach them that

He proves *His own* presence, and is not amenable to their small proofs,—before they can gain any permanent hold of those great spiritual realities to which they have made it their triumphant occupation to pave these narrow and dismal approaches?'

XI.

ROMANISM, PROTESTANTISM, AND ANGLICANISM.

THEOLOGICAL creeds seldom escape the fate of "holy places." The more sacred is the presence which has departed or is departing from them, the more keenly do the occupants feel, and the more reluctant are they to express, the sense of vacancy which steals over them. And the greater the glow of trust with which they formerly held possession of their post, the more sullenly do they fortify the empty sepulchres, the more passionately do they dispute the line of the deserted walls. It is so with Romanism. And the same thing has happened, nay, happens every day, with Protestantism. It was a saying of Luther's, that the very people who, in his lifetime, would not touch the kernel of his teaching, would be greedy after the husks of it when he was once dead. And so it was, and so it is, and so it will be. The seed of a great faith falls into men's hearts, and God "giveth it *another* body, as it pleaseth him;" the husks alone are treasured up, *unchanged*, and last the longer without suffering transformation " into something rich and strange," that the germ of their organic life has altogether disappeared, even if it has not been anxiously excavated, and its place supplied by the mineral, inorganic cement of theological learning. It is this husk-theology which both shelters within itself, and provokes into activity outside itself, the spirit of scepticism. The dogmatism of half-belief which gradually steals upon the first downright confidence of full belief, leans with a less and less sincere weight on the object of its faith, till at last the bold sceptic who stands upright on his own strength, and will not affect to lean at all, becomes, and is conscious of being, a really stronger man in his isolation and his weakness than those who are painfully endeavouring to avoid putting any strain on the weak props of a decaying faith. An attempt to appreciate the essence of the two opposite faiths, and the two opposite forms of scepticism which still contend for the body of the Anglican Church, will help me to estimate more fairly the true position and prospects of the various parties in that Church than would be possible if I were only to criticise the consistency or inconsistency of their present theological positions.

Forty years ago, Roman Catholicism was almost a fable in England. Children were told about it as a branch of ancient history, and taught to connect that superstition very closely with the inability to read and write and think. The Catholics in England "were found in corners, and alleys, and cellars, or in the recesses of the country, cut off from the populous world around them, and dimly seen as if through a mist, or in twilight as ghosts flitting to and fro!" Suddenly there rose up, on the chosen ground of classical learning and among the ablest thinkers of the day, a rumour that Protestantism was reaping what it had not sown—that it could not have originated the faith which it had inherited. Restless, scrupulous, self-tasking, reasoning, subtle-minded men affirmed that, though the tendencies of their whole nature seemed to converge upon the Christian Revelation as the very focus of their highest *needs*, yet that they could never have accepted its fact as their highest *certainty* without a constantly-renewed testimony from an authority above that of individual conviction. They were sure that it was easier to recognise a divine authority than to grasp or compass for themselves divine truth. They thought they could perceive where they ought to obey, far more easily than where they ought to believe. And they maintained, too, that the power to obey must be granted first, as the simpler and most practical necessity of life, and that it would draw after it the fulness of belief. Nevertheless, they were not unembarrassed. They felt that they could scarcely faithfully obey on a *venture* what they did not confidently believe to be divine, though they were clear that a fuller confidence of belief was to be the reward of their obedience.

And so they vacillated long, unable to find satisfying conviction without a rule of action they could wholly accept, and painfully deploring that they had not early and always had a strict and indisputable law of discipline over them, which might have yielded as its natural fruit the faith they now groped after with uncertain hands. And then there grew upon them, more and more powerfully, the fascination of that mighty power, who through the march of centuries, had advanced with a measured tread of her own, unborrowed from her children—a step of which every footfall was a fiat, and the rhythm a faith. It was obviously easy to throw a temporary spell over minds in such a mood; but what is the charm which has power to retain them, after experience of Rome's coarse splendours, and of her vigilant and oppressive rule?

Rome alone has presented her theology to the world in a wholly institutional form. What Protestants believe, Rome embodies in a visible organism. While they derive the life of the church from their faith, Rome derives her faith from the life of the church. Romanism was a vast organization almost before it was a distinct faith. Rome did not incarnate her dogmas in her ritual, but distilled her dogmas out of her ritual. She had, indeed, knitted in with her spiritual agency many an act both of conscious and unconscious faith; she had built up her great missionary system on many assumptions both of truth and duty; but on the whole, she acted before she thought, and interpreted her faith under the inspiration of her achievements. Her theology flashed upon her, as it were, as she beheld the ecclesiastical form and order which was growing up out of her own unconscious energy. She solved the mystery of her own success by believing that her institutions were even fuller of the divine power than her thought, that she could more easily draw God down into the bosom of the church by her life, than she could lift up the church to God by her meditation. Wherever the drift of Christian practice seemed to point towards a development of the church's influence, there was a hint which she followed up eagerly to its limits, as the directing finger of a divine hand. And then contemplating her own fresh conquests from a heathen world, under the inspiring consciousness of being set to guide the mightiest and holiest of the world's forces, she did not hesitate to affirm that God was in her institutions, that He was acting through her agency, that He was really placing His divine influences at her disposal, and that in contemplating the orderly system of ecclesiastical life which was rising under her creating hand, she beheld the divine disposition of His living power. Thus, for example, the Christian practice of baptism was, in her hands, an agent of great social influence; and as she witnessed its results in consecrating new multitudes to Christ, and was conscious that her own faith grew in gazing at the act (instead of the virtue of the act having arisen from her faith), she at once affirmed that God had granted a mighty regenerating power to her *hand*, which did not proceed from, but afterwards passed into her *spirit;* that a grace was granted to her institutions from which her faith was nourished.

Again, the words of the last supper enjoined, as she supposed, the sacrifice of the mass. Eagerly Rome saw and used the mighty social influence of that divine institution. But here again she seemed to gather faith from the power of the rite. She administered it in weakness, and yet she was the almoner of power; the faith was multiplied in the giving, so that while it seemed too little for a few, it fed multitudes, and she gathered up more than she had divided; it seemed that no virtue went out of her, yet richly it streamed in; in the act itself was the birth of faith; the power of God was in the elements themselves, for the grace and peace, which had not passed through the spirit of the church, returned upon her: and so she gazed till she could see the bread and wine no longer, though their external qualities remained; the essence was transmuted before her eyes into the life of Him who first consecrated them; the outward signs were but transparencies, through which the living glory gleamed; that seeming film of physical quality held fast the very presence of the Eternal, and God was perfectly blended with that sign of Himself which He had chosen.

This is the doctrine which marks the whole character of the Roman Church. Faith is nourished from the divine institution, not the divine institution by the faith. The Roman theology claims for the entire ritual of the church that it is one vast transubstantiation. Every rite which other Christian sects regard as suggesting and shadowing forth the spiritual life of faith, Rome regards as itself the shrine of divine power, as itself radiating light and heat. She believes that the church's ministrations impart more grace to her ministers, than her ministers can impart to their ministrations.[1] God's power is held to be in the church's actions, and from that centre it flows out on the whole church, alike strengthening the feeble knees of the worshipper, and lifting up the drooping hands of the priest. According to the sacramental system of Rome, neither is it the unity of human faith which binds together the church in one, nor is it the merely inherited commission of the church which holds together human faith; but the vivid electric spark of divine grace shooting, in eternal miracle, through her whole frame, is the true pulse of her immortal life; and this, though it is called down at the bidding of the priesthood, does not proceed *out of* their life, but into it, where its heavenly fire is no less needed than in the body of the church at large.

There is something in the sacramental system essentially congenial to the Roman character. We read Roman history, and ask ourselves why the records of the greatest nation of the world are so dull and inanimate, why a people that could *act* so mightily, puts forth so slight a charm over the student's mind? The answer

---

[1] Technically, the grace received *ex opere operato* is more than that received *ex opere operantis*.

is exactly this :—That they were a working nation, engraving for themselves monuments everywhere, but without any play of national mind distinct from, and out of relation to, the external tasks on which they were engaged. Had they possessed richer inward resources of self-occupation, they would have had a more interesting history, it may be, but not such a career. The very essence of their history is, that they were insatiable in their appetite for new materials to organise—new matter to mould. The Romans had no spontaneous mental or spiritual occupations apart from their will. As a nation they hated external tranquillity, and could find nothing satisfying but administrative and military exploit. Mental life, out of relation to political, social, or domestic *institutions*, they had almost none. They had little lyrical movement of spirit like the Greeks, little deep enjoyment of sympathy and sentiment like the Germans. They were made to *mould* others; and their only reverence for what was divine, was reverence for a moulding power, that shaped order and law out of social and material chaos. They could barely conceive of a free divine spirit in close *mental* contact with man, like the Jews. With a large and vivid receptive, but not a creative imagination, they could believe in a current of divine power moving under the surface of human or material agencies, but they were not drawn directly to the personal Spirit of God. Art fascinated them, but for poetry they were unfit; law was their occupation, yet they did not love to trace it to its purely moral sources in conscience; religious rites subdued them, but they shrank from analysing the spiritual life in which those rites were rooted. Hence, a sacramental system was of the essence of their religion. They sighed for a divine *administration*, but not for vivid, conscious *communion* with the Spirit of God. To find so rich a fountain of strength for the life of new and purer institutions as Christianity at first afforded, gave them a stern and holy joy. But still they retained their character of workers. They did not seek to be spirit to spirit with God; they adored Him in His acts; they sought for Him in a ritual. In this respect it is most true that the Catholic Church has never changed since first the ancient world began to suspect that the lost sceptre of the Cæsars had passed into a Roman bishop's grasp. She has ever claimed these outward ordinances —these gradually raised historical habitations of faith— not only as part and parcel of its essence, but as the organic influences which are mighty to *generate* it, as being its very bone and flesh—its body, not its raiment —as dying with it in its death, and as raised again in its resurrection.

The danger of the Roman side of faith is as obvious as its social power was once great. It began in humility, but it passed early into scepticism and arrogance. It originated in the wonder and the gratitude with which the church perceived the rapid growth of her influence, and perceived also that her own faith was marvellously strengthened by the very act of claiming for others the blessings of her divine message. But there was another side on which her strength was very near to weakness, and her faith to scepticism. Close to her power of social influence, was a passion for social ascendancy. Close to her faith that God was the strength of all her actions, was a disposition to dwell on her actions as though they were necessary to God. She was willing to recognise her own dependence, but most unwilling to suppose that He could ever choose any other instrument. It was natural to her to believe that all real power, as essentially orderly, could be organised and codified, and reduced to a system; and on this followed the natural temptation to claim for her own acts, as fixed *physical occasions* of spiritual influences, the right of being their *exclusive* cause. After proclaiming that a divine influence attended her ministry, which was in no way due to her own power, she fell into the snare of prizing her instrumentality as if it had been the very centre of that influence, and so gradually forgot the essence of her former faith. By dreaming that she held a monopoly of ecclesiastical instrumentality, she gradually came to believe that she could say "Come" or "Go" at pleasure to the very Spirit of God, and be obeyed.

The noble part of the church of Rome's testimony to the church of all ages, is her teaching that the faithful action of man does meet with a response from the reciprocal action of God—that it is not the mere lifting up of the human heart, but the actual descent of God's Spirit, which enlarges the life of duty and fosters the growth of faith. Protestantism has been inclined too often to overlook the double element that must exist in all real religion. Belief must lose its reality directly it is assumed either that man is absorbed into the divine agency, or that the activity of God is far removed from all definite relation to human acts and prayers. Rome has testified against both errors, but she has rendered her testimony feeble by virtually denying that beyond her own narrow dominions there is any recognised access to that free Spirit which "bloweth where it listeth," and by arrogating to her ministers the haughty privilege to signalise, by mere *outward* acts of their own, the certain approach of God.

I cannot present any passage which more strikingly realises to the mind the *institutional* conception of the Catholic worship, as intended to preach to the eye the visible descent of Christ to His church, than by quoting the following passage from a religious tale by Dr. Newman. It at once draws out all the implied faith, and also illustrates the corruptions by which Rome came to confound a church with a priesthood, and a real presence with a local form. What is most remarkable, is that so great a mind as Dr. Newman's should deny that Protestant communions ground their worship on faith in a positive *action* of God, only because they conceive that action to be directed to the spirits, and not to the altars of their churches:—

"The idea of worship in the Catholic Church," Willis replied, "is different from the idea of it in your church, for in truth the *religions* are different. Don't deceive yourself, my dear Bateman," he said, tenderly; "it is not that ours is your religion carried a little farther, —a little too far, as you would say. No, they differ in kind, not in degree; ours is one religion, yours another. . . . . . I declare, to me," he said, and he clasped his hands on his knees, and looked forward as if soliloquizing, "to me nothing is so consoling, so piercing, so thrilling, so overcoming as the mass, said as it is among us. I could attend masses for ever and not be tired. It is not a mere form of words,—it is a great action, the greatest action that can be on earth. It is not the invocation merely, but, if I dare use the word, the evocation of the Eternal. He becomes present on the altar in flesh and blood before whom angels bow and devils tremble. This is that awful event which is the end and is the interpretation of every part of the solemnity. Words are necessary, but as means, not as ends; they are not mere addresses to the throne of grace, they are instruments of what is far higher, of consecration, of sacrifice. They hurry on as if impatient to fulfil their mission. Quickly they go, the whole is quick; for they are all parts of one integral action. Quickly they go, for they are awful words of sacrifice, they are a work too great to delay upon; as when it was said in the beginning, 'What thou doest, do quickly.' Quickly they pass; for the Lord Jesus goes with them as He passed along the lake in the days of His flesh, quickly calling first one and then another. Quickly they pass; because as the lightning which shineth from one part of the heaven unto the other, so is the coming of the Son of man. Quickly they pass; for they are the words of the Lord descending in the cloud, and proclaiming the name of the Lord as He passes by, 'The Lord, the Lord God, merciful and gracious, long-suffering and abundant in goodness and truth.' And as Moses on the mountain, so we too 'make haste and bow our heads to the earth, and worship.' So we all around, each in his place, look out for the great Advent, 'waiting for the moving of the water.' Each in his place, with his own heart, with his own wants, with his own thoughts, with his own intention, with his own prayers, separate but concordant, watching what is going on, watching its progress, uniting in its consummation;—not painfully and hopelessly following a hard form of prayer from beginning to end, but like a concert of musical instruments, each different, but concurring in a sweet harmony, we take our part with God's priest, supporting him, yet guided by him. There are little children there, and old men, and simple labourers, and students in seminaries, priests preparing for mass, priests making their thanksgiving; there are innocent maidens, and there are penitents; but out of these many minds rise one great eucharistic hymn, and the great Action is the measure and the scope of it. And oh, my dear Bateman," he added, turning to him, "you ask me whether this is not a formal and unreasonable service. It is wonderful!" he cried, rising up, "quite wonderful. When will these dear good people be enlightened? O sapientia fortiter suaviterque disponens omnia, O Adonai, O clavis David et expectatio gentium, veni ad salvandum nos, Domine Deus noster!"

Exactly the same conception of the Roman idea of worship, as a great and *visible* divine action, to be livingly impressed on the eye of the worshippers, is thus graphically given by a very different witness, who had himself renounced the priesthood and the communion of Rome:—

"If mental incitement, though attended by the most thrilling and sublime emotions, though arising from deception, could be indulged without injury to our noblest faculties,—if life could be made a long dream without the painful starting produced by the din and collision of the world. . . . . the lot of a man of feeling brought up in the undisturbed belief of the Catholic doctrines, and raised to be a dispenser of its mysteries, would be enviable above all others. . . . . . . A foreigner may be inclined to laugh at the strange ceremonies performed in a Spanish Cathedral, because these ceremonies are a conventional language to which he attaches no ideas. But he that from the cradle has been accustomed to kiss the hand of every priest and receive his blessing—that has associated the name and attributes of the Deity with the consecrated bread—that has observed the awe with which it is handled—how none but a priest dare touch it—what clouds of incense, what brilliancy of gems surround it when exposed to the view—with what heartfelt anxiety the glare of lights, the sound of music, and the uninterrupted adoration of the priests in waiting, are made to arouse the overpowering feeling of God dwelling among men—such a man alone can conceive the state of a warm-hearted youth, who for the first time approaches the altar, not as a mere attendant, but as the worker of the greatest miracles. . . . . .

"When the consecrating rites had been performed—when my hands had been anointed—the sacred vesture, at first folded on my shoulders, let drop around me by the hands of the bishop—the sublime hymn to the all-creating Spirit uttered in solemn strains, and the power of restoring sinners to innocence conferred upon me—when at length raised to the dignity of a 'fellow-worker with God,' the bishop addressed me in the name of the Saviour, 'Henceforth I call you not servant, but I have called you friend,'—I felt as if, freed from the material part of my being, I belonged to a higher rank of existence. . . . . . . In vain did I exert myself to check exuberance of feeling at my first mass. My tears bedewed the *corporals* in which, with the eyes of faith, I beheld the disguised Lover of mankind, whom I had drawn from heaven to my hands."[2]

Here is clearly enough indicated where it is that the original faith of the Roman church has so often passed into the dreariest and most superstitious scepticism. She began by ascribing all her power and faith to the free and immanent agency of Christ, but too soon evinced the disposition to confine His agency to the narrow limits of her power and faith. Real, simple reliance on Him would have rendered it impossible for her to lay down exactly where His life and power was *not*, and where, on the other hand, she could undertake to *secure* it. In proportion as she claimed a plenary and irrevocable commission, she withdrew her dependent trust, and by believing more in herself, was compelled to

---

[2] Don Leucadio Doblado's 'Letters from Spain,' p. 122, and following.

believe less in her Lord. And, accordingly, as she enlarged the arrogance of her assumptions, she narrowed the channels of His mercy, and enforced in one breath the doctrines that she can command, at will, the bodily presence of the Lord on her altars, and that she can excommunicate, at will, the spirits of her children from some of His richest blessings. Is not this indeed a terrible combination of much creed with much scepticism—a living trust metamorphosed into an immeasurable distrust—that repels no teaching so zealously as the doctrine that God is greater than the church, that He is neither imprisoned in its limits nor bound by any covenant to sustain its arrogant decrees?

One more characteristic point of faith (with its allied scepticism) in the Church of Rome, I will briefly delineate before I pass on. I have touched upon her characteristic faith in the reciprocal action of God and His church, too soon passing into the limitation that God's Spirit is confined to the organization she has chosen to sanction; I must indicate the corresponding phase of her faith in human nature, which was, in its turn, too soon narrowed into self-idolatry, by confounding human nature with the ecclesiastic nature under her own sway. I have said that Rome acted first and thought afterwards. She distilled her Christian theory out of her Christian institutions. And what is the rule by which she has tested her institutions, and therefore, in the last result, her dogmas? It is by their adaptation to the mind of the universal church. Neither ancient[3] nor modern Rome has had any strong love for truth *as truth*. The distinction between absolute truth and truth of moral *effect*, or, in other words, social and political "pietas"—was never clearly apparent to the Roman character. And every devotional writer in the Roman Church speaks as if it were his *duty to believe* as true, all the rumours of a devotional tendency afloat in his communion, until they are proved to be false. The definition of divine truth coming nearest to the real conception formed of it by the Roman Church, would be, 'that body of theoretic assumptions which would be needed completely to justify, on intellectual grounds, all those institutions, special and general, by which practically she has been enabled to win hearts and guide nations.'

Now, ill as this definition would define pure moral truth, yet it has been based originally on a very deep and just faith in the affinity of human nature for pure religion and its deep love of moral excellence. The faith that all great controlling power, all authority which

---

[3] "Religion in the mind of Q. Fabius," says Dr. Arnold, "was not a mere instrument for party purposes: *although he may have had little belief in its truth, he was aware of its excellence,* and that a reverence for the gods was an essential element in the character of a nation, without which it must assuredly degenerate." I quote this only to show the general impression of Dr. Arnold as to the fact that religious Romans were more concerned for the *moral tendency* of their divine traditions, than for their truth. I do not know any special ground for the doubt implied in the case of Fabius. Livy's language would give strongly the opposite impression. See Book XXII., c. 9.

permanently sways multitudes, is of God—that the mighty *vox populi* is only uplifted with one accord when the *vox Dei* has spoken—that there is a species of mere *authority* so overpowering that it is its own evidence of being founded in *truth*—is a faith, which, however liable to misconstruction, is a true source of freedom. For teaching that the widest, most universal springs of faith in man, are those which most directly touch the nature of God, it tends to liberate us from the galling servitude of private prejudice, to make us suspect as false that which we cannot show to be *human*, and to move with a new elasticity and ease among the various windings of social faith.

But, in order that the *vox populi* may be any sign of the *vox Dei*, in order that the social power and influence of an institution may be any sign of its divine origin, the common cry must go up spontaneously, and without ulterior aim, out of the popular heart, *revealing* a new union, and flooding the inner life of society with a startling sense of an unsuspected oneness. Then, indeed, is the *vox populi* a response to the *vox Dei*, but not unless it be thus a revelation of the hidden and deeper sources of life,—not if it be only the result of combination, instead of its cause. If you can explain it in the vulgar method by merely pointing to a common and visible self-interest, or even to a clearly recognized class of common aims and purposes, then there is no sacred mystery in this uplifting of a common voice. If it arise wholly as the consequence of social relations, as the result of persuasion, or of discussion, or of any existing relations, then it sheds no light on the divine origin of society. It must be a secret spring of union, not an incidental result of union, still less the sedulous pursuit of a coincident self-interest, if it be one feature in that common humanity by which we are taught to feel that we are all children of one God. "Great is Diana of the Ephesians," was no *vox populi*, but merely a *vox argentariorum*—a voice of silversmiths. It was an official cry, the clamour of consentient self-interests, issuing from the artificial mouthpiece of *esprit de corps*. "Crucify him! crucify him!" was no *vox populi*, rather was it a *vox diaboli*, at least a *vox pontificum*—a voice of chief priests. Class-watchwords unfold no new union. They are no message from the awakening life of our common humanity. They are merely the strong language of official conventions crying out against an approaching dissolution.

Now here, again, is the second well-marked point on which the faith of the Roman Church contracted into the virtual scepticism and the deep distrust of a tyrannical and suspicious corporation. She professed to accept the *mind of the church, i.e.*, the testimony of all places, and all classes, and all times, which had been powerfully influenced and subdued by her teaching, as a test of the faithful development of the Christian spirit into Christian institutions; and then, again, of the true evolution of Christian doctrine out of those institutions. As a positive criterion of truth, this was a hazardous principle at best;

for, while the really universal spirit of religion in man is almost unerring in its moral admirations, it is frequently partial even to idolatry, and utterly unfit to judge of the true or false *historical* faith on which Christian institutions must rest, so long as their moral elements are noble and fascinating. What the *vox populi*, rightly questioned, *rejects*, is not and cannot be divine truth. But what it *accepts* may be divine only in its moral essence, and even there needlessly partial, and may be, moreover, surrounded with an unreal vesture of historical fact to almost any extent. But all these causes of probable alloy become sources of certain falsehood, if from the tribunal of all men really subdued by Christian influence, an appeal lie to the judgment-seat of a narrow *class* with special privileges, special interests, more than human influence, and less than human experience.

And this is the case of the Roman Church. The church early began practically to mean the priesthood, and, ere long, many of the living human fibres which united the priesthood with the church at large were severed, and the former was constituted into a disciplined missionary army of arbitrary and ghostly magicians. The principle of church development was exchanged for a principle of hierarchical encroachment; and the genuine faith in man as the image of God, which was the root of the former, for the superstitious and sceptical veneration for the priesthood as knowing more of God than other men, which was the foundation of the latter. Let me glance at its actual working in one of its least repulsive aspects, the history of that long "development" which ended in the Papal decree on the original freedom of the Virgin Mary from the moral infirmities of man.

The tenderness of the human relation between Jesus and His mother early captivated the mind of the church. Mary herself is said even to have "anticipated" the development of the doctrine in the words of the Magnificat, "For behold from henceforth all generations shall call me blessed," and the people soon began, not merely to call her blessed, but to regard the image of feminine purity and love which is shadowed forth in the gospels with an affectionate partiality that eventually shaped itself into fable as to her subsequent lot. The *vox populi* was true as ever in its moral sentiment, but already beginning to clothe its feelings in unreal history, and to give them that preponderance which uncultivated nature assigns to what it can fully comprehend as well as love. "The Christians of the first four centuries were ignorant of the death and burial of Mary."[4] Ephesus and Jerusalem alike claimed her empty tomb. The following is Dr. Newman's own account of the growth of fable concerning her:—

"Her departure made no noise in the world. The church went about her common duties, preaching, converting, suffering. .... At length the rumour spread through Christendom that Mary was no longer upon earth. Pilgrims went to and fro; they sought for her relics, but these were not; did she die at Ephesus, or did she die at Jerusalem? Accounts varied, but her tomb could not be

---

[4] 'Gibbon,' vol. iv. p. 345, of Milman's edition.

pointed out, or if it was found, it was open ; and instead of her pure and fragrant body, there was a growth of lilies from the earth which she had touched. So inquirers went home marvelling and waiting for further light. And then the tradition came wafted westward on the aromatic breeze, how that when the time of her dissolution was at hand, and her soul was to pass in triumph before the judgment-seat of her Son, the apostles were suddenly gathered together into one place, even unto the Holy City, to bear part in the joyful ceremonial ; how that they buried her with fitting rites ; how that the third day, when they came to the tomb they found it empty, and angelic choirs with their glad voices were heard singing day and night the glories of their risen Queen." " But however we feel," adds Dr. Newman, after narrating the tradition, " towards the details of this history (*nor is there anything in it which will be unwelcome or difficult to piety*), so much cannot be doubted from the consent of the whole Catholic world and the revelations made to holy souls, that, as is befitting, she is, soul and body, with her Son and God in heaven, and that we have to celebrate not only her death but her assumption." [5]

And thus the Roman Church has ever tested these traditions, asking little about the marks of historical accuracy, but much about their social influence. "St. Epiphanius does not affirm that she ever died," says another esteemed Roman Catholic writer, "*because* he had never found any mention of her death, and because she *might have been* preserved immortal and translated to heaven without dying. Much more ought *piety to incline* us to receive with deference a tradition so ancient and so well recommended to us as is this of the corporal assumption of the Virgin Mary,—an opinion which the Church so far favours as to read from the works of

---

[5] 'Discourses addressed to Mixed Congregations,' by John Henry Newman.

St. John Damascen and St. Bernard an account of it in the breviary, as *proper to edify and excite the devotion of her children!"*

This principle of assuming and usually regarding as *true* all that the ecclesiastical tact of the day feels to be socially "desirable" is, as I have said, of the very essence of the Roman Church. The image of the Virgin Mother was engraved deep on the mind of the first Christian population. The authorities of the church understood, and probably were themselves influenced by its power, and encouraged the development of this partial reverence. When Nestorius denied that Mary should be called the "mother of God," the church appealed not merely to the *vox populi*, but to the *vox Ephesi* to support the privileges of their local saint, and Mary was lifted to the dignity of her new title on the shoulders of an Ephesian mob. In the same century, St. Augustine indicates how powerfully the popular affection had influenced his own mind, and will not deny but that she might have had grace to remit *all* sin, who was chosen to be the mother of the Redeemer. Here, then, the voice of the technical ecclesiastical church is beginning to theorize and justify the practical development. The people loved her image and magnified her story. The church was bound either to moderate the growing enthusiasm or to find it some special doctrinal sanction. Immunity from actual sin was Augustine's suggestion. And it rapidly spread. It suited the ideas of the age. No one asked after evidence. Historical verifications were not then in request. But a passionate idolatry for this sweet vision of the church grew with its growth. And when the priesthood of the church was severed from the human life of the church, more and more did any merely human ascendancy, like Mary's, seem to the mind of that body to be insecure while it rested simply on human relations, and, therefore, to need a preternatural justification. This is what the sacerdotal mind constantly dwelt upon. Her human relation to Christ was not enough. "A Mother without a home in the church, without dignity, without gifts, would have been, as far as the defence of the Incarnation goes, no Mother at all. She would not have remained in the memory or the imagination of men." This was the sacerdotal conviction. And hence grew in the twelfth century the Franciscan suggestion of the "Immaculate Conception." She must have been, they maintained, not only free from sin, but miraculously exempt from the *tendency* to sin. And even St. Bernard, who opposed this "preservative addition" to the old worship with all his power, could write in this strain: "Nothing more delights me, yet nothing terrifies me more than to dwell on the glories of the Virgin Mary." St. Bernard had come to accept the first suggestion of immunity from actual sin; he stumbled only at the second, which a few years ago received the seal of Papal enactment.[6]

---

[6] See the 'Bishop of Oxford's Sermon;' Butler's 'Lives of the Saints;' and Dr. Newman's 'Two Sermons on the Glories of Mary.'

It is, I believe, quite unjust to say that if the same process of development proceeds, centuries later may witness Mary's elevation to the "intrinsic attributes of the Blessed Trinity, namely, infinite power, infinite wisdom, infinite love," which were ascribed to her, as Mr. Gladstone once told us, in his own hearing, by a preacher of the Franciscan order many years ago. "Archangels' gifts are restrained within the bounds of what is finite, while hers touch the bounds of the infinite—*toccano ai cancelli del infinito.*"[7] For though individual preachers are ignorant, the Church has always been true to her own logic, and the complete subordination of Mary to her Son is at the very root of the recent development. She was glorified *for the sake* of her Son, and the Roman Theology never breaks with its own motives. Still, the developing "mind of the church" is a sacerdotal mind; as, by the declaration of the dogma of Papal infallibility, is now formally admitted.

Here I must leave the Church of Rome, content with having thus slightly indicated her two most characteristic features of faith and scepticism. Her belief that the increase of her faith does not begin from within, but from the gracious action of God in her spreading social institutions, borders close on the scepticism which claims for those institutions a charmed life—a divine right in God,—close on that scepticism which, as she herself

---

[7] 'Gladstone's Church Principles considered in their Result,' p. 353.

expresses it, gives her "the custody of the sacraments," which means, in other words, the custody of God. The faith which sees in the universal voice of the Church the divine witness of the living word of God, borders close on the scepticism which anxiously substitutes for it the testimony of a class which has been worse than *arbitrarily* chosen, because it has been artificially trained.

Dr. Newman is right in saying that the Protestant Christianity implies a different idea of worship, and is in many remarkable features a different religion from the Roman Christianity. The Roman is an embodied faith, laboriously providing all kinds of visible media for bringing man into union with God, and variously skilful in adapting these media to their ends. Baptism, Confirmation, Penance, Mass, Ordination, Extreme Unction, Vows, Indulgences, Invocation of Saints,—at every point the massive masonry of the Roman ritual overarches and closes in the religious life of the individual soul,—human agency everywhere appearing on behalf of God. The Protestant faith is a protest not merely against the abuse of this machinery, but against the machinery itself. It was suited to the plastic, all-embodying genius of Rome. It is not suited to the freer mental genius of the German nations, whose strength is far more dependent on inward conditions, and who have formed their freshest springs of active energy almost entirely in the free life of meditation, in the lonely inspiration of poetry, in the force of *personal* affections. Art and Rhetoric, indeed,—in which genius is directed to outward ends,—are, as I have before hinted, mainly of Roman Catholic parentage. But Poetry and Philosophy, in which genius finds all its conditions within itself, are, on the other hand, mainly Protestant. And so, too, while Law is the child of Rome, the life of Conscience and of conscious affections has found its most genial climate in the character of the northern races.

Isolate the mind from visible agencies and the Roman Catholic has hardly a religious life to live. But the religion of Protestantism is in its primary nature separated from visible agencies. Springing up in secret struggles, it is matured by thought, watered by personal emotion, and rooted directly in God. It has been the child of Conscience, the pupil of Philosophy, the companion of Poetry, the parent of Freedom. Not that I ignore its relation to the Bible. But I am speaking of an inborn character in the nations which embraced it, which, after ripening long in silence, must have led to some far angrier flood of religious resentment against Roman bonds, had there been no simultaneous republication of a Gospel which gave grandeur to rebellion and set a limit to the spirit of destruction. The access to the Scriptures was no more the actual *cause* of Luther's spiritual revolution than were the pillar of cloud and the pillar of fire the cause of the departure of Israel from Egypt. But for the Scriptures, indeed, Luther and his followers might have perished in the deserts of fanaticism after their deliverance from Rome. But the pillar and the cloud which guided the Reformers' steps were not revealed until the sands of the untravelled waste were already flying around their path, and the brick-kilns of their taskmasters were lost behind them in the distance.

The Bible led on the Reformers indeed ; for the Bible was one long record of similar protest and reformation, from the reformation in the desert to the reformation of John the Baptist. Moses, Samuel, Elijah, Isaiah, and all the prophets, up to John the Baptist, were all engaged in one great effort to pierce the dull hearts of Israel with a personal knowlege of the living God, and to penetrate them with the conviction that ecclesiastical institutions were but miserable "holes in the rocks" which might hide God from them, but could not hide them from God when He should arise to "shake terribly the earth." Yet not the less was Luther's movement a moral necessity of the nations and the age, which must have come, even without the restoration of the Bible, though it may be in very different shape. Not the less had it characteristics of its own, which showed themselves by the remarkable course it ran and by the peculiar elements it alone assimilated freely from the newly-recovered stores of spiritual food. Luther's own character is the key, not only to his work, but to his powerful influence over the north, and to the limits which that influence speedily reached. I am very far from assenting to Macaulay's utterly sceptical suggestion that Catholicism and Protestantism must always divide the world. But I do believe that the Christianity which alone can conquer the earth will be a faith neither so entirely rooted in inward and personal emotions as that of Luther, nor so studiously reflected in secondary agencies and external institutions as that of Rome.

It is not easy to regain fully the sense of profound despair with which Luther regarded the external spiritual appliances of the Roman Church while he was still a member of her communion. Some appreciation of it can be gathered from the passionate fervour of abhorrence which he afterwards expressed (quite free, as I believe, from personal irritation), of the chains from which he had broken loose. "I have no better 'work,'" he once said, "than indignation and zeal; for whether I want to compose, write, pray, or preach, I *must* be indignant; then all my blood is freshened, my understanding is sharpened, and every miserable thought and temptation flies away."[8] Never for a mind like his could such a dreadful Sisyphus-punishment have been invented as the task of rolling disordered human nature with Roman levers up the holy mountain of the Lord. Not by mere patient effort, not by any process of incessant resolve, not even by any merely general trust in divine help, did ever such a mind as Luther's attain tranquillity and self-command. Collisions with sin

---

[8] 'Tischreden,' vol. ii. p. 215, ed. Förstemann.

which shook his stormy nature to its very centre passed and returned but to find him, as he thought, on the same level of the eternal ascent—no nearer to the cloudless and stormless climate of Christian peace. Was there no free act of the spirit which was able to gather up and illume, in one lightning-flash of thrilling conviction at once the summit of distant hope, the mighty arm of power by whose help it should be reached, and the path of sanctification, now so toilsome, winding on through shadows and beside precipices to the everlasting home? Was there no "spirit" to the cramped and microscopic "letter" of human duty, the possession of which would be a master-key to the minute provisions of a moral law, and secure freedom and joy, in the place of scruple, anxiety, and pain? Was there no access to a surer prophecy of final victory than any painful scrutiny into the small and doubtful variations of earthly conflict?

These were the great problems which occupied the whole soul of Luther, and which were at once characteristic of the revolution which he led and of the nations who were included in it. And he solved the problem by maintaining that there was such a spiritual principle of freedom, the essence of all good works, in the act of *faith;* which meant, with him, the personal apprehension of Christ's living presence with the heart, and the entire surrender to His power.[9] This one act included

---

[9] Whatever comments theologians may wisely make on Luther's many unguarded expressions, there can be no doubt that this, and

all belief, all hope, and all the holiness within the reach of man on earth. It contained the whole Christian life in germ. It was the only spring of holiness, and the only sign of the promised peace. To do right with the spirit bent downwards upon the duty seemed to him impossible, for the only *possible* right act in man was the turning of the heart to God, and from that flowed by His decree all that there was of right in any other. The act of faith was the one glimpse of glory, and opened the dark passages of the soul for the entrance of the divine life. One good work, and only one good work, Luther admitted as the root of the partial goodness in all others—the unbarring of the prison-door, the glad reception of the Light. One act, and that a joyful and free act of the spirit, he thus substituted for all the toiling duties of the law. No longer with downcast face were men to raise the heavy burdens of life, and fight again its often-fought battles; but, averting their eyes from the punctilious pleadings of the law, they were to draw their impulses from the God who had the keeping of their heart, and whose prompting love

---

nothing less than this, was in his mind in all his expressions on justifying faith. The late Archdeacon Hare's defence of him on this point is triumphant, if any careful reader of Luther could ever need to have his convictions strengthened. It was Luther's distrust and dread of the admission of free will in man that made him occasionally use expressions which seem to imply less than a *self-surrender*. He preferred to think of it as a yielding to *irresistible* grace. But no one can read his 'Table Talk' without a moral certainty that he included in the act of faith, the placing the mind in a living union with Christ, the delivery of the helm into His hands.

Luther held to be the very righteousness of which conscience was to him only the blanched and formal outline.

The law of conscience Luther regarded as an exacting law which it is impossible to fulfil, and which is meant only to spur on the agonized soul to seek a personal refuge. But when God entered the heart in the act of faith, then the law was no longer a law of condemnation; in part it was *fulfilled* rather than *obeyed* by the new influence of the divine love; and in part, so far as it presented an ideal yet imperfectly attained, its sting might be taken away by the belief that where the life was constantly committed into God's keeping, He would not be strict to mark anything that did not imply a resumption of individual self-will. And yet Luther found it impossible really to separate in experience and thought the divine *life* and the overbearing law of conscience. "To separate rightly the law from the gospel," he once said (and by the gospel he always means the revelation of God to the heart), "is easily enough learnt, as far as words go. But when it comes to the experience of heart and life, then it becomes so high and difficult, that we are all at sea, and seem to understand nothing about it." "Yes," he said, on another occasion, in that style of coarse reproach to the Antinomians, too characteristic of him, "there is *no* man who can rightly distinguish between the law and the gospel. And this is no wonder, seeing that Christ in the garden knew not how to do it, and could not distinguish, since He needed to be comforted, and to be taught the gospel by the angel—He on whose head the Holy Ghost had sat bodily, as a dove. Therefore these fanatics are but coarse, shameless fools, who imagine they understand and know all about it, when they have only read a page or two, as if they had eaten up the Holy Ghost, feathers and all."[1]

Luther proclaimed, then, that the act of faith was the one inlet of divine *love* into human life, while conscience only convicted man of an imbecility. Conscience was the mere serving of a writ upon a helpless prisoner; faith unbarred the doors and guided him on his way. Yet he held that faith *fulfils* what conscience *demands*, and in the secrets of the inner life he admits that it is impossible to unravel the promptings of the two. The peculiarity of his faith lay, not in denying validity to the moral law, but in appealing from it *as law* to the personal love of God. He will admit no power in the will to fulfil such a law. Nor would he willingly admit that he might be unconscious of that grace of God which assisted him to fulfil such a law. All holiness that he admits at all must come fresh out of *conscious* trust in the perfect God. That is the only untainted spring of action in the Lutheran theology.

Hence the deepest characteristic of the original Protestantism lay in this, that it withdrew its life from all the complicated and stagnant channels of ecclesiastical action, to draw it afresh at the divine sources of action,

---

[1] 'Tischreden,' vol. ii. p. 132, ed. Förstemann.

in emotion, meditation, poetry, prayer. Rome had sickened men with their own corrupt wills, and had exhausted their belief that they had even the smallest power to co-operate with the pure Spirit of God in His influences for good. In religion the whole current of thought went to magnify the divine agency and to depreciate the human. Thirsty, and faint, and weary, choked with the dust of ritual service, they needed to be baptized in divine waters, to lose themselves once again in the cloud of mystery, to recover the freshness of inspiration and the "wise passiveness" of loving dependence. And this was Luther's aim. He cast away the artificial pruning, and training, and clipping contrivances of Rome, not because he did not see evil in man, but because he found no tendency in such contrivances to subdue that evil. He thought ill enough of human nature, but he was sure that the only remedy lay in yielding up that nature more entirely to the inward activity of God. Nor did any fruit of mere nature, however cankered, seem to him so unsightly as the blighted fruit reared in the forcing-houses of the church. He knew that the Spirit of God had as much real access to the life of nature as to the life of the cloister or the convent; and as the only true holiness sprang from the moulding influences of His Spirit, so it seemed to him indifferent whether sin manifested itself in the untutored growth of the natural man, or was diverted into the less obvious channels of ascetic pride, secret doubt, or ecclesiastical formalism.

Every vein of subsequent Protestantism might be quarried out of Luther's massive nature, but all these veins together would hardly furnish out another Luther. He was the genius of the great German reaction against a religion of will. Like Protestantism he spent all his strength in the fervour of his trust, and yet would fain ascribe to that trust a purely involuntary character. His action, or his action on the world at least, flowed spontaneously from the exuberance of his trust; and the action of his soul in clinging to God he would not have to be an action at all. What was greatest in him, and most Protestant too, was the perfect clearness of heart with which he estimated the relation between God and his own instrumentality in setting forth the truth of God. He not merely said, but *realised*, that the Lord he preached would declare Himself without *his* aid ; and that were it not so, He were no Lord at all. There was no anxiety about success. In the spirit of true Protestantism, he was anxious that those who had felt the power of God should acquit themselves of their obligation to reveal it,—not be solicitous about it, as if there were no other channel for the Eternal Word. Smaller men are anxious to mould their age—to construct some artificial reservoir for perpetuating their faith before they die. As if there *could* be any such reservoir except the living Spirit of God,—as if any faith which is not ever springing fresh out of that infinite life would not stagnate or dry up before their own bodies had crumbled into dust! It was not thus with Luther. He had no cast-iron views of faith. He was not a semi-Protestant, with a Romanist reserve, that God could not get on, after all, without a formula and a human representative. "We tell our Lord God," he said, "that if He will have His church, He may uphold it; for we cannot uphold it, and even if we could, we should become the proudest asses under heaven." [2]

Therefore he could stand free and declare the Lord who was in him,—planning nothing, dreading nothing. The vast strength of his nature was all due either to the warmth of his impulses and the vividness of his sensibilities, or to the power of his trust. It was all natural or supernatural; none of it was of the stern voluntary cast of Rome—none of it of the preternatural, fanatic cast of a "child of destiny." He had none of the inflexible marble strength of iron *purpose*—nothing of the blind impetuosity of men possessed by their own notions. His most stormy force, as the late Archdeacon Hare most truly said, was never *violence*.[3] The gusts of such

---

[2] 'Tischreden,' vol. ii. p. 330.

[3] After quoting Luther's saying that he would not be deterred from riding to Leipsic, though "it were to rain pure Duke Georges for nine days, and each of them were nine times more furious than this," Archdeacon Hare remarks: "To our nicer ears such expressions may seem in bad taste; be it so. When a Titan is walking about among the pigmies, the earth seems to rock beneath his tread. Mont Blanc would be out of keeping in Regent's Park; and what would be the outcry if it were to toss its head and shake off an avalanche or two! Such, however, is the dulness of the elementary powers, they have not apprehended the distinction between force and violence. In like manner, when the adamantine bondage

a spirit might well shake the earth, but it was, as it were, an accident of his power, not its aim. These whirlwinds of vehemence issued from the depths of a spirit in which elements were stirring such as had scarce existed in any other man; but they were not summoned forth by the cold resolve of a determined will. They "proceeded" from him—they were not "created" by him. The vast social power of Luther, and the social power of his religion, was the mere natural expansion outwards of inward, elastic, uncontrolled affections; all its voluntary power was spent in the act of faith, and even this was claimed as involuntary.

Luther (in this, too, the very genius of Protestantism) had a breadth, and tenderness, and vigour of nature, physical and moral, which set the problem of self-discipline, the misery of inward disorder, in its full difficulty and its sharpest outline. His was a nature in which the flames of inward strife were easily kindled, and the occasion of no common anguish. He knew only too well that the seed of evil was not in the outward mould of his nature, not in the forms of human desire and affection, but deep below them, at the very sources of the will, and *therefore* he protested against every attempt to force nature into new channels. The rich endowments of the natural man he neither trusted nor

---

in which men's hearts and minds had been held for centuries was to be burst, it was almost inevitable that the power which was to burst this, should not measure its movements by the rule of polished life."—'Vindication of Luther,' p. 172.

dreaded. He admitted their rights, and left them to find their own channels in the world. This alone might have given the Protestant faith its physical superiority over the Roman (which depresses nature, and shears away her overflowing energies). But this alone would not, and will not, now or ever, give Protestantism its moral superiority. It was the complementary truth, that though the life of sin cannot be reached from below by any blockade of nature—by any hermetical sealing of its outlets,—it *may* be reached from above through the opened heart of trust, by unroofing the soul to the clear, calm love of God, that has given Protestantism its moral power. Wherever this faith has faded away, any moral superiority of Protestant nations is due to the mere vital force of unimpeded national characteristics; only where it remains, and so far as it remains, does the true spirit of Luther still preach to us that trust is stronger than action—that the shortest, nay the only way to conquer sin is to wrestle with God for His blessing first,—that it is both arrogant and hopeless to wrestle in our own strength with sin that we may be blessed by God.

There is scarcely anything so melancholy, even in the perversion of the Roman Church, as the perversion of the early Protestant theology. Protestantism began by teaching men that their religious faith must be individual and distinct. And thus the centres of life were multiplied, and the unity of disease was interrupted. But if the fall to pseudo-Protestantism was less general than that of Catholicism, it was a fall from a greater height.

Yet it was only a fall from a precipice on the very edge of which Luther stood. "Only believe that your sins are forgiven, and they are forgiven," said Luther, meaning as his whole life and teaching show, that to believe this was impossible without a moral delivery of the whole spirit into God's hands. In his thought, the one great conflict of life was to believe this; and how did he set about it? Not, certainly, by convincing himself that highly probable reasons could be accumulated in favour of this proposition; but by throwing into the act of trust all the intensity of moral and spiritual power which the pious Romanist would have spent on duty,—by making trust the first right action and the postulate of all right action,—by withstanding, as the most awful sin, the thought that God had provided no way of escape to each of His children, from the evil of their own nature,—by summoning up before his heart the infinite treason of doubting that God's desire for our holiness is immeasurably deeper than our own,—in short, by absorbing every other moral and spiritual struggle into this most central and passionate of struggles with his distrust of God, knowing perfectly, that wherever that enemy is absolutely beaten, there can be no choice for any other enemy but instant flight.

Before Luther's intense thought every scene of moral conflict, however apparently trivial, was at once transfigured into that final battle-field. Every temptation dilated before his inward eye into the threatening form of that one great Tempter, and with passionate defiance he drove before him, at the first symptom of danger, the enemy he durst not delay to crush at once. This, and nothing less, was what Luther implied in the assertion, "Only believe that your sins are forgiven, and they are forgiven." Yet though he was safe, he was, as I have said, near the margin of a great abyss. In his passionate eagerness to vindicate all the mercy and the love of human salvation for God, he *theoretically* denied that man could even co-operate with the Spirit which drew him on to spiritual victory. All was God's doing, he ejaculated, as with a soldier's heart he cast himself sternly into the thickest fray. Man could only be helplessly grateful and believing. And that which Luther said in theory, but by his life belied, men were soon found to accept in theory and in practice too. And thus came that horrible corruption of his faith which may be called the doctrine of passive salvation by correct notions concerning the nature and policy of God. And it is with this corrupted form of Protestantism that the ordinary bibliolatry which is its complement is associated.

I know well that every great and good man, who, like Luther, overleaps the mark in vindicating for God's grace the absolute and unmixed authorship of man's salvation, repudiates, like Luther, the practical inference that the faith by which he is saved is mere inevitable acquiescence in the authoritative statements of a supernatural oracle. Nevertheless, the one doctrine *cannot* be preached by large minds without the corresponding attenuated form of it immediately spreading among narrow minds. The way by which natures of small calibre are most often enlarged so as to receive a wider faith, is through the ennobling life of effort after a voluntary co-operation with the Spirit of God. And if they be taught that this is impossible, that they can only attend upon it,—that if they are to be chosen they will be chosen,—nothing can prevent them from accepting the practical inference, and contracting into mild content with such degree of general conviction as they happen to attain, and substituting a little leisurely reading and "inquiry" for the throes and the travail of spirit from which a faith like Luther's was generated. Deny the active and voluntary element in faith,—deny that men have real voluntary power to follow the promptings of the Holy Spirit by cleaving to God, and throwing themselves upon His purifying mercy and love as the last hope of their soul,—and you open the way for all the dryness and sterility of the Protestant orthodoxy, because not being able to move their own affections, men will naturally suppose that their only road to a fuller conviction is through the intellect, and so lose the rich elements of new spiritual life which are really opened to them through the secret history of the will. And then all the vast issues of trust and distrust are narrowed into the miserable controversy about accurately hitting the true mark in *doctrine*, and about the sufficiency or insufficiency of certain records of inspired life and history to insure this fine skill in archery.

If ordinary men once cease to believe in the divine

and supernatural freedom of their own inward responsible relation with the Spirit of God, they lose the principal experience in which He can become to them a *present* reality; for very few are originally constituted for a life of deep religious emotion, such as would pour conviction on their spirits, without the experience of duty and sin. And then, as a necessary consequence, revelation becomes —*not* an unveiling to us *now*,—but a declaration that such an unveiling has happened once and will again— that there is a God still living *behind* the veil of nature, if we could but see Him. And of course the evidence of this truth becomes a question for natural theology, and the mode of His government a point of investigation for biblical criticism.

What the life of the church was to Rome, the life in the Bible was to Luther and his first followers. To the Roman Christians God was first *realized* in the social power and external organization of the church. Looking on all power as capable of incarnation, they could not believe fully in divine power till they saw it embodied in the young and expansive energy of a social institution. It explained their yearnings, their hope, their trust. But in the age of Luther it had become a weary and feverish dream, explaining nothing, most difficult to explain itself. Moreover, the too individual cast of the Protestant character needed the history of the highest individual life in order to reflect its own questionings, and to resolve the mystery in which it was shrouded. Luther came to the Bible, and there he found the history of a class of men more near to the German nations in the mould of their moral nature, in the intensity of their conscience, in the close *personal* relations they sustained to the infinite God, than any the world had ever known. And, moreover, he found them one after another struggling for life and for salvation with Pharisaism, which was the very prototype of the extreme Roman formalism. He found the history of simple families of which God had been the real bond and living head. He found the history of a selfish and wilful nation, whose every crime was chronicled, not from the historic point of view as the mere breaking foam of popular passion, but as a sinful resistance to their spiritual King. He found the history of statesmen who rendered the strictest account of their government and their misgovernment in prayer to God, and who asked counsel of His Spirit ere they advised an alliance, or proclaimed a war. He found there, amidst many similar histories, the inward and outward experience of one, who, like himself, had to break a yoke of ordinances, to resist and upbraid his own people, to destroy for others and lose for himself the tradition of unity with an ancient church, to announce the abrogation of the dead tribute of actions, and to demand in its place the surrender of the citadel of the heart, and then to see with anguish that his own disciples had been held more securely to their allegiance by the outward bond than by the inward trust. Such a history of individual religion, unrolled to the yearning eyes of a nation thirsting vainly for an inward religion, was in the highest sense a *revela-*

tion. It made clear their own wants; it made clear their new life; it reflected their spiritual experience; it brought close home to them the divine answer to that experience. Jerusalem seemed to live again in the heart of Germany, and with startled hearts the people saw their own life repeated, but also, closely mingled with it, that personal life of God in which they were longing to put their trust.

Here, then, was a ground of fact for their desires. Here was a protection against fanaticism. Here was God elsewhere revealing Himself to be that which they found Him to be in their own hearts. The Bible, however, was thus fresh and pure as a revealing authority only while the hearts of men were thus deeply stirred with the want of a diviner life. The time came when the faith in a revealing history was as much disguised and overlaid with practical scepticism as ever was the Roman faith in a revealing church. The intensely inward character of the personal trust of the great Reformers laid too great a strain upon the spiritual capacity of the people, and their faith gradually relapsed into a passive dependence on the one outward prop left to them in the canon of Scripture. Instead of reverencing the Bible for its power of revealing a present God, they elevated it into the entire substance of the revelation. Thousands desired a belief for which they felt in their own hearts little or no support, and they unconsciously sought to shift the ground of the Reformation so as to relieve themselves from choosing between the alternatives of retrogression and positive doubt.

And thus arose that large class of Protestant sceptics, who fortify their belief in the Bible just as the Romanists fortified their belief in the church, as the only stronghold of their faith. They have faith in a *past* revelation. They pray with eyes ever bent upon that blue streak in the eastern horizon, where, once at early dawn, the very sun of heaven was visible; but if they are told that its glory is still undimmed, that, would they but look upwards, they might see it now riding clear on high, they make it painfully evident that their faith is jarred and shaken by the unreasonable assertion, and that to their minds it only throws a mist of doubt upon the past reality of the morning glory, when so clear an optical illusion can deceive an experienced eye at noon. Thus the faith in the Bible was gradually overlaid with an active hostility to every present medium of revelation, and it became necessary to proclaim this " preservative addition " to the biblical orthodoxy, that the Bible was the *only* mirror of the purposes and character of God.

But no sooner was the Bible held to be the only accessible abode of the divine Spirit, than it became suddenly more and more difficult to discover the divine Spirit even in the Bible. The light and shade of human sentiment and human purpose are as clearly distinguishable in the Hebrew history as in modern life. The sacredness once driven out of the latter, it becomes more and more impossible to vindicate it wisely for the former. And thus the declining faith of Protestantism reaches its last stage, in which one class passing into absolute scepticism, affirms that God neither *is* present in humanity nor ever was, while another class, less sincere, and almost equally untrue, substitutes the *history* of a revelation for the living God, and pretends to find Him more clearly manifested in the minutest of its moral incidents, and the least sacred portion of its literature, than in all subsequent or present history,—more clearly in the Song of Solomon than in the farewell thoughts of Socrates,—nay, more clearly in the mention of a patriarch's age, the dimensions of the ark, or a verse of a genealogy, than in all the tried and tempted life of man's daily experience.

This citramontane bibliolatry, which fairly rivals the ultramontane ecclesiolatry,—going out of its way to brand as the worst kind of *sin* any hesitation as to the literal dictation of the Bible by the Holy Ghost,[4]—has borne bitter fruit in the English church. Our national Establishment boasts a considerable portion among her

---

[4] At a May meeting held by the so-called Evangelical party some years ago, a Cambridge professor was branded as putting forth books *only fit for Holywell-street*, because he had called in question the scientific truth of the Mosaic account of the creation. The allusion was to the Rev. Baden Powell's book on the "Unity of Worlds," in which he states the well-ascertained incompatibility of the Mosaic account with the facts of modern geology, and gives it as his view that moral and spiritual, not scientific truth, is all that can be looked for in the Bible. Wherever the Bible is deified, science is treated as calumny against God. As the modern bibliolaters in Germany candidly say, "Die Wissenschaft muss verdreht werden."

clergy and laity, of that class who, as Luther predicted, greedily gather up the doctrinal husks of his faith, and who yet, had they been living when he broke his bonds, would not so much as have touched the kernel. Luther believed in a Bible that referred him back to the Christ living in his heart; the English biblical orthodoxy believes in a God who refers us finally to the Bible. And this ossification of the revealing power necessarily corresponds to a petrifaction of the revealed truth. Whatever be the nature of that faith in the atonement of Calvary which has taken so high a place in the theology of the Reformation, there is a very broad distinction to be drawn between those who conceive that it works its ends through the *existing trust*, that is, by the present *living* influence of Christ over the heart, and those who regard belief in it as the technical condition of a pardon by virtue of which they escape a penalty, and are included in the muster-roll of a favoured class. The former regards that faith as the means of bringing man into new relations with a divine Person, the latter regards the belief as completing the conditions of an old contract. The bibliolatry which relegates the Holy Spirit to the province of explaining to us the Bible, necessarily contracts the meaning of salvation by faith, from salvation by a living act, into salvation by acquiescence in the terms therein proposed.

Where there is no belief in the divine revelation *in* man, all the sacred part of faith consists in taking the Bible upon trust, instead of trusting in a present Christ;

it becomes necessary that the whole spiritual portion of the negotiation should be conceived as completed within the limits of the Bible ; that nothing but the *formal* signature should be left for the recipient. Were it otherwise, it would be necessary to assume a real living communion of the soul with God, independently of the sacred volume, and so a new and powerful innovating element would be introduced by which its absolute and supreme authority might be undermined. Thus the passionate faith of Luther is degraded into the acceptance of an artificial contract of which all the truly divine operation had taken effect centuries ago, the only new element now added being the admission of a new name. Instead of trust being the *power* by which the sinful spirit comes under a new influence, it is only the occasion on which the envelope of Christ's death is extended to the guilty.

The orthodox theory of substitution carefully excludes the supposition that the spiritual union with Christ is the purifying influence which renders possible the favour of God; and maintains that His suffering was the essential ground of our liberation. The following is the language in which the modern remnant of Protestant faith is measured out to spirits eager to find all the truth which any formula still retains. The speaker is the Dr. Candlish who undertook to expose Mr. Maurice's heresies to the Young Men's Christian Association, as the representative of evangelical orthodoxy :—

" The will of God is not only not changed by the Atonement—which of course is an impossibility—but it does not find in the

Atonement any reason for a different mode of dealing with man from that which, irrespectively of the Atonement, might have been adopted as right and fitting. The wrath of God is not turned away from any: it is not quenched. But what! some one says, would you really have it quenched? That wrath against the unlovely, which is the essential attribute of all love worthy of the name,—would you have it quenched in the bosom of Him who is love, so long as anything unlovely anywhere or in any one remains? No. But the object against which the wrath burns is not merely an abstraction; it is a living person—myself, for example. And that wrath is not merely indignant or sorrowful dislike of what is unlovely in me on the part of a Father whose nature is love;—but holy displeasure and righteous disapprobation on the part of One who, however he may be disposed to feel and act towards me as a Father, is at all events my Ruler and my Judge;—whose law I have broken and by whom I am condemned. There is room here for his *arranging* that, through the gracious interposition of his own Son, meeting on my behalf the inviolable claims of justice, his wrath should be turned away from me;—and if from me, from others also, *willing to acquiesce in the arrangement.* If a moral government according to law is conceivable, such a procedure is conceivable under it."

"Willing to acquiesce in the arrangement!" If ever there were a hollow ring about theological doctrine,—if ever there were an empty husk from which the kernel had dropped,—it is in such a formula as this. From the opinion,—I will not call it a faith,—that rigorous spiritual justice concerns the external *act* of punishment, irrespectively of the recipient,—from the doctrine which professes to excuse men, once for all, from all the requisitions of divine law on grounds wholly disconnected with their own spiritual life, has come all that unreal and external conception of duty and sin,—that chronic *suspiciousness* of nature without open war with it,—that askance glancing at the joys of life without either hearty acceptance or manly resignation of them,—that way of living half to the carnal and half to the spiritual man which combines the perils of ascetic and of epicurean practice,—that official life with the Redeemer and actual life with the world,—which naturally flow from a theory of purely artificial righteousness and from gratitude to God that we are permitted to produce a proxy in the most personal relations of spiritual life, in short, that He is pleased to admit a double dramatic fiction as the ground of a real reconciliation with Himself. Well may Mr. Maurice indignantly deny that this is either a Christian or a Protestant doctrine.

And from this point of view it is far from difficult to understand the nature of that Puseyite reaction in our Establishment which has taken hold of so many minds little inclined to go back into the Roman church. The Lutheran assertion, that a living trust in the Christ within man is the only pure fountain of action,—that this alone can produce a holiness unstained by human pride,—had relapsed into a confidence in the terms of a technical agreement, in which Christ and men are the contracting parties. This was the result of laying too much stress on the *consciousness* of the act of faith,—the effect of putting a strain on the inward attitude of the heart which it cannot in most men bear, and which produces artificial reaction. It cannot be wondered at, then, that a large party looked eagerly for a more comprehensive church, which should nourish the unconscious life of man, and recur to action as the school of faith, instead of looking on conscious faith as the only holy spring of action. This is the strength, I believe, of that Puseyite reaction towards the sacramental system of grace by outward ordinances, and towards the doctrine that the privileges of Christ's church are not necessarily confined to those who individually and inwardly " close with Christ," which has taken so strong a hold upon a portion of our Establishment. Puseyism is very far from being at one in principle with Romanism. It is only a *conservative* movement towards ancient doctrine,—while Romanism has a principle, a life, an idea of its own. Like all conservatism, it is negative, arising in a dislike towards present tendencies, a preference for old customs, of which it shares the sentiment and understands the truth. Puseyism is no distinct faith; it is a compromise between Protestantism and Catholicism; it desires to combine the advantages of both. Archdeacon Denison says, "The Roman Church is Catholic but *not* primitive; the English church is Catholic *and* primitive." In other words, Puseyism is the Body Catholic bereft of its present mind, or the Body Protestant acting under the inspiration of a past mind.

Puseyism owns positively no *living* authority at all; it has no principle of development; it is radically averse to all principles of development; its desire is to live by the customs and observances of a past age. It talks, indeed, of the authority of the church. But if you come to look into the meaning of what is said, you find it to mean only that clerical gentlemen,—especially bishops,—are rather more likely to understand what was the ancient practice and the ancient creed than any one else. But it is very far from recognizing any practical and present dogmatic authority even in bishops or archbishops. On the contrary, Archdeacon Denison evidently thinks that he could start a Church Catholic of his own; and that once having the apostolic succession and the "custody" of the sacraments, the Puseyites need no sanction from any overruling ecclesiastical mind to enable them to set up for themselves. Puseyism recognizes the sacramental channels of grace, but has no local and present power by which it can decide the issues of a present controversy. Its only proposal for a bridge over a yawning schism is to suspend above it a narrow causeway attached to a "catena" of the fathers, but unfortunately it has no solid buttresses of critical authority by which the catena itself can be hung.

Puseyism is to Romanism what an hereditary aristocracy is to the encroaching power of the first lords. It holds its own only by prescription, and has no life within it by which it can annex new territory. Romanism has a present principle of expansion, as well as a claim to inherited possessions. We can neither wonder at Puseyites for going to Rome, nor at their remaining in the church. Rome is the only church with a power of *movement* which holds their sacramental system; and consequently where men crave to see their principles active, conquering, unfolding to present exigencies,—they go to Rome. But the greater portion of the Puseyite party desire nothing so little as any sign of movement. They dread and fear Rome exactly for the same reason for which they dread and fear Protestantism. They desire the "primitive" in form as well as essence. They reverence authority as a cohesive, not as a moving force. They are all for what the mathematicians call the principle of the Conservation of Areas. They eulogize authority when it denounces change. They condemn it as not "primitive" when it issues a new decree. They would love to have a government that makes fast everybody else's thoughts in the stocks first, and then takes its place beside them.

Finally, in protest at once against Puseyism and Bibliolatry, there has arisen of late years, that school in the church from which all its richest life in the future bids fair to spring, unless the entangling formularies, of which they seek to gain the deepest and truest meaning, should prove too literal and fettering to leave consciences at ease while faith reasserts her freedom. The following are amongst the last words of one whose large wisdom and profound faith endeared the Church of England to many of us who find much in her to which we cannot assent, and yet can look with no hope so strong elsewhere. I quote from the last charge of Archdeacon Hare:—

"As time advances, circumstances change; new wants spring up, and multiply; that which may have been perfectly suited for one form of society, for one mode of human thought and feeling, becomes, in certain respects, inappropriate for others. According to the old illustration, the clothes of the boy will not fit the man; and the attempt to force them on him will only disclose their unfitness more and more. Nor, when manhood is attained, is the progress of change arrested—it is continually going on; wherefore fresh adaptations are continually needed. Now, let anybody call to mind what the English nation was in 1660, when the last revision of our Common Prayer Book took place, or in 1604, when our Canons were framed, and what it is now, in the middle of the nineteenth century. How enormous is the difference in the extent of the empire, in the mass and distribution of the population! And it is scarcely less in their social, moral, intellectual condition. Hence those forms and rules, which were drawn up with immediate adaptation to the former age, can hardly be equally well adapted, in all respects to the latter. Indeed, this truth was fully recognised and acknowledged by the framers of our Liturgy themselves. Being men of a living faith, they knew that whatever lives must move and work, must shed its leaves and its plumage; and that while it assimilates new elements, it parts with those which had previously been assimilated. They knew, too,—and their work had directly taught them,—that even Religion itself, through its manifold relations with man, had entered into the region of human mutability, and that, in addition to the other causes which might produce a necessity for change, it was corruptible through the corruptibleness of mankind. . . . . . On the other hand, as of course it would be impossible to prohibit our Ecclesiastical Synod permanently from the examination of our Liturgy and Articles, it may be after a time, when it felt itself at home in the work, and looked around on the manner in which the nation is divided among so many religious denominations, it might take thought whether a large number of the Nonconformists in the land might not be gathered into the unity of the Church. However inaccurate the official Religious Census may be in a multitude of its details, the broad fact is undeniable, that a vast part of the nation—if not half, a third or a fourth—are not joined with us in that unity: and every true lover of the Church, all who remember our Lord's earnest prayer for that unity, all who bethink themselves how St. Paul speaks of it, all who see daily how our work is cramped and hindered by the want of it, must needs yearn for the reconciliation of our brethren who are now worshipping apart from us."

The movement which Archdeacon Hare led and represented,—which began with him in the reassertion of Luther's Protestantism, probably in too unqualified a form,—but which, in passing out of his hands into that of his disciple, Mr. Maurice, has received that more practical mould which was wanting to rescue it from the risk of its former perversion, has not yet probably attained its destined power.

Mr. Maurice seems to me still to follow Luther and his friend too strictly in the theory of faith, though no one assigns a richer *practical* influence to the power of the will in co-operating with God than he. He still preaches that the act of grace by which God reconciles man to himself, is perfect without relation to our surrender to its influence, and this he would sometimes seem to deprive of all element of freedom. Such at least is the general tenor of his teaching,—that the reconciliation is complete,—that no free and individual act of will in us is a necessary condition of its inclusive power. Practically no one will accuse him of holding the *results* of such a teaching. But I believe the true safeguard against Puseyism on the one hand, as against Calvinism on the other, is to preach what may be termed the sacramental power of common every-day duty—to preach that a real eucharistic grace goes forth from the unconscious action to the spirit—unless that influence is destroyed by " receiving it unworthily," *i. e.* by a conscious self-trust.

Luther was wrong in saying that all pure life goes forth out of conscious faith. Rome and the Puseyites are right in affirming that unconscious actions are often the sustaining power of faith, and that God may feed us with Himself through common bread and wine taken in humble thankfulness for His incarnation. Common minds, and English minds especially, are not equal to a constant strain on their conscious relation to God. Many can do their duty who cannot do it out of a life of faith,—*i. e.* out of conscious and living dependence. But Luther was right in asserting that all *conscious* trust in ourselves is tainted with sin, that all conscious attitudes of our moral nature, must be attitudes of trust in One higher and purer than ourselves. The unreality of Puseyism lies in its restricting the real communication of an unconscious divine influence to symbolic and ritual actions; the unreality of Lutheranism in restricting it to conscious spiritual attitudes of mind. Mr. Maurice has got hold of this truth practically; he does not yet seem to hold it consciously. He is so afraid of conceding *any* power to the human will (even a power of co-operation in working out its own salvation), that he has hardly either met the falsehood of the vicarious theory, or gleaned from Puseyism its truth, with that full success for which there are ample resources in the tendencies of his noble and genial faith. The true adjustment of the relative claims of responsible action and conscious trust, is reserved for a theology that can enter at once into the Roman and into the German faith—while guarding against the official, ritual tendencies of the one, and against the too introspective spirit of the other.

In this respect the late Mr. Robertson, of Brighton, appears to me to have taken a maturer line of thought than any of his fellow-labourers. Greatly Mr. Maurice's inferior in theological depth and in breadth of historical culture, yet with a mind that was never satisfied without sounding the deepest truths which the formularies of the English church enshrined, he had perhaps attained a fuller conviction than any of his brother clergymen that these formularies do not comprehend the whole truth, especially in reference to that deepest question of theology, the relation of faith to action.[5] With a thoroughly Catholic spirit, that accomplished man had a clear appreciation that the theology of Luther had injuriously affected English religion, and had led to an insincere compromise between the religion of law and duty which is the nation's natural worship, and the religion of incessantly conscious trust at which they were taught to aim. He was content often to build faith upon duty, and not inclined to insist with Luther and his modern English disciples on the partial truth asserted in the Articles, that duty must spring out of a clear life of faith. Indeed, I believe that "the tongues of many stammerers would speak plainly" as his, but for the constant reminder, that not out of the abundance of the heart, but out of the abundance of the formula, the English clergy are bound to speak. The land of formula from which they are forbidden to stray, is rich and plen-

---

[5] See especially the apparently not very perfect record of a fine sermon on the Roman character.

teous in all manner of wisdom, as they are not slow to discern. But the range of the prisoner on parole is not freedom, though the hills which mark his limits are but faintly visible in the blue horizon. Not till the church has "set their *heart* at liberty," will the life of the highest and best in our communion cease to be the *most* painful and constrained.

END OF VOL. I.

LONDON:
PRINTED BY WILLIAM CLOWES AND SONS, STAMFORD STREET,
AND CHARING CROSS.

www.ingramcontent.com/pod-product-compliance
Lightning Source LLC
Chambersburg PA
CBHW051723300426
44115CB00007B/446